MY PAST AND THOUGHTS

MY PAST AND THOUGHTS

The Memoirs of Alexander Herzen

VOLUME VI

Translated from the Russian
by Constance Garnett

faber and faber

This edition first published in 2008
by Faber and Faber Ltd
3 Queen Square, London WC1N 3AU

A CIP record for this book is available from the British Library

ISBN 978–0–571–24546–8

CONTENTS

TRANSLATOR'S NOTE

THIS volume concludes the 'Memoirs of Herzen.' Nothing in the complete Russian edition has been omitted except two or three pages, which are practically repetition of earlier passages, and a brief section, Aphorismata, the humour of which has so evaporated with the lapse of time that it could hardly be made intelligible to an English reader.

I have ventured to add to the volume Herzen's famous letter to Michelet, which is of interest in view of what has actually happened in Russia during the last ten years.

INTRODUCTION

HERZEN'S own story of his life as a connected narrative breaks off with his arrival in London in 1852. A full description of his later years is given in the Reminiscences of Madame Ogaryov-Tutchkov, from which the following extracts are taken. As the latter is the central figure in the picture of those years, some account of her is essential.

Natalya Alexyevna Tutchkov was born in 1827, and came of a distinguished family. Her grandfather and his four brothers were highly cultured men, remarkable for their gifts and their character. Her father was a friend of the Decembrists, was slightly implicated in the conspiracy, and was for a time under arrest. When released, he settled on his estate in the province of Penza, where he was elected Marshal of Nobility and did much good work for the welfare of the peasants and the administration of the district. His two daughters, Elena and Natalie, had a happy childhood. In 1846 Ogaryov, an old friend of their father's, came, after seven years' absence, to his estate near the Tutchkovs. He saw a great deal of them, and the young girls became very fond of him. In 1847 the Tutchkovs went abroad, and Ogaryov gave them a letter of introduction to the Herzens, who were at that time in Rome.

The Herzens welcomed them warmly, and Natalie Herzen and Natalie Tutchkov became deeply attached to each other. Natalie Herzen called the young girl 'Consuelo di mia alma,' and many of her letters are addressed to her. She is said to have expressed a wish that in case of her death Natalie Tutchkov should have charge of her children.

After the happy time in Italy they all returned together to Paris, where they witnessed the terrible days of June 1848. Herzen (volume iv. pp. 11-13) describes

the mournful parting between his wife and her 'Consuelo'; the Tutchkovs went home to their estate in
Penza, where Ogaryov was a frequent visitor. His
affection for Natalya Alexyevna soon passed into love,
and he tried to obtain a divorce from his first wife, Marya
Lvovna, *née* Roslavlov, who had left him several years
before, and was living in Paris with the well-known
painter, Vorobyev, but out of spite she refused to release
him. In the end Natalie Tutchkov decided to dispense
with the legal ceremony, and in 1850 settled with
Ogaryov as his wife. In those days such a step required
a good deal of courage, and her parents were greatly
distressed, though they, like every one else, indeed, had
a warm affection for Ogaryov. Not long afterwards
Marya Lvovna died, and the Ogaryovs were legally
married.

Herzen had, on his first arrival in London in 1852,
settled near Primrose Hill with his son Sasha (Alexander),
a boy of twelve, and his friend Haug. The latter
had quarrelled and left him by 1854. The two girls,
'Tata' (Natalie) and Olga, had joined him with their
governess, Malwide von Meysenbug, an excellent woman,
well known in her own day as the authoress of *Memoirs
of an Idealist*, but now remembered only for her correspondence with Nietzsche and Wagner.

Herzen repeatedly wrote to Ogaryov, begging him to
come to London. At last Ogaryov, who had been living
since his marriage in the province of Simbirsk, where he
had a paper-mill, decided to go to England. It took
him some time to obtain permission to leave Russia, but
"on April the 9th, 1856," Madame Ogaryov writes,
"we crossed from Ostend to Dover on a very rough sea;
it was all I could do not to be ill. Ogaryov is a very good
sailor. When at last the steamer came to a standstill
before the dark, endless cliffs of Dover, dimly visible
through the thick yellow fog, my heart sank: I felt every-

thing about me somehow strange and cold; the unfamiliar language . . . everything overwhelmed me and made me think of my home and my family so far away. . . . We found our luggage, took a cab and drove to the station; there we hardly had time to have our things put in and to take our seats when the train moved off with incredible swiftness—it was an express: the objects beside the line flashed by, making an unpleasant impression on unaccustomed eyes. I was vexed that we had not managed to get breakfast. It was so important for Ogaryov, who might easily have had an attack from exhaustion and impatience to see his friend.[1] Four hours later we saw London—grand, gloomy, for ever wrapped in a fog, like a muslin veil—London, the finest city I had ever seen. We hurriedly got into a cab and set off to seek Herzen at the address given us by Dr. Pikulin: Chomley Lodge, Richmond. But a cab is not an express train, and we needed all our store of patience; at last we arrived in Richmond; in spite of the rain, the place made a great impression on me; it was buried in verdure, even the houses were covered with ivy, wild vines, and other creepers; in the distance we caught sight of a magnificent immense park; I had never seen anything like it! The cab stopped at the gate of Chomley Lodge; the cabman, muffled up in a great-coat, with a number of collars each wider than the one above it, gave a loud ring at the bell. A woman came out; scanning us with evident curiosity, for we probably looked very different from Londoners, she bowed very civilly to us. To Ogaryov's enquiry whether Mr. Herzen was living here, she replied with alacrity:

'Yes, yes, Mr. Herzen used to live here, but he moved a long time ago.'

---

[1] Ogaryov suffered from some form of epilepsy.—(*Translator's Note*.)

'Where to?' Ogaryov asked dejectedly.

'Where is he now?' she rejoined. 'Oh, a long way from here; I 'll fetch you the address.'

She went off, and returned with the address on a scrap of paper. Ogaryov read, Peterborough Villa, No. 21 Finchley Road, London. The cabman bent over the paper and evidently read it for his own benefit.

'Oh . . . oh!' he said, shaking his head, 'I'll drive you back to London, and there you must take another cab, my horse wouldn't get so far, it's at the opposite end of the town, and he's tired already, here and back again's a tidy journey.'

We sighed disconsolately and accepted his decisions without protest. When we were back in London Ogaryov owned that he would be glad to have a hasty meal, while our luggage was being transferred to another cab; and we succeeded in obtaining something to eat. Then we got into the second cab and drove off again on the hard resounding road; we did not talk on the way, but looked anxiously out of window, only from time to time exchanging the same thought: 'What if he is not there either?' At last we arrived. The cabman climbed down from the box and rang the bell. We had a view of No. 21 above the gate; the neat, prosaic brick house stood in the middle of a flower-garden, surrounded by a high stone wall with bits of broken glass on the top of it; the wall made the little garden look like a deep bath. Herzen could not bear it and never sat in the garden. The cook, François, a little, bald, middle-aged Italian, opened the door of the house, looked at our trunks, and closed it again; probably he was going to tell his master of what he had seen. The impatient cabman rang again more loudly. This time Francis came out briskly, ran down to the garden gate, gave us a careless bow, and said in French:

'*Monsieur pas à la maison.*'

'How annoying!' Ogaryov answered quietly in French, and he gave me his hand to step out of the cab, then bade the cabman lift down the luggage and carry it into the house; then he asked him his fare and paid it. François followed us in great perturbation. In the hall Ogaryov turned to François and asked:

'Where are the children?'

Herzen was standing at the top of the stairs. Hearing Ogaryov's voice, he ran down like a boy of twenty and rushed to embrace him, then he turned to me. 'Yes, Consuelo?' he said, and kissed me too.

At the sight of the general rejoicing, Francois at last recovered; at first he stood thunderstruck, thinking the Russians were taking the house by storm.

At Herzen's summons the children appeared with their governess, Mal wide von Meysenbug. The younger, Olga, a little girl with regular features, seemed lively and somewhat spoilt; the elder girl, about eleven, was rather like her mother in her dark-grey eyes, the shape of her forehead, and her thick eyebrows and hair, though this was fairer than her mother's. There was a rather diffident, forlorn look in her face. She could not readily express herself in Russian, and so was shy of speaking. Later on she liked talking Russian to me at bedtime, and I used often to sit by her little bed while we talked of her dear mother. Herzen's son, Alexander, a lad of seventeen, was delighted to see us. He was at that stage when boyhood is over, but the youth is not yet a young man. Until he left London, I was like an elder sister to him, the friend to whom he confided all that was in his heart.

For the first days after our arrival in London Herzen bade Francois admit no visitors whatever; even the presence of Malwide was irksome to him: he wanted to talk with us of all that had been aching in his heart these last two years; he told us all the details of the terrible blows he had endured, told us of his wife's illness and death.

Often the children or Malwide came in and interrupted our conversation, and he preferred to begin talking when they had all gone to bed, so we spent several nights without sleep, and the dawn found us still up. I was only anxious on Ogaryov's account, but it could not be helped. Afterwards, when he had relieved his heart and shared his sorrowful memories with us, Herzen regained his liveliness and activity. He went about London with us, showing us what had struck him at first, among other things the London public-houses, where people sat partitioned off from each other like horses in stalls, and the markets on Saturday nights lighted up by torches, where only the poor make their purchases, and where we heard on all sides: 'Buy, buy, buy!'

A few days after our arrival, a little lodging, consisting of two rooms, was found for us with a Mrs. Bruce, a few steps from Herzen's house. . . . We were very comfortable with that worthy woman, but we spent the greater part of our time at Herzen's. There we met *émigrés* from almost every part of Europe; there were Frenchmen, Germans, Italians, Poles, but at that time only one Russian, Ivan Ivanovitch Savitch, a cousin of the Savitch who suffered for his political views, I believe, when Herzen was a student; that is, many years before. Yet Ivan Ivanovitch, simply because he was his cousin, felt that he was under suspicion, and so was afraid to return to Russia. He had suffered great hardships and privations, but when we arrived he had work as a private teacher, and rarely asked for help from Herzen, who assisted all the *émigrés* indiscriminately. . . ."

"*Soon afte*r our arrival the news came that the daring revolutionary, Orsini, had escaped from an Austrian prison and would soon be in London. . . . A few days afterwards Herzen, on returning from his daily excursion into town, told us that Orsini had arrived, that he had seen him, and that Orsini would be dining with us next day. I had heard so much about him that I looked forward with interest to seeing him.

We were by then living at Herzen's; this is how it came to pass. One day Ogaryov and Herzen had gone to town together, and I was alone in my lodging. Suddenly Miss Mills, the old housemaid, appeared with Herzen's two little girls. The elder, Natasha, with a happy face, threw her arms round my neck and said: 'She has gone and taken all her things.' Miss Mills told me that Fräulein Meysenbug had left the house. I could make nothing of it and went back with the children; we were met by their brother Alexander. He looked distressed, picked up little Olga and kissed her; his eyes were full of tears.

'What is it for? what is it for?' he said.

Herzen was quite incensed at this typically German proceeding.

'She might have explained and talked things over,' he said.

Nothing would induce him to go and ask her to come back.

She lived henceforward in lodgings, and we moved into Herzen's house and said good-bye for ever to our dear Mrs. Bruce.

But to return to Orsini. He arrived at the hour fixed. He was a typical Italian: tall, with black hair and eyes, with a small black beard and regular but rather marked features. Most likely he was even handsomer in Italian military uniform, but in London he was in a frock-coat, and he wore it with the peculiar *chic* with which all military men wear civilian dress. When he talked, he impressed one by his extraordinary earnestness, vivacity, and fervour, and at the same time by knowing where to

draw the line and avoid saying more than he meant to.
I asked him about his escape from prison, and he readily
told me what he could. . . ."

*   *   *   *   *

"I remember that we spent not more than six months
at Peterborough Villa. Herzen was fond of changing
from one house, and even from one neighbourhood, to
another:[1] he soon became aware of all the inconveniences
of any house he had taken, and could not bear seeing the
same faces in the omnibuses that plied backwards and
forwards between the centre of the city and the suburb.
Peterborough Villa had besides a great drawback. It
was not a detached house, but was joined by a party wall
to another next door to it. On Sundays various circles
gathered at our house: Czernecki and Tchorszewski
invariably, Germans, Italians, Frenchmen. Sometimes
one of them would bring a new casual visitor. Gradually they all grew lively, some one would begin playing
the piano, sometimes they sang in chorus. The children,
too, took part in the singing, and soon there would be
laughter and an uproar of merriment. Then a knocking
at the wall would remind us that it was highly reprehensible to spend a Sunday like this in England. That
used to make Herzen very indignant, and he would
declare that there was no living in England except in a
house standing quite apart and alone. He commissioned
his friend Saffi, who often took long walks in the remoter
parts of the town, to look out for a detached house for
him. When Saffi at last found Tinkler's or Laurel
House (it was called by both names), he invited Herzen

[1] Herzen lived twelve years in London, and during that time took
no less than seven different houses: (1) 'a house in one of the
remotest parts of the town, near Primrose Hill'; (2) Chomley
Lodge, Richmond; (3) Peterborough Villa, Finchley Road; (4)
Laurel House, Fulham; (5) Park House, Putney Bridge; (6)
Orsett House, Wimbledon; (7) Elmfield House, Teddington.—
(*Translator's Note.*)

to go over it with him, and they were both very much pleased with it.

Laurel House was in every respect the opposite of Peterborough Villa. With its iron roof painted red, it looked more like an English farm than a town house, and on the side next the garden it was entirely covered with greenery; ivy twined from the bottom to the top of its walls; in front of the house there was a big oval lawn with little paths round it; there were bushes of lilac, fragrant syringa, and other flowering shrubs on all sides; there were masses of flowers, and there was even a little greenhouse.

Dear house, how happy we were in it, and how rapidly and successfully all that made the life of the two friends developed in it!

Every day Herzen's elder daughter and I used to gather two nosegays, putting a big fragrant white lily in the middle; one was for the drawing-room, the other for Ogaryov's room. . . ."

"We moved into our new abode and settled in happily. Herzen could go into London by rail, the station was only a few paces away. And when he was too late for the train, he could take the omnibus which went from Putney Bridge to the City every ten minutes.

Herzen used to get up at six in the morning, which is very early for London habits; but, not expecting the same early rising from the servants, he used to read for some hours in his study. He read for a little while, too, when he went to bed; and we sat up till after eleven, sometimes even later, so that he had hardly six hours' sleep. After dinner, as a rule, he was at home, and then he usually read aloud something from history or literature within the grasp of his elder girl, and, when she had gone to bed, he read aloud books suitable for his son's age. Herzen followed every new scientific discovery and read everything new in the literary way that appeared in any European country or in America.

At nine o'clock in the morning coffee was served in the dining-room. Herzen used to drink a whole glass of very strong coffee, in which he would put a tablespoonful of cream; he liked very good coffee. Then he read *The Times*, made his own deductions, and told us various bits of news. He did not like the politics of *The Times*, but thought it essential to read it. Then he went into the drawing-room, where he worked without a break till lunch. Between one and two there was lunch, consisting of two dishes, almost always cold meat and something left from the previous day's dinner. A jug of pale ale and a little claret or sherry stood on the table. Herzen was very fond of pale ale and drank it every day. Ogaryov was always late in the morning; by the time that he came down to the dining-room Herzen had always left it. But at lunch we all gathered together, the door was thrown open into the garden, and the children ran off to play in the open air. Then the friends talked of their work, of the articles they had to write, and so on. Sometimes one of them brought a finished article and read it aloud.

One day, soon after we had moved into Laurel House, Ogaryov said to Herzen after lunch, in my presence: 'You know, Alexandr, the *Polar Star* and your *Past and Thoughts* are all very good, but that's not what's wanted; it's not talking with our own people; we ought to bring out a journal regularly, once a fortnight, or once a month; we could state our views, our hopes for Russia, and so on.'

Herzen was delighted with the idea. 'Yes,' he cried eagerly, 'we will bring out a journal, we will name it the *Bell*, the bell that calls men to council, we two together just as we were only two together on the Sparrow Hills—and who knows, perhaps some one will answer our call!'

From that day they began getting ready articles for the *Bell*; soon afterwards the first number of the Russian paper appeared in London. Trübner, who always bought Herzen's works, or took them on commission, took the *Bell* also. He sent it about in all directions, and soon it was heard of even in Russia. About that time Turgenev arrived from Paris. Ogaryov and Herzen told him the joyful tidings, and showed him the first number of the *Bell*, but Turgenev did not at all approve of the plan. As a refined writer with rare gifts and exceptionally elegant taste, he was delighted at the publication of the *Polar Star* and *My Past and Thoughts*, but, never in close sympathy with political views and movements, he refused to believe that two men living isolated in England could carry on a real correspondence with their far-away country, could find in themselves anything to tell or could understand its needs.

'No, it's impossible,' said Turgenev; 'give up this fantastic notion, don't waste your energies; you have plenty of work as it is, *the Polar Star* and *My Past and Thoughts*, and there are only you two.'

'Well, the thing is begun now, and we must go on with it,' they answered.

'It won't and can't be a success, and literature will lose a great deal,' Turgenev protested hotly.

But the friends did not take his advice, whether from a presentiment that the *Bell* would rouse many from their slumber and find contributors, or from simple obstinacy, I cannot say.

With Turgenev, Vassily Petrovitch Botkin, author of the *Letters from Spain*, came to see us. I knew something of him from Herzen's description and from the sketch 'Basil and Armance,'[1] but I must own that he seemed to me more eccentric than I had expected. He could speak of nothing without theatrical affectation, and was, more-

---

[1] See vol. ii. p. 403. — (*Translator's Note.*)

over, a great gourmand, and moved, one may say, to
tenderness at the sight of dishes which he particularly
liked. He presented a complete contrast to our household, in which no one cared enough even to order the
daily dinner. François himself chose the menu and
cooked the dinner for eight o'clock in the evening. When
anything was particularly nice we all praised it, but no
one except Herzen criticised the cooking, and he only
very rarely.

After lunch Herzen and Ogaryov went off, each in
accordance with his tastes and inclinations. Herzen
would go by train or omnibus as far as the crowded
streets, and there stroll about, looking at the brightly
lighted shop windows, and he watched and observed a
great deal that went on in the street. He went into
different coffee-houses, generally asked for a tiny glass
of absinthe and a syphon of Seltzer water, and read there
newspapers of all kinds. . . . He often brought home
with him savouries or sauces, the choice of which he did
not care to leave to François' taste. Often, too, he brought
us something we particularly liked, a lobster, or a special
cheese, occasionally curaçao, or sweet things for the
children, crystallised fruits or dried cherries. When
he was in a very good humour, he liked to make us all
guess whom he had met in London. I could read his
mobile, expressive features so well that I could always
tell; and so he would exclude me, and I was always
left to guess last.

When Ogaryov went out of our peaceful suburb,
Fulham, he tried to find still more solitary places for his
walks. He lived in his inner life, people worried him,
but he was fond of them in his own way, was particularly
compassionate and excessively kind to every one. Instinctively he held aloof from his fellow-men; but
when chance threw him into contact with them, he was
so good-hearted and unconstrained that none of the

people who talked to him imagined how oppressive they all were to him. Herzen, on the contrary, was fond of people, and though he was sometimes irritated if some one came at the wrong time, his interest was quickly aroused and he was glad to see them. Company was necessary to him, he was only afraid of bores.

On Sunday everything in England is locked up. The whole of London is transformed into a sort of huge cupboard; shops, bakeries, coffee-houses, restaurants, even the milkshops, are closed. Silence reigns in the streets, the only movement is in the parks, and even there it is not like week-days. Here and there in the distance one sees preachers surrounded by dense crowds of people listening with strained attention in unbroken silence. The children walk decorously, not one bowls a hoop nor tosses a ball in the air—and all this irritated Herzen. He did not like going out on Sundays, and was obliged to keep in hiding from the unceremonious visitors who called all day long from early morning. On such days he stayed longer at work, while the two elder children and I entertained the boring visitors in the garden. Little by little more interesting people began to arrive, the bell never stopped ringing; then Herzen at last joined us. When he came out everything was transformed and animated; there was a continual flow of entertaining talk, discussion and interesting news, mostly political. He was for his circle what the sun is for nature. As a rule he had extremely good health. . . . Once he caught a very bad chill and had a high temperature and shooting pain in his side; both Ogaryov and I were much alarmed and sent at once for our doctor and friend, the exile Deville. The latter was very fond of Herzen, and came several times a day while he was ill, but in less than a week the patient was on his legs again."

     *   *   *   *   *

"At that period so many Russians came that the servants

were constantly making mistakes; at last Herzen arranged
that all newcomers should be shown into the other half
of the drawing-room, where I saw them and learned
who they were, how long they were to be in London,
and so on. Those who had come only for a day or two
on purpose to deliver manuscripts, had to see him at once,
for they always had a great deal they wanted to tell him
by word of mouth. . . . When people arrived who
were already known to him personally, or through their
works, Herzen was overjoyed, and gladly left his work
for their sakes; in such cases I called him to see them at
once, but as a rule I gave him the visitor's name, etc.,
and then asked them to come when he was at leisure,
that is, at two or three o'clock in the afternoon. Then
after sitting a little with his visitors, he would suggest
going with them into London, for he needed fresh air
and exercise after his sedentary work.

Herzen used to try to keep Russians away on Sundays,
for we sometimes had so many visitors on that day that
it was impossible to be sure that no spy made his way in
with them. But it was not easy to induce the Russians
to be careful; they often would come on Sundays all
the same, and were often unnecessarily open with everybody, mentioning their own surnames, though all of us
made it a rule when introducing visitors from Russia to
Poles or other Russians, to say: 'Our fellow-countryman
whose name I have forgotten, or I have not heard,' and
when introducing them to foreigners, we said: 'Un
compatriote, le nom de famille est trop difficile à pro-
noncer, trop barbare pour les oreilles occidentales,
appelez-le par le nom de baptême—M. Alexandre,' or
some Christian name.

I believe that not a single person came to harm through
carelessness on the part of Herzen or any of his household. He always refused to give a note in his own hand-
writing addressed to anybody in Russia, and did not like

giving his portrait, maintaining that to do so was unnecessary imprudence.

Unhappily I cannot say the same for Bakunin; later on, when he came to London, he was guilty of thoughtless actions which had deplorable consequences; he was like a child playing with fire."

*   *   *   *   *

"One day a short, rather lame Russian came to see Herzen, who had a great deal of conversation with him. Now that he is no longer in this world I may reveal a secret known only to me, I may tell the reason which brought him to London. After his first visit Herzen said to Ogaryov and me: 'I am very glad N. has come, he has brought us a treasure, only not a word must be said about it in his lifetime. Look, Ogaryov,' Herzen went on, handing him a manuscript, 'it's the Memoirs of Catherine the Second, written by her in French; look at the spelling of the period; it's an authentic copy.' By the time the Memoirs of Catherine were published, N. was in Germany. From Germany he wrote to Herzen that he would like to translate these Memoirs into Russian. Herzen was delighted to send him a copy, and a month later the translation was published by Czernecki; I don't remember who translated the book into German and English, I only know that the Memoirs of Catherine the Second appeared simultaneously in four languages and made an extraordinary sensation throughout Europe. The editions were quickly exhausted. Many people maintained that Herzen had written the Memoirs himself, others were puzzled to think how they came into Herzen's hands. Efforts were made to discover who had brought them from Russia, but that was a secret known only to N. himself and three other persons who had been trained to silence under Nicholas the First.

I forgot to say when speaking of Herzen's character, that he was very impressionable. Though as a rule of a serene and at times even gay and mirthful disposition, he was apt to become suddenly gloomy if anything disagreeable happened. Such depression was frequently caused by his carelessness, which grew upon him in the trifling affairs of daily life; he was very precise in business, and never forgot anything relating to the printing-press, to money matters, or to any questions affecting people. When he set off after lunch to London he would think he had remembered everything; his letters and his proofs were ready—he would say good-bye, looking cheerful, but five minutes later there would be a terrific ring at the bell: this was Herzen back again with a gloomy face and a voice of exasperation. 'I have forgotten everything,' he would say in despair, 'and now the train will be gone before I can get back to the station.'

'Well, go by the omnibus, then,' his son would tell him, unable to help smiling at his despair.

We all rushed to look for what was lost, ran to the drawing-room where he had been writing, or to his own room, and sometimes came back unsuccessful; no letters, no proofs! Occasionally it turned out that they were in his pocket; unluckily, he had so many pockets in his coat and in the cloak which he wore over it to keep off the London dust; then Herzen, more wrathful than ever, would have to cross Fulham Bridge to the omnibus office, and just as he approached it would see one going off, and have to wait there ten minutes for the next."

     *   *   *   *   *

"At Laurel House Ogaryov and I once got up some theatricals for the children. . . . I made two red shirts for Herzen and Ogaryov. Sasha put on a fur-lined coat inside out to represent a bear, and Ogaryov, in a red shirt, was the bear-leader. The red shirt was very becoming to him. With his big fair beard and curly head he looked a typical Russian peasant. On the other hand, the red shirt did not suit Herzen at all, he looked like a foreigner in it.

Not supposing that he would mind, I blurted this out, and Herzen would never put on the red shirt again."

      *   *   *   *   *

[Somewhere about 1856 Herzen sent his son, who had been a brilliant student of natural science in London, winning a silver and then a gold medal in examinations, to Geneva to study under his old friend, Karl Vogt. After six months in Geneva, the young man entered the University of Berne, and there lived in the family of old Professor Vogt. In 1859 Herzen's cousin,[1] Madame Passek, visited Berne and saw the young student there. She writes:]

"In Berne we stopped for a few days at the Hotel au Faucon, and at once sent a note to Alexandr's son, who was about to take his final in medicine at the University of Berne, and was living in the family of Professor Vogt, a man greatly respected by every one. A few minutes later he arrived; he was a young man with long fair hair, kind, pleasant face, and blue eyes like his mother's. He had left Russia as a child of seven, but had not forgotten us; he was glad to see us, and at once made such friends that with all the ardour and simplicity of youth he confided to us his love for Emma, the thirteen-year-old granddaughter of the Vogts. He said he had asked his father's permission to propose to her formally and after the engagement to wait till she came of age; but his father would not consent, and was vexed at his falling in love so young. 'I reminded my father,' he said, 'that he was not much older than I am when he fell in love and married; he did not like this, and now we are having a disagreeable correspondence.'

'But why is your father against your love?' I asked. 'The Vogts are an excellent family, he respects them, and is a friend of their son, the famous naturalist, Karl Vogt.'

[1] See vol. i. p. 67.—(*Translator's Note.*)

'Well, you see, he has got it into his head that I should marry a Russian, should live for Russia, love Russia. But how can one love what one doesn't know? I hardly remember Russia, it is a foreign country for me, and what can I do for it? I am not a politician, I am a man of peace. If I had a plot of land in Switzerland, Emma, and my books, that would be enough for me.'

'Do the Vogts know of your love for Emma, and what is their attitude?'

'They know and strongly disapprove—that makes my position all the more difficult.'

We spent about a fortnight in Berne; Alexandr's son spent whole days with us. Through him we got to know the Vogts; they treated us like old friends and often kept us to dinner. We dined at their famous round family table, which had served several generations of Vogts and Vollens. . . . The gifted zoologist, Karl Vogt, came to see his parents while we were in Berne. He was a man of clear, realistic intellect and of the happiest disposition. He did not waste his energies in yearning for impractical ideals; he was passionately fond of nature, work was for him a pleasure, not a task, and he did not ask from man or nature more than they could give. . . . In Berne Alexandr's son introduced us to Emma. With her grandmother's permission he brought her from Zurich, where she was at boarding-school. She was still a child, fresh and rosy, with bright, merry blue eyes—still a chrysalis, as Herzen said of her.

After a fortnight in Berne we moved to Geneva. . . . Our young friend soon came to see us there, and told us that he had formally proposed to Emma, had informed her grandparents, and obtained their consent, and had, as her recognised betrothed, been with her to call on all their friends and relations. He had done all this without his father's knowledge, and now asked me to break the news to him and try to settle it all peaceably.

It was settled peaceably—in appearance; but Alexandr was planning to put an end to the engagement.

When his son came to London, however, with his fiancée to introduce Emma to his family, Alexandr met them at the railway station with a carriage and drove the betrothed child to his house; everything there had been prepared for her reception, and all the time she spent with him she was surrounded with tenderness and attention; but this was all.

When Emma's parents arrived in London, Alexandr received them rather coldly, and advised them to take their daughter, till she came of age, to live with them in South America, where they were returning shortly. At the same time he sent his son on a scientific expedition to Norway and Iceland, undertaken, I believe, by Karl Vogt. During the years of parting the young people wrote to each other; the letters from America did not always reach their destination: the correspondence grew slacker and slacker, and finally ceased.

I have heard that Emma married a rich banker in South America; Alexandr's son settled in Italy, where, later on, he married; he has nine charming children, owns a villa near Florence, is devoted to farming, does scientific work, and is well known as a naturalist. The dreams of the boy of twenty have come true."[1]

[It seems probable that Natalya Alexyevna had cherished a girlish adoration[2] for Herzen during the time she spent in his company in Italy and in Paris. Now that she was

[1] Natalya Alexyevna's version is slightly different. She gives Emma Vogt's age as sixteen, and says that when the girl's parents were returning to America Herzen begged them to leave her in London, 'but they insisted on taking her with them.' Neither Madame Passek nor Madame Ogaryov can be relied upon for perfect accuracy, but I think the latter is the more trustworthy.

[2] This is how I interpret the cryptic passage on page 113, vol. iv.— (*Translator's Notes.*)

in daily contact with him, this early passion revived, and
soon eclipsed her feeling for Ogaryov. About the same
time (possibly earlier) Ogaryov formed a permanent con-
nection with an Englishwoman, Mary (her surname is
never given), by whom he had two sons, Henry (born
1857) and 'Toots.' She seems to have been a kind,
good woman, but not of much education nor of intellectual tastes. Herzen's enemies have not hesitated to
accuse him of treacherously seducing the wife of his best
friend. It must be borne in mind that Ogaryov remained on the warmest terms with Herzen, continuing
to live in his house so long as they were in England, and
no trace of resentment can be discerned. It is, indeed,
quite possible that his wife's defection may have been
rather a relief than a subject of regret to him. Moreover, the initiative and the responsibility seem to have
been hers. At first no one but Ogaryov and Herzen's
elder children understood the real position, and Natalya
Alexyevna's daughter, Liza, as a child looked upon
Ogaryov as her father. Twins, a boy and girl, were born
in 1861. Herzen seems to have found little happiness
in this new union, which was a constant source of anxiety
and misery. He was morbidly sensitive in regard to the
irregularity of the position, but accepted the tie as a
binding obligation and responsibility. Except for short
intervals of absence on business, or on visits to his children
or his friends, he lived with Natalya Alexyevna to the
end of his life, though he does in his letters to Ogaryov
talk of escaping from his bondage.

In 1858, just after the birth of Liza, Natalya Alexyevna's mother arrived.]

"Herzen now thought our house overcrowded, and
shortly afterwards took another, called Park House, also
in Fulham and not far away, with a big garden and a fairly
large vegetable patch. My mother moved with us and

spent six weeks there. Though Park House was in some respects very superior to Laurel House, I regretted the beautiful flower-garden we had left. There was a very spacious verandah along one whole side of the new house looking into the garden, and there we used to spend the greater part of the day. On the ground floor there were the kitchen and a little room for washing up the crockery, and another tiny closet with an open rack in which the plates were stood to dry without being wiped. These adjuncts to the kitchen are usual in all English houses; in fact, Herzen used to say that English houses were so exactly alike in the arrangement of the rooms and even of the furniture, that he could find any room and any object in them with his eyes bandaged. . . ."

[The difference between the Russian and the English attitude (at that period) in regard to law and punishment is well illustrated by the following domestic incident.]

"We had four servants in Park House. . . and on Saturdays, as in all English houses, a charwoman came to scrub and clean everything, even the front doorsteps. Mazzini recommended Herzen an Italian cook, Tassinari, a revolutionary and ardent patriot. . . a stout, fresh-looking man, in spite of his grey hair and long white beard, with a clever, expressive face and big bright black eyes. He was an excellent cook, and Herzen was well satisfied with him. . . but he had one great defect, jealousy or envy—painful as it is to admit it, those two feelings are closely akin. The Irish housemaid, who was very much with us, as she looked after my little girl, aroused this feeling particularly. He was always finding fault with her, would not give her lunch in the morning if she did not come in at once when the bell rang, and so on. We brought from Laurel House with us a middle-aged German called Trina, who took the children out and read German with them. She had been with us for six months, and seemed to be fond of us. One day Jules, our manservant, said to me: 'Isn't it sad for poor Trina, madam; last Sunday she was taking the wages you paid her to her sister's, and in the crush in the omnibus she had her pocket picked.'

'Why didn't she tell me?' I asked.

'I expect she didn't like to,' answered Jules.

I went to Ogaryov and Herzen; they gave me the money and I handed it to Trina. She thanked me, but seemed overcome with confusion and did not look me in the face. I imagine it was a clever trick on her part. Not long after this, Trina was suddenly taken ill with acute rheumatism, and could not move hand or foot; we sent for a doctor and a nurse, but she soon begged to be taken to the hospital. Herzen hired an omnibus, she was with the greatest care carried down on a mattress and driven at a walking pace to the hospital. Some months later, when she had completely recovered, she came back to us. That was just when we were leaving Laurel House. Then Jules lost his silver watch; he could not imagine who had taken it, but was inclined to suspect the gardener and his wife. I was very much annoyed at this suspicion, but I had no positive proofs by which I could convince Jules that he was mistaken. We had been for nearly two years at Laurel House, the same gardener had been there all the time, and nothing had ever been missed. After her return Trina went on visiting her sister, who kept, I believe, a baker's shop; she even took to asking me to let her stay the night there, as it was a long way off; this was very inconvenient, but I put up with it, as I liked her.

One day, when Trina was at her sister's, Tassinari came into the dining-room looking worried. 'Madam,' he said, they came yesterday from the chandler's, where we have an account; you know they are also carriers, that is, they deliver parcels all over the town.'

'Well, what then?' I asked.

'You will see in a minute,' our cook answered. 'Do you know this address, madam?' and he handed me a piece of paper.

'It's Trina's sister's name,' I answered, glancing at it.

'They let us know,' Tassinari went on, 'parcels are very often sent from Park House to that address, and that there is often something that clinks in the parcels. It's always the same box; it comes back empty and is sent off from here full. . . . I told them to keep back the box, which was to be sent to that address yesterday; would not you like to look what there is in it, madam?'

'Of course not,' I answered warmly, 'you can't open another person's boxes. Trina is sending something to her sister,' I said, with a simplicity certainly excessive at my years; but the thought that she was capable of stealing did not enter my head; besides, I imagined this was another instance of Tassinari's fault-finding ways. The Italian smiled.

'Then shall I ask Monsieur Herzen?' and he went off and knocked at the drawing-room door.

Herzen listened to him and gave him leave to bring in the box. Tassinari was triumphant; he quickly reappeared with the box, deftly unfastened the lid, and began picking things out with a gleeful face; there were curtains, ribbons, children's smocks, and I don't know what else; I stood overwhelmed.

'Herzen,' I said, 'could Trina really . . . ?'

He looked at me with sympathy for my distress.

'She could,' he said.

He told Tassinari to pack the things in the box again, and put it in the other half of the room, then dismissed him.

'When Trina comes,' said Herzen, 'show her that box; we shall see what explanation she gives. Of course, it is all very clear and simple, but what matters is this: by English law we are bound to prosecute a thief, or we are liable to a considerable fine, and nothing would induce me to hand over a thief to the police. Let her go back to Germany, for we can't give her a character. . . .'

It was a long time before Trina returned; I suppose she was waiting for the arrival of her box. At last she came into the drawing-room, with apologies for having stayed away so long, but turned pale and said no more when she saw the box on the table. After listening to her protestations that she had done wrong only once, I gave her Herzen's advice to go back to Germany, which she at once agreed to do. Three days later she left our house, together with the Irish housemaid, who had been in the secret, and had carried the box to the chandler's."

       *   *   *   *   *

"Malwide von Meysenbug had all this time been living apart from us, sometimes in lodgings and sometimes with friends, but she looked forward to an independent life and to visiting Paris and Italy, where she had never been. She suggested that she should take Herzen's younger daughter, Olga, with her on a visit to Madame Schwabe, the widow of a wealthy banker with a large family and a splendid estate in England. As Madame Schwabe was going to Paris for the winter, Malwide asked Herzen to let Olga go with them. . . . Soon afterwards Malwide left Madame Schwabe and settled alone with little Olga."

[Olga, who was devoted to Malwide, remained with her permanently. In a letter from Fräulein von Meysenbug to Wagner she gives a charming picture of the little girl's enthusiasm at a performance in Paris of one of Wagner's operas, and her audible indignation when some of the audience hissed the new music]

"Among the Russians who came to see Herzen at Park House, I cannot pass over Alexandr Serno-Solovyo-

vitch, at that time a very young man. Herzen liked him
very much: it was evident that, in spite of his youth, he
had read and thought much; he was intelligent and
interested in all the important questions of the day. I
don't remember where the rest of the family had gone,
but I know they were obliged to be out one day when
Serno-Solovyovitch particularly wanted to see the
Zoological Gardens. I went with him, taking Natasha,
Olga, and my baby Liza. Serno-Solovyovitch inspected
the Gardens thoroughly, and was very charming and
attentive to the children. He spent a few days more
in London, continually seeing Herzen and Ogaryov,
and showing them the greatest warmth and respect. At
that time his bad qualities were slumbering, and circumstances had not yet arisen to develop them. I shall have
to speak of him later. . . . It is painful to think how
this intelligent and cultured man perished in a strange
land without being of any service to his country, brought
to ruin by vanity, envy, and despair; but I must speak of
him not so much on his own account as because in his
relations with him Herzen's innate characteristics — a
magnanimity, kindness, and compassion almost passing
belief — were so strikingly displayed."

[In the summer of 1859 Natalya Alexyevna, hearing
from her sister, Madame Satin, that she was visiting
Germany with her children, went to Dresden with her
baby Liza and Natasha Herzen, then to Heidelberg
with her sister, where she saw many old friends and met
Madame Passek for the first time, and then to Berne to
stay with the Vogts. On returning to London the following winter she found Herzen and Ogaryov installed in
Orsett House, a large house of five storeys, in Westburn
Terrace, Wimbledon.]

"Herzen told me that while I was away an artist,

Madame O'Connell, a complete stranger, had written asking him to give her five sittings. At the first sitting she had been extremely kind, and had told him that having heard a great deal about him she wanted to paint a portrait of him for posterity. . . . What became of the portrait I do not know."

[In the summer of 1861[1] Herzen went with his daughter Natasha to Paris to see Olga, who was ill, and there]

"After long years of separation he met his cousin, Tatyana Passek.[2] He told us a great deal about this, and said that the Yakovlyevs[3] had treated her very badly and taken possession of her share of the family property. When she had been in need of money, Herzen had lent her what she wanted and had never asked for repayment. In his views he had moved far away from the friend of his youth. Madame Passek was religious, and regarded the monarchy as the salvation of Russia.

They disputed hotly, both stoutly defending their convictions, and parted with a smile, conscious that only the grave could reconcile their divergent views, and that as long as they lived they would be warriors in opposing camps."

"Soon after Herzen's return from France, he received visitors who greatly interested us all—Sergey Ivanovitch Turgenev and Lyov Nikolaevitch Tolstoy. The former we had known for years, and we were used to his caprices and little peculiarities; the latter we saw for the first time.

Not long before leaving Russia, Ogaryov and I had

---

[1] See vol. v. p. 245.   [2] See vol.i. chapter iii.
[3] Yakovlyev was the surname of the two brothers, Ivan, Herzen's father, and Pyotr, Madame Passek's father.—(*Translator's Notes*.)

read Tolstoy's *Childhood, Boyhood, and Youth*, and tales of the Crimean War, with enthusiasm. Ogaryov was constantly talking of these tales and of their author.

When we came to London, we hastened to tell Herzen about this new and exceptionally gifted writer. It turned out that Herzen had read several of his works already, and was delighted with them. He particularly admired the boldness with which Tolstoy spoke of feelings so subtle and deeply concealed that no one had put them into words, though many had perhaps experienced them. As regards his philosophical views, Herzen thought them feeble, misty, and often unsupported by evidence.

'Tolstoy is in our house!' Natasha and I thought, and we hurried into the drawing-room to have a look at the illustrious fellow-countryman, who was being read by all Russia. When we went in Count Tolstoy was carrying on a heated argument with Turgenev. Ogaryov and Herzen, too, were taking part in the discussion. At that time (1861) Tolstoy looked about thirty-five; he was of medium height, his features were ugly, there was a piercing and yet dreamy look in his little grey eyes. It was odd that his face never wore that expression of child-like good-nature sometimes seen in Turgenev's smile, and so attractive in him.

As we went in, the usual introductions began. Of course, Tolstoy had no idea that we were so excited at seeing him that we hardly dared to speak to him, but only listened to what he said to other people. He came to see us every day. It was soon obvious that he was far more sympathetic as a writer than as a thinker, for he was sometimes illogical; in defence of his fatalism, he often had heated arguments with Turgenev, in the course of which they said extremely disagreeable things to each other. When there was no discussion going on, and when Tolstoy was in a good humour, he would sit down at the piano and sing us the soldiers' songs composed in the Crimea during the war:

> 'On the eighth day of September,
> How the devil brought us here
> To camp upon the mountains,' etc.

We laughed as we listened, but in reality it was painful to hear of what was done in the Crimea—the light-hearted way in which the fate of thousands of soldiers was entrusted to incompetent generals, and the incredible amount of thieving that went on. Even lint was stolen and sold to the enemy, while our long-suffering soldiers were dying."

"Every year Turgenev paid one or two visits to London.

Once he came to see us soon after writing *Faust*. He read it aloud to us, but neither Ogaryov nor Herzen liked it; the latter was, however, very reserved in his observations, while the former criticised it very severely. From that day Turgenev lost all liking for Ogaryov.

I remember on one visit to London Turgenev was particularly good-humoured and sweet to Herzen.

'Do you know,' he said to him, 'I have not come alone this time. Simply to see you, a queer fellow has set off on his travels, without knowing a word of any foreign language, and begged me to take him to London. Isn't that heroic? Guess who it is. But I tell you what,' he went on, 'perhaps you had better call on him first: Ogaryov may not care much about seeing him; there were some misunderstandings. . .'

'Goodness,' said Herzen, 'surely it's not Nekrassov? He knows no foreign language. What makes him suppose I should care to see him after the message he sent Ogaryov through you, Sergey Ivanovitch?'

'But you know he has come all the way from Russia on purpose to see you!'

'He can go back again,' said Herzen, and he was not to be moved. He was always far more ready to resent a slight to Ogaryov than to himself.

For three days Turgenev went on trying to persuade Herzen to see Nekrassov, but he was forced in the end to submit, and to take the latter back without obtaining an interview."

*   *   *   *   *

"When they met in Paris in 1869, they talked about literature, and Herzen asked Turgenev what he was writing.

'I am writing nothing,' he answered, 'I am no longer read in Russia; I have begun writing in German for Germans, and publishing in Berlin. . . .'

Turgenev joked, but he was inwardly sore at the estrangement of his fellow-countrymen. From the age of five-and-twenty he had been the spoilt darling of fortune; his fame had grown steadily; later on, thanks to Viardot's translations, he became no less famous in Europe, and the doors of all the best salons of Paris and London were thrown open to him; he was being spoilt by success, when his own country suddenly drew back and turned away from him, and what for? His faithful picture of Nihilism in *Fathers and Children.* He wrote as the nightingale sings, with no idea of wounding any one's vanity; he wrote because writing was his vocation, but the younger generation in Russia saw a spiteful intention in it, were resentful, and were up in arms against Turgenev. These strained relations with his own people lasted for several years.

Herzen disliked the anti-aesthetic side of Nihilism, and was surprised at the indignation of young Russia with Turgenev. He used to say to Russians: 'Why, Bazarov is the apotheosis of Nihilism; the Nihilists never rise to his level. There is a great deal of humanity in Bazarov; what is there for them to be offended at?'

Herzen and Turgenev had both fallen on evil days; they were both ostracised by social opinion in Russia at that time, Turgenev for his vivid presentation of Nihilism, Herzen for his sympathy with Poland. The latter's views and principles always led him, of course, to espouse the cause of the weaker, but he had taken no part in Polish affairs. There were, however, evil-disposed persons who hinted that he had done so, and this was enough to make almost every one abandon him."

"In 1861, not long before the Emancipation of the Serfs, Herzen had a letter with the London postmark, and from a Russian, asking permission to call on him. The letter was simply written and dignified, though not free from mistakes in spelling. Herzen, as always, answered that he would be glad to see a fellow countryman. A young man appeared and explained that he was a peasant of the Simbirsk province, and that his name was Martyanov. He was a tall, graceful, fair man, with regular features and a rather cold-looking, ironical expression that seemed full of a sense of his own dignity. He was engaged on translation of some sort, and had been for some time in London. At first Herzen was rather mistrustful of him, but soon Martyanov's character showed itself so clearly that it was unthinkable to suspect him of being a spy. He was of an unusually straightforward disposition and of sharply-defined views; he believed in the Russian peasantry and in the Russian Tsar. He was not very talkative as a rule, but at times he spoke with great enthusiasm.

Sad to relate, this perfectly loyal Russian citizen came to a sad end. After the Emancipation of the Serfs, the Polish demonstrations and the pacification of Poland, Martyanov decided to return to Russia. At the frontier he was detained and sent to Siberia. What for he never knew.

The rumours of the Emancipation of the Serfs were at last confirmed, ceased to be rumours and became truth, the great and joyful truth. As he was reading the *Moscow News* in his study one day, Herzen ran his eyes over the preamble of the manifesto, gave a violent tug at the bell, and, keeping the paper in his hand, ran out with it on to the stairs, shouting loudly in his resonant voice:

'Ogaryov, Natalie, Natasha, come, make haste!'

Jules was the first to run out, asking:

'Monsieur a sonné?'

'Je ne sais pas, peut-être, mais que diable, Jules, allez les chercher tous, vite—vite; qu'est-ce qu'ils ne viennent pas?'

Jules looked at him with surprise and pleasure.

'Monsieur a Pair bien heureux,' he said.

'Ah! diable! je crois bien,' Herzen answered carelessly.

At that instant we all ran up from different directions, expecting something out of the ordinary, and from Herzen's voice something good. He waved the paper at us, but would not answer our questions till he was back in his study with us following him.

'Sit down and listen,' he said, and he began reading the manifesto. His voice broke with emotion; at last, he passed the paper to Ogaryov. 'You read it,' he said, 'I can't go on.'

Ogaryov read the manifesto through in his quiet, gentle voice, though he was inwardly as rejoiced as Herzen; but his feelings were always differently expressed.

Then Herzen suggested that they should go together for a walk in the town; he wanted air and movement. Ogaryov preferred his solitary walks, but on this occasion he readily agreed. At eight o'clock they came back to dinner. Herzen put a little bottle of curaçao on the table and we all drank a glass, congratulating each other on the great and joyful news.

'Ogaryov,' said Herzen, 'I want to celebrate the great event. Perhaps,' he went on with feeling, 'there may be no happier day in our lives. You know we live like workmen, nothing but toil and labour; we ought sometimes to rest and look back over the distance we have come, and to rejoice at the happy solution of the question so near our hearts; perhaps we, too, have done our bit towards it.'

'And you,' he went on, turning to Natasha and me, 'must get ready some coloured flags and sew big letters in white calico on them; on one, "Emancipation of the Peasants in Russia, February 19, 1861," on another, "Russian Free Press in London," and so on. We will have a dinner for Russians; I 'll write an article about it and read it aloud; I have the heading already: "Thou hast conquered, Galilean." Yes, the Tsar has conquered me by accomplishing the great task. At the Russian dinner I will propose in my own house a toast to the health of the Tsar. Whoever removes the obstacles that hinder the advance of Russia towards progress and prosperity is not acting against us. In the evening we will invite not only Russians, but all foreigners who sympathise with this great event, all who are rejoicing with us.'

At last the day for this festival was fixed. . . . Flags were made, English words were sewn on them, and little glass lamps of different colours were procured for illuminating the house. Prince Golitsyn,[1] hearing of Herzen's plan, undertook to write a quartet, which he called 'Emancipation,' and performed it on the occasion.

On the morning of the festive day we had not very many guests, only Russians and Poles. Among others there were Martyanov, Prince Pyotr Dolgorukov, and Count Uvarov. Tchorszewski came later than the rest; I remember we were all in the drawing-room when he arrived.

[1] See vol. v. p. 82. — (*Translator's Note.*)

'Alexandr Ivanovitch, it is not a day for rejoicing; Russians are shedding Polish blood in Warsaw!' said Tchorszewski, breathless.

'What?' cried Herzen.

'Impossible!' exclaimed the others. Tchorszewski took out of his pocket photographs of the slain which he had just received from Warsaw.

'There have been demonstrations there,' he told us; 'the Poles were praying in the street; all of a sudden the word of command rang out, and Russian bullets felled several men who were kneeling in prayer.'

All pressed round Tchorszewski and examined the photographs. Herzen was pale and silent. His face was overcast, the serene and happy expression was replaced by a look of anxiety, trouble, and sadness.

Jules announced that dinner was served. We all went down to the dining-room, every face looked troubled. . . . When champagne was handed round, Herzen stood up and proposed a toast to Russia, to its prosperity, its progress, and so on. We all stood glass in hand, every one responded warmly, and other toasts were proposed. . . . Herzen made a short speech, of which I remember the first sentence: 'Friends, our day of rejoicing is darkened by unexpected news; blood is flowing in Warsaw, Slav blood, and it is shed by brother Slavs!'

There was a hush, and all sat down again in silence.

In the evening the house was lighted up; flags fluttered on it; Prince Golitsyn conducted his quartet in the drawing-room. In response to Herzen's invitation in the *Bell*, there was a great gathering not only of our Russian and Polish friends, but also of the Italian *émigrés*, Mazzini and Saffi among them, the French exiles, among whom Louis Blanc and Talandier were conspicuous, as well as Germans, English people, and numbers of Poles and Russians whom we did not know.

At moments it seemed as though Herzen had forgotten

the events at Warsaw and recovered his gaiety. Once he even stood on a chair, and with great feeling said: 'A new era is coming for Russia, and we shall be in Russia again, friends; I do not despair of it, the nineteenth of February is a great day!' Kelsiev and some fellow-countrymen whom we did not know responded. There were so many people that nobody could sit down. Even outside our house there was such a huge crowd that policemen had to stand there all the evening to protect the place from thieves.

A photographer took a view of our house lighted up and decked with flags. The figure of Prince Yury Golitsyn was seen on the steps. This photograph was reproduced on the cover of the published quartet 'Emancipation.' I preserved a copy, but it was taken from me, together with my books, at the Russian frontier.

A few days after this celebration, Herzen wrote the article headed 'Mater Dolorosa,' in which he expressed his sympathy with the oppressed Poles, and published it in the following number of the *Bell.*

Martyanov came to Herzen after reading this article and said:

'You have buried the *Bell* to-day, Alexandr Ivano-vitch; no, you can't revive it now, you have laid it in its grave.'

And so the first blow to the *Bell* was given it by Herzen himself through showing sympathy to suffering Poland. Russian *amour-propre* was wounded, and little by little every one turned away from the London publi-cations. The second blow to the *Bell* was dealt later by Bakunin.

One day after dinner the postman rang the bell, and Herzen opened a huge letter. It was from Bakunin, who wrote describing his escape from Siberia and the sympathy shown him in America.

Bakunin expressed a hope that he would soon be in London and helping his friends in their propaganda, writing for the *Bell*, and so on. Herzen pondered after reading the letter, then said to Ogaryov:

'I must own I am afraid of Bakunin's coming, he will be sure to ruin our work. You remember what Caussidière —or Lamartine, was it?—said of him in 1848: "Notre ami Bakounine est un homme impayable le jour de la Revolution, mais le lendemain il faut absolument le faire fusiller, car il sera impossible d'établir un ordre quelconque avec un pareil anarchiste."'

Ogaryov agreed. He, too, thought that Bakunin would not be satisfied with their propaganda, but would insist on activity after the pattern of Western European revolutionary movements. Moreover, Bakunin had always figured abroad as the champion of Poland. Herzen and Ogaryov sympathised with the sufferings of Poland, but disliked the aristocratic character of the Poles, their attitude to the lower classes, and so on. As for Bakunin, he saw nothing. . . .

I very well remember Bakunin's first appearance in our house.

It was between eight and nine in the evening, every one was sitting at table, but, as I was not very well, I was having dinner lying on the sofa. There was a loud ring at the bell, Jules ran upstairs to the front door, and in a few minutes came back with the visitor: it was Mihail Alexandrovitch Bakunin. I don't remember whether I have spoken before of his appearance. He was very tall, with an intelligent and expressive face; in his features there was a great likeness to the Muravyovs, to whom he was related. Every one stood up as Bakunin came in. The men embraced each other, Herzen introduced the children and Malwide, who happened to be dining with us. After greeting all the rest, Bakunin came up to me. He recalled our meeting in Berlin not long before the

Dresden barricades, when he was captured and handed
over to the Austrians.

'That's bad—lying down,' he said to me briskly;
'you must get well; we must be acting, not lying down.'

Bakunin sat down to the table, the dinner began to be
very lively. Afterwards he told us about his imprisonment in Austria. . . . I should like to repeat his account
of it, as far as I remember it.

Chained to the wall in an underground dungeon, he
was brought to such a pitch of misery that he resolved to
commit suicide and tried sucking phosphorus off matches.
This, however, had no satisfactory result; it gave him a
pain in his stomach, but he remained alive. After a year
and a half or two years of this existence, one night,
Bakunin told us, he was awakened by an unaccustomed
sound. Doors were being noisily opened and shut,
locks grated; at last footsteps approached nearer, and
various officials entered his cell: the governor of the
prison, warders, and an officer. They ordered Bakunin
to dress. 'I was tremendously delighted,' said Bakunin;
'whether they were taking me to be shot or transferring
me to another prison, anyway it was a change, and so
anyway it was for the better. I was taken in a closed
carriage to a railway station and put in a closed com-
partment, with tiny windows at the top. The compart-
ment must have been shunted, when we changed to
another train, for I was not led out at any station. . . .
To get a breath of fresh air, I said I was hungry, but that
did not lead to the desired result, they brought me food
to the carriage. At last we reached our destination. I
was brought out in fetters from the dark railway carriage
into the bright winter sunshine on the platform. Casting
a cursory glance round the station, I saw Russian soldiers;
my heart throbbed joyously, and I understood what was
happening.

'Would you believe it, Herzen, I was as delighted as

a child, though I could not expect anything good for myself. I was taken to a room apart, a Russian officer appeared, and they began transferring me as though I I were an inanimate object; official documents in German were read. The Austrian officer, a spare, lean man, with cold, lifeless eyes, began demanding the return of the chains riveted on me in Austria. The Russian officer, a very young, shy fellow, with a good-natured expression, agreed at once. The Austrian fetters were removed and Russian ones put on. Ah, dear friends, the chains seemed lighter, I was glad of them, and smiled happily to the young officer and the Russian soldiers. "Ah, lads," I said. "so I may die in my own country." The officer interposed, "You are not allowed to speak." The soldiers looked at me with silent curiosity. Then I was put in a closed carriage like a hen-coop, with little openings at the top. It was a very frosty night, and I was unused to fresh air. You know the rest; I wrote that I was confined in the Peter-Paul Fortress and afterwards in the Schlüsselburg, that Nicholas commanded me to write an account of my doings abroad. I complied with his desire, and at the end of my confession added: "Sire, for my openness, forgive me my German sins." On the accession of Alexander I was sent to Siberia; that blessed news reached me in the Solovetsky monastery. In Siberia I was very well off. Muravyov is a very sensible man—he did not worry me, but it is a true saying: you may feed the wolf, but he 'll still yearn for the forest. Though it was a shame to do it, I had to deceive my friends, to break away to freedom.'

But Herzen's foreboding was soon justified. With Bakunin's arrival the Polish note began to be more conspicuous in the Free Russian Press. At first Bakunin published his articles in the *Bell*; but Herzen, noticing this tendency in them, suggested that he should bring them out as separate pamphlets or print them in the series called 'Voices from Russia,' as their views diverged, and Herzen did not want to publish articles in the *Bell* with which he was not usually in complete agreement. What was most unfortunate was that Ogaryov was nearer in his ideas to Bakunin, and the latter acquired a great influence over him. And Herzen always gave way to Ogaryov, even when he recognised that Ogaryov was wrong.

While Bakunin was in London there came among other visitors from Russia an Armenian called Nalbandov. He was a man of thirty, ugly, awkward, shy, but kind-hearted, sensible, and full of sympathy for everything good. He was a wealthy man. . . . After completing his studies, I believe, in the University of Moscow, he had travelled for his own pleasure, and had been in China; on his return to Russia he heard of the *Bell* and of Herzen, and made up his mind to visit London. The first time he came to see Herzen he could scarcely speak for shyness. Afterwards, however, delighted at the friendly welcome given him, he used often to visit us. Bakunin completely took possession of him; every day he used to go about London with him, and he insisted on Nalbandov having his photograph taken. This was done in a very original way: Nalbandov had his photograph taken, back view, reading a newspaper. This queer man spent two months in London, well pleased with his stay in England, and took no part at all in the work of Russian propaganda. Yet on his way back to Russia he was arrested and clapped into some fortress in the East, where he was probably forgotten. He was ruined by the carelessness of Bakunin, who sang his praises in a letter to some relative in Russia. Bakunin's letters were, of course, opened in the post; word was sent to the frontier, and Nalbandov paid for his friendship with Bakunin. We heard no more of the fate of this truly good and worthy man.

Sad to say, Nalbandov was not the only one who

suffered from Bakunin's recklessness. The latter had a really childish inability to control his tongue.

After the Warsaw risings, when repressive measures were being taken by the Russian Government for the pacification of the country, Herzen was visited by a Russian officer, Potyebnya, who had left his regiment, but continued living in Warsaw, where he showed himself everywhere in public places, sometimes in civilian dress, sometimes disguised as a Polish monk. Occasionally he came across fellow-officers, but nobody recognised him. Potyebnya was a fair man of medium height and attractive appearance. Herzen and Ogaryov liked him very much and tried to persuade him to remain in London, but he would not. It was said that he was in love with a Polish woman, and so had gone over to the side of the Poles. He came several times when in London; the last time he said: 'I shall not fire on Russians, I could not bring myself to it.' 'Do stay with us,' said Herzen. 'I cannot,' he answered, with a mournful smile.

Potyebnya was extraordinarily nice with children. My eldest child, a little girl of four, was very fond of him. She was often present when they were talking, busy with her playthings, and we thought she noticed nothing. But we were once struck by a saying of hers to Potyebnya. It was on the last evening that he spent in Orsett House. The young officer had taken the child on his knee and was talking to her. Suddenly she said:

'Dear Potyebnya, don't go away, stay with us.'

'I can't,' he answered, 'but I will soon come back; I am not going far, only to the South of France.'

'Oh no,' she said; 'you are going to Poland, and they 'll kill you there.'

Then Herzen cried out: 'If you won't listen to us, listen to the child, who makes such a dreadful prophecy.' But Potyebnya could not be shaken in his determination, and he went back to Poland next day. A Russian bullet laid him low soon afterwards."

[In 1863 Bakunin left London with the expedition described by Herzen in volume v. pp. 169-175, and was stranded in Sweden.]

"Bakunin went to Stockholm to complain of the captain's treachery. He heard that the King's brother was a very cultured and liberal man, and hoped with his support to force the captain to continue the voyage. But Bakunin's hopes were not realised. There was a highly cultured society in Stockholm and great sympathy for every liberal movement. He was throughout his stay well received by the King of Sweden's brother, and fêted by Stockholm society as the Russian agitator of 1848. Dinners and evening parties were given in his honour, his health was drunk, and people were delighted to get the chance of seeing him, but he received no help as regards the captain. The other *émigrés* determined on bold action; they hired boats and attempted to continue on their way. But a terrible storm blew up, and all those luckless and foolhardy men perished. . . .

While Bakunin remained in Sweden hoping that another expedition would be arranged, his wife arrived in London from Siberia. I was not at home at the time; I had, on the advice of our doctor, gone to Osborne for the sake of the children. . . .

One day Herzen was sitting at his writing-table when Jules announced that a very young and pretty woman was asking to see him.

'Ask her name, Jules, I am always telling you,' said Herzen, with some impatience.

Jules went out, and at once came back with a look of astonishment on his face.

'Eh bien?' said Herzen.

'Madame Bakunin! comment, monsieur, est-ce possible?' said Jules incoherently, as he probably compared husband and wife in his mind. Herzen had heard that Bakunin had married the daughter of a Polish clerk in Siberia. 'Surely she has not turned up?' he thought. Making himself a little tidier, he went into the drawing-room, where he saw a fair, very young and handsome woman in deep mourning.

'I am Bakunin's wife; where is he?' she said. 'And you are Herzen?'

'Yes,' he answered. 'Your husband is not in London.'

'Where is he?' she repeated.

'I have no right to tell you that.'

'What, not me, his wife!' she said in a tone of offence, and she turned crimson.

'We had better talk about the Bakunins. When did you leave his brothers and sisters? What on earth is the name of their place? You have stayed in the country with them—what are the names of his brothers and sisters? I have forgotten and mixed them all up. . . .'

Madame Bakunin gave the name of the country place, and answered all the questions correctly. The Bakunins had helped her to obtain a passport and had provided the money for her journey. . . .

At last Herzen was convinced that she really was Bakunin's wife, and suggested that she should stay in our house and for the time occupy my room. Calling my maid, Herzen told her to look after Madame Bakunin, which was rather difficult, simply because the latter did not know one word of English.

But all the same Herzen did not tell her where Bakunin was, which offended her very much, and left a shade of dislike for him in her heart.

By the time I came back from Osborne she had moved into lodgings, where she remained till she left London.

We were very good friends, but she got on best of all
with Varvara Timofyevna Kelsiev.[1] She told the latter
a great deal about her life and her marriage. 'I liked a
young doctor much better,' she said, 'and I believe he
was attracted by me, but I preferred to marry Bakunin
because he is a hero and has always been for Poland.
Though I was born and grew up in Siberia, I love
my fatherland; I wear mourning for it and always
shall.'

There was a great deal that was childish and naive in
her, but at the same time much that was sweet and sincere.
Then a telegram came from Bakunin addressed to me:
'Natalya Alexyevna, I commend my wife to you, take
care of her.' Soon afterwards, however, he sent for her
to Sweden, and a great many of us went to the station
with her to see her off to Dover. Before she left London,
Madame Bakunin invited us all to dinner and regaled us
with Polish dainties, which were very nice and greatly
delighted our Polish friends, Czernecki and Tchorszewski.
The latter, however, was such an admirer of female beauty
that, however bad the dinner, he would have been in
raptures if the hostess were handsome."

*   *   *   *   *

"One summer we spent at Torquay. Malwide von
Meysenbug came from Italy with Olga, and I went down
from London with Natasha and my baby, Liza. Ogaryov
and Herzen could only come for visits, for they had to
be in London to look after the Russian Free Press, and to
receive the Russians who used to come to interview the
editors of the *Bell*, bringing a great deal of material for
publication. That summer Tatyana Petrovna Passek
decided to visit Herzen. She arrived in London and
telegraphed to him; he hurried back from Torquay and
met her at the station. We were all delighted to see her;
she had the gift of winning people by her gentleness and

[1] See vol. v. pp. 105 and 106. — (*Translator's Note.*)

typically Russian good-nature. Unluckily, she only paid us a brief visit. Soon Malwide went back to Italy with both Herzen's daughters; on the way they visited Nice, where the girls' mother was buried. . . .

In 1862, or 1863, we decided to leave London, as Herzen thought it would be cheaper and more comfortable to live in a suburb. There was, only fifteen minutes by rail from London, a little place called Teddington, consisting of a long street with country houses in large luxuriant gardens, and several smaller houses, with little shops of various sorts. . . . There Herzen found a fairly roomy house with a big garden, and we all moved into it, taking with us Varvara Timofyevna Kelsiev and her little girl, Marusya. The printing-press was moved to a little house not ten minutes' walk from us. There Czernecki was installed with the companion of his life, Marianna; they had no children.

Our new house had only one drawback: behind it there was a factory from which often came a smell of burnt tallow. But the doctor assured us that this would do the children no harm, and so we meekly put up with the unpleasantness of it. The only one of our intimate circle left in London was Tchorszewski, and he came to Teddington at least once a week, partly on business, and partly from affection for the family, of which he was like an indispensable member. His devotion to Herzen and all of us was beyond all bounds, and he proved it indeed after Herzen's death."

[At Elmfield House, Teddington, they were visited, as described in volume v. p. 111, etc., by Gonchar, who took Madame Kelsiev and her little girl Marusya with him to Tulcea, the colony of Russian raskolniks to which Kelsiev had previously gone, and there the mother and child died. (See volume v. p. 115.) Soon afterwards Garibaldi's visit took place, as described in volume v.]

"After being a year in Teddington we spent a summer by the sea at Bournemouth. Malwide von Meysenbug joined us there with Herzen's daughters. This was the last time we were all together in England; but I will say nothing of that stay, as nothing of general interest occurred. After living in Italy neither Malwide nor the girls were willing to hear of a change. Sometimes Herzen spent a month or two with them in Italy. . . .

On our return to London Herzen began to make plans for transferring the printing-press to Geneva. From the time of the Polish rebellion the circulation of the *Bell* had dropped; fewer manuscripts were sent us from Russia than before. This was obviously a grief to Herzen. 'We are old,' he used to say; 'the Nihilists look upon us as reactionaries; it is time to retire, it is time to set to work on some big job.' But Ogaryov did not lose heart. He thought that in Switzerland there would be more people coming fresh from Russia, and that the Free Press would begin to flourish again.

While Herzen and Ogaryov were settling things up and preparing to go, I went to Paris with my children, thinking that it would be easier for my relations to come there from Russia to see me.

Then a calamity befell me from which I could not recover; for several years afterwards I moved about from place to place and could nowhere find peace."

[In 1864, in Paris, Natalya Alexyevna's two younger children, the twins, died of diphtheria.]

"At midnight, on the 15th of December 1864, Herzen and Ogaryov, accompanied by some other persons, whom I did not notice at the time, put me with my daughter Liza into the train for Montpelier. Some of the company commended us to the care of the guard, others gave us letters of recommendation to doctors and various other persons.

Yielding to necessity, I set off with a heavy heart on this long journey alone with my child; but I knew Herzen could not take us. He promised to join us shortly at Montpelier. The doctors insisted that we should leave Paris as soon as possible, for diphtheria was raging there. The well-known writer and journalist, Emile Girardin, had just lost from this epidemic his only daughter, a child of my Liza's age.

Herzen did in fact arrive in Montpelier soon afterwards. Doctor Coste, who was attending us, beamed all over with enthusiasm ith when he saw him. A few days later he took Herzen in the evening to the 'Cercle Démocratique'; there many people were eager to make his acquaintance, warmly shook his hand, and talked of his writings. Herzen was much moved when, on his return, he told me of the warm welcome given him; indeed, he was extremely popular at that time in France, north and south alike, with all classes of the population.

From Montpelier Herzen went to Geneva, and there meeting his son brought him to Montpelier. Alexandr Alexandrovitch spent two days with me and then went back to Florence.

At the end of the winter we went to Cannes, and from there again to Nice. In Cannes we made the acquaintance of Dr. Bernacki;[1] he was recommended to us in the hotel when my daughter had some trifling ailment. Bernacki turned out to be a great admirer of Herzen; he was a Polish *émigré*, an elderly man whose patriotism was as keen as ever, though he had lived in France since 1830. He had married a widow, who died, leaving him her son. Herzen saw all Bernacki's surroundings; life is hard for the rich Slav temperament in the narrow, petty life of the French bourgeois. Bernacki brought up and at last married this son who was not his own, and all his love was centred on the latter's children.

[1] See vol. iv. chap. iv.—(*Translator's Note.*)

In the spring of 1865 we moved from Nice to a villa, Château de la Boissière, near Geneva."

[Here the whole group, including Malwide, Herzen's two elder daughters, and Ogaryov, were for some time together again.]

"Prince Dolgorukov left London soon after we did, and he too settled in Geneva. . . . He was an intelligent man, but had a great deal of *amour-propre*, and, as I have said already, his views were absolutely different from Herzen's, yet he seemed drawn to the latter by a strange, inexplicable, and irresistible attraction. The prince's harsh, hasty, and despotic temper caused him continual difficulties abroad.

At the Château de la Boissière there was rather a curious incident with Prince Dolgorukov. I was not in the house at the time, but I well remember Herzen's humorous account of the quarrel between Prince Dolgorukov and our servant, Jules.

Dolgorukov, Vyrubov, and some other guests were dining at the house. When they got up from the table, Dolgorukov went out of the dining-room meaning to give some order to our cook. He had to go down some steps to reach the kitchen; there he halted, listening to a conversation in which he caught his own name; Jules in a loud voice was complaining of the prince, saying that he gave the servants far more trouble than all the rest of the visitors. Instead of calling Jules and pretending to have heard nothing, Dolgorukov pushed open the door and, drawing the blade out of his swordstick, began waving it in the air while he scolded and shouted at Jules. The latter gave him back as good as he got and raised his fist to strike Dolgorukov. Hearing a great uproar below-stairs, and knowing the prince's troublesome temper, Herzen, calling Vyrubov to follow him, hurried down to the kitchen. . . . He seized Dolgorukov's arms, and asked Vyrubov to hold Jules; the prince was led away to the dining-room, where, frantic with rage, he snatched up a decanter and smashed it into splinters on the table, then seized a chair and threw it on the floor so that it was broken to pieces. Herzen gazed at him in mute amazement. The prince, choking with fury, at last articulated: 'Never again will I set foot in your house,' and went off.

But he could not do without seeing Herzen; and a week later wrote asking him to dismiss Jules for his impertinence. Only on this condition, said the prince, could he visit Château de la Boissière again.

To this missive Herzen replied that he was very sorry for what had occurred, but that it was against his principles to dismiss a servant simply for impertinence, the more so as he 'considered the prince more to blame than Jules, since the latter could not be compared with Dolgorukov as regards culture and education, and, moreover, the prince had begun the quarrel.' 'We sometimes perhaps complain of servants in their absence,' wrote Herzen, 'though we have many interests, and our relations with our servants do not take the most prominent place in them; but as for them, they may well pour out their indignation with us pretty often to relieve all the unpleasantness of their lot in life.'

By degrees the prince began to calm down. He told his cook to meet Jules in the market and to ask the latter to come to him. Jules was buying provisions in the market when the prince's man went up to him with this message. Jules followed the man, set down his basket in the hall, and not without surprise walked into Dolgorukov's study. The latter, on his entrance, stood up and came to meet him. In response to our cook's bow, the prince held out his hand.

'Je veux, Jules, me réconcilier avec vous, voulez-vous?' said the prince.

'Je veux bien, je veux bien, monsieur le prince,' Jules answered good-humouredly, 'il ne faut pas se fâcher toujours.'

'Alors buvons à notre réconciliation,' said the prince, filling two glasses with some good red wine and offering one to Jules. They clinked their glasses, and drained them.

From that time forward Prince Dolgorukov took to visiting Herzen again, and never referred to the past.

When we settled in Geneva there were a great many Russians there; almost all of them were Nihilists. They took up an extremely hostile attitude to Herzen.

The greater number of them lived either in the Russian hotel or in a boarding-house kept by Madame X., a Russian who had several years before visited Herzen in London, accompanied by her husband and the writer Mihailov. Since then there had been many changes in her life; her husband had long before returned to Russia, lived somewhere in the wilds, and wrote constantly for the reviews. Mihailov had been exiled. A year or two after parting with Mihailov, she had succeeded not only in forgetting him, but in replacing him by the younger Serno-Solovyovitch.

I permit myself to speak of the relations of Madame X. with Mihailov and Alexandr Serno-Solovyovitch, because every one knew of them at the time, and she made no secret of them. . . . Serno-Solovyovitch was younger than she was: hasty, jealous, and hot-tempered, he had stormy scenes with Madame X., and she began to be afraid of him. When a son was born, to put an end to all relations with him she made up her mind to send the baby off to her husband X. to be brought up. Two other Russians assisted her in this, to my thinking, in-human action: I cannot see what right a mother has to rob a father of his child, unless she keeps the child herself. Serno-Solovyovitch was beside himself at the child's being sent away, he threatened to murder Madame X., broke into her room, and really did become alarming, 'You have taken everything from me,' he said with despair, 'now I have nothing I care for.' I do not know how Madame X. managed it, but for the sake of her own peace and comfort she got Serno-Solovyovitch put into a lunatic asylum. Probably his friends helped her. O Pushkin! how right you were! it is easier to defend oneself from foes than from friends!

One evening Herzen, Ogaryov, and I were sitting in the dining-room; suddenly the door was thrown open, and a man with a face of despair ran in, looked about him, then fell on his knees before Herzen. It was Serno-Solovyovitch; I recognised him.

'Get up, get up, how can you!' said Alexandr Ivanovitch in a voice full of emotion.

'No, no, I won't get up. I have wronged you, Alexandr Ivanovitch, I have slandered you, I have slandered you even in print. . . . and yet it is from you I ask help. Protect me from my friends, they will shut me up again that *her* mind may be at rest. You see I have run away from the madhouse and come straight to you, my enemy.'

Herzen and Ogaryov raised him up, shook his hand, assured him that they harboured no malice against him, and kept him in the house, but earnestly begged him not to go where he would be irritated (namely, to Madame X.'s).

They looked on him with all-forgiving compassion, and as I watched them I thought that the first Christians must have loved and forgiven like them.

Serno-Solovyovitch was fond of children; he liked to walk about the garden and play with my little girl Liza. Malwide and Olga had not yet arrived, and Natasha was with her brother in Berne at Marya Kashparovna Reihel's. Suddenly we received from Malwide a telegram:

'We will stay on longer as Serno-Solovyovitch is with you.'

Herzen answered by telegram:

'As you like; Natalie is not afraid of him; he is playing with Liza in the garden.'

On the morning after the first night that Serno-Solovyovitch slept at the Château de la Boissière we all got up early and met in the dining-room; we hoped that he was still peacefully reposing in freedom, and yet we were a little uneasy. Suddenly Jules came in with the coffee and said:

'You told me to keep an eye on our visitor, but really no one could do that. He was there all the time,' he went on anxiously,' but now the room is empty, he's not there, M. Herzen,' he said in despair.

After waiting some time we began breakfast, but Herzen was gloomy. 'He will murder her,' he said, 'and I shall never forgive myself for not keeping watch over him myself!'

All at once we caught the sound of footsteps coming nearer and nearer, and Serno-Solovyovitch walked into the dining-room, looking almost cheerful. He apologised, and told Herzen in a low voice that he had gone out to buy a paper collar and cuffs, as he felt uncomfortable at sitting down to table in a lady's company without. We felt as though a weight had been lifted off us when he came in.

But not long afterwards Serno-Solovyovitch's self-control gave way, he went where he was irritated to frenzy, and he was taken back again to the asylum.

Later on he was discharged, and then he joined a society of working-class Socialists; but his success with them did not fully satisfy him. He felt that he was severed from his own country and grew more and more gloomy. He wrote a great deal about socialism, but was dull and depressed, and held aloof from every one. . . .

He ended by suicide—and what a terrible end! He sought death in three ways: he poisoned himself, cut his veins, and stifled himself with charcoal fumes. He had suffered enough, and so escaped to freedom.

While we lived near Geneva, Madame X. was only twice in our house, and then not as an acquaintance but on business. I found her very unattractive, and could not understand how it was she had so much influence over undoubtedly good men. Various persons came to see us from her boarding-house, chiefly men, though I remember one very handsome young woman, who had married a very young Prince Golitsyn in order to go abroad to study. She saw him for the first time in church and never saw him again. Such marriages were a fashion at that time and were treated as a joke, but later on, so it was said, this reckless marriage was the cause of great sorrow to Golitsyn: he fell in love, and could not marry the girl he loved!

*   *   *   *   *

Herzen did not like living in Geneva; the *émigrés* were in too close proximity; having nothing to do, they had plenty of time for gossip and tittle-tattle; their antagonism to Herzen, an antagonism for which envy of his material resources was chiefly responsible, irritated him extremely, and his irritability was increased by the state of his health, which began to fail from the year 1864.

The Château de la Boissière was abandoned; I sought solitude in Montreux with my little girl and her governess, Miss Turner. Mal wide went back to Italy with Olga. Herzen remained with only Natasha in Geneva; he moved into lodgings on the Quai du Mont Blanc, while Ogaryov settled at Lancy, almost outside the town. Living at Geneva was not a success; little good work was done, and we had not what the English call a *home*.

I was drawn to Nice again, to the newly-dug graves.[1]
Herzen was fond of the scenery of the south; besides,
he had in Nice many precious memories, and his wife's
grave, which he never forgot. Sending Natasha to
Italy, he accompanied us to Nice, and stayed there for a
time himself.

Whether I wanted to or not, I had to make some
acquaintances for my daughter's sake; a gloomy environment is bad for a child. She used to play in the public
gardens every day with some children; she soon made
friends with them, and so I came to be acquainted with
two or three families. I arranged with a dancing-
mistress to form a class, and had no difficulty in finding
some among my little girl's friends who were glad to
join it. And so the children came to us twice a week.
Among others, we made the acquaintance of the family
of Garibaldi (a cousin of the celebrated Garibaldi), whose
amiable wife and children were in friendly relations with
us till I went back to Russia for good.

At that time Herzen was still in Nice. He wrote a
great deal in Nice—there was no one to hinder him;
then he used to go and read the papers at Visconte's;
after dinner he liked to go a walk alone with Liza; sometimes he took her to the theatre, and enjoyed her sallies,
her apt remarks, and intelligence. He was then writing
for the *Week* the series of articles entitled 'To Pass the
Time.' It was a comfort to him to be writing and being
printed in Russia. He was fond of reading aloud what
he had written before sending it off."

[Ogaryov was now settled wth Mary and their two
children, Henry and 'Toots,' in Geneva.]

". . . . While Herzen was in Nice, a telegram arrived

---

[1] The two children who died in Paris were buried at Nice.—
(*Translator's Note.*)

from Tchorszewski, telling him that Ogaryov had broken his leg, and begging him to come to Geneva as soon as possible. I was not in the house at the time, and on returning home I found Herzen sitting on a chair in the hall in a dazed condition; I was astounded at his being there and looking so overwhelmed. He handed me the telegram without a word. Glancing at it, I said: 'Well, Herzen, you must make haste and go; let us look at the time-table and pack up your things; you must not delay.'

But Herzen sat mute as though he did not hear what I said. 'I feel,' he said at last, 'that I shall never see him again.'

However, I managed to pack what was needed, and to see Herzen off at the station; I felt that if anything could relieve his mind it would be seeing Ogaryov. Such an accident was a serious thing at his age. Herzen wrote afterwards, describing with what terror and anxiety he travelled to Geneva; how, meeting Tchorszewski at the station, he had not courage to ask 'Is Ogaryov alive?' At last Tchorszewski, of his own accord, said that he thought that there was no ground for anxiety in Ogaryov's condition. Doctor Meyer had set the bone and put the leg in a splint. Ogaryov had borne the operation with the greatest fortitude.

I have searched in vain for the letter in which Herzen described this unfortunate accident. I remember that he wrote that Ogaryov was taking an evening stroll in the outskirts of Geneva, when he had one of the fits to which he was subject. On recovering consciousness, he got up and tried to go on, but, as it was by then dark, he did not see the ditch, stumbled, broke his leg, and was sick from the pain; after lying there for a while, he tried again to get up, but could not. Then he began to call to passers-by, but nobody came to him. As ill-luck would have it, he was lying in a pool just outside the lunatic asylum, and this was why everybody hurried away when he shouted, supposing him to be a lunatic.

Seeing that no one would come, Ogaryov, with great presence of mind, took a knife and a pipe out of his pocket, cut off his boot, then lit his pipe, and lay there, I believe, till next day. Early in the morning an Italian who knew Ogaryov passed by, and, though the latter was lying at some distance from the road, the Italian noticed him, and began looking more closely; then Ogaryov called to him. The Italian went up, said he would fetch a carriage, and took him home, Ogaryov suffering great pain when moved."

[Some months later—Natalya Alexyevna rarely gives dates—when Ogaryov was able to hobble about, and the accident was almost forgotten, there was a family gathering again.]

"Tchorszewski took an old château called 'Prangius,' about an hour and a half's drive from Geneva; here, for the last time, the whole family were together again; Liza and I, Malwide and Olga and Natasha. . . . Rather later Ogaryov joined us with little 'Toots.' Last of all, Alexandr (Herzen's son) arrived with his young wife. They were only just married, and Teresina did not yet speak French, so we all had to talk Italian to her, which curtailed conversation a good deal. Teresina liked going for walks, sometimes with Herzen, sometimes with me."

[At the end of the summer.] "Alexandr and his wife went to spend the whole winter in Berlin for the sake of his work. . . . Olga and Malwide went back to Italy, where they were now so used to living that they liked nothing else so well. . . . Herzen was intending to go to Vichy for the first time. Ogaryov returned to Geneva with little 'Toots,' who had amused us all with his

liveliness and originality. . . . But before going to
Vichy, Herzen went with us to Lucerne, and from there
he was summoned to Berne, as Prince Dolgorukov, who
was lying there seriously ill, wished to see Herzen once
more before his death."

"After spending some time in Geneva we went to
Paris, where Vyrubov and Herzen's French friends
were very anxious that he should settle with all the
family. . . . To Herzen's great delight we found
Sergey Petrovitch Botkin[1] and his family in Paris.
Botkin still hoped at that time that Herzen's vigorous
constitution might successfully combat the diabetes from
which he was suffering, but this hope was not realised;
doctors cannot foresee the fatal accidents which have sometimes a decisive effect on disease.

We had rooms in the Grand Hotel, on the fourth
storey. Botkin was as charming and attentive as ever.
There was such serenity and kindness in his beautiful
smile that I thought him handsome; I particularly liked
to see his eyes rest upon Herzen with such unfeigned love
and admiration. Alexandr Ivanovitch was glad to be
with him too; he actually seemed better when Botkin
was present, for the latter had a charming and encouraging
effect on him.

We were sitting in the little drawing-room talking
almost light-heartedly of how we should probably be able
to make a home here; here there would be suitable and
even interesting society for Natasha; and as regards educational facilities, we could find everything that could be
desired. . . . All at once Herzen was handed a letter
from his son, telling him that Natasha was very seriously
ill, and begging him to go at once to Florence.

Knowing his daughter's strong constitution, Herzen
was perplexed, and sent a telegram asking what her ill-

[1] The famous doctor.—(*Translator's Note.*)

ness was. When he received the reply, he handed me
the telegram in silence, then said: 'I would rather have
heard she was dead.' The telegram read: '*Dérange-
ment des facultés intellectuelles*.'[1] These terribly alarming words seemed to paralyse him. He remained sitting
with a pale face, in a sort of stupefaction, not attempting
to get ready: it was obviously impossible to let him go
alone, and indeed he said himself: 'We had better all
go together.'

I hurriedly packed the most necessary things and, not
staying to say good-bye to any one in Paris, we paid our
bill at the hotel and went off to the station on the chance
of getting a train—they go pretty often. We had not
to wait, but to hurry: Herzen took the tickets, while I
looked after the luggage, and Liza, who was then ten,
went to the buffet to buy some provisions for the journey.
We travelled without stopping. It was very exhausting
for us all, especially for the child. As though she understood the gravity of the reason for our journey, she did
not complain, and was impatiently eager to arrive and
see Natasha. Herzen was silent almost the whole way;
his anxiety and impatience were apparent in his careworn
face. At last we reached Genoa; from there Herzen
went on alone, telling us to remain in Genoa till we heard
from him: if Natasha were fit to travel, Herzen would
bring her, and we would all return together to Paris; if
the doctor decided that she must stay on in Florence, he
would let us know, and we would join him there. Next
day we found a letter and a telegram for us at the post
office. The telegram only told us to await the letter;
in the letter we were directed to go at once to Florence,
which we accordingly did.

When the train stopped at the station we saw Herzen

[1] As a matter of fact, Natalya Alexandrovna Herzen's illness was
what would now be called a 'nervous breakdown,' and was followed
by a complete and permanent recovery.—(*Translator's Note*.)

and his son, who had come to meet us. They took a carriage, and we drove to the villa that young Herzen had bought. There we saw Teresina with her first-born, a charming baby whom Herzen found enchanting; then we went in to Natasha, who was very glad to see us. However, Herzen thought it more comfortable for the patient and for all of us to be in the town, and so next day we moved with Natasha to the Hotel de France. . . . There we spent about a fortnight; again I had to part with Liza, whom I put for the time in the care of Malwide and Olga, while I remained with Natasha. There was nobody to nurse her but me. Malwide would not undertake to look after the invalid, and I did not care to leave her to strangers. It is true that before I came the doctor had called in an acquaintance, a Miss Reynolds, to nurse her, but though she was experienced, she only irritated the patient. What was needed was not experience but love.

Anyway, my coming was crowned with success; the patient began to recover, sleep and appetite returned, but I looked in vain for any sign of joy in Herzen's gloomy face: he seemed crushed, and had not the strength to hope or to believe in his beloved daughter's recovery. He lived in a state of morbid apprehension. The doctor sanctioned Natasha's leaving Florence. . . . Liza and Natasha set off with us for Paris. Only Herzen's son saw us off. For some reason Malwide and Olga did not come to say good-bye.

This time we did not hurry; we travelled very slowly. We stopped several times on the way to rest. We spent a day in Genoa; I remember that there Herzen was writing to Florence, and he said to me: 'What am I to say to Olga and Malwide: ask them to come to Paris or leave them in Italy? They so dislike coming away!' But I advised him to send for them, because I saw that Natasha still needed me, and Herzen himself was too

unhinged to be fit to look after Liza. He could not be
with the patient either; her overwrought nerves could
not stand her father's resonant voice.

We stayed two days in Nice, then rested at Lyons, and
at last reached Paris, where we went to the Pension
Rovigan. But it was not sufficiently comfortable for our
invalid, and so in his daily walks about the city Herzen
looked out for a spacious flat where there would be room
for us all. Soon after our return to Paris Malwide and
Olga arrived, though they certainly were very unwilling
to come. They were sorry to exchange Florence for
Paris. Then we moved into a big flat in the Pavilion
Rohan, No. 172 rue Rivoli, into that fateful house in
which he who, forgetful of himself, thought and lived for
his country, for humanity, and for his family, after some
five days' illness left us for ever."

[Herzen had been suffering from diabetes since 1864,
but the doctors thought his strong constitution would
enable him to resist the disease, if only he received
no shocks. The alarm caused him by his daughter's
illness made him worse. In January 1870 he had an
attack of pneumonia, of which he died four days later
at the age of fifty-eight. He was buried in Nice beside
his wife and children.

That his life with Natalya Alexyevna was not a happy
one can be seen from his correspondence with Ogaryov.
They made more than one attempt at separation, but
Herzen could not bear parting from Liza. There seems
to have been something morbid and unbalanced in
Natalya Alexyevna's character. Even Liza, to whom
she was devoted, was after Herzen's death on very bad
terms with her. They lived near Herzen's other children
in Italy, but Liza did not always get on well with them,
in spite of the unvarying patience and affection of Natasha
Herzen. Brilliantly intelligent, vain and capricious, Liza

committed suicide in 1875, at the age of seventeen, after
a dispute with her mother, who wished her to break off
an undesirable intimacy. Natalya Alexyevna went back
to Russia and lived in seclusion in the country. Later
on she adopted the daughter of a niece. The girl was
consumptive, and for the sake of her health Madame
Ogaryov took her to the Black Forest, where the adopted
daughter died. Natalya Alexyevna just succeeded in
reaching Russia before her own death in 1913.

Ogaryov, who had become more or less of an invalid
from the time of his accident in 1866, was still living in
Geneva in 1873, when his old friend, Madame Passek,
visited him there. Not long afterwards he moved to
England with 'Mary,' who faithfully cared for him to
the end. Once a wealthy man, he had lost or given away
all he had and was maintained in his last years by Herzen's
children. He died at Greenwich in 1877, and is buried
at Shooter's Hill.

The following extracts from letters written by Herzen
to Ogaryov throw light on the former's state of mind
during his last years.

"NICE, *May* 31, 1868.
"Ah, you dear, absurd person, you will hardly believe
me, I laugh at you and at myself quite genuinely—with
no tinge of anger or anything of the sort. I knew all
along and wrote to you in Geneva that whether it's
Lausanne or Prangius—it's a terror to you (you accepted
the suggestion too hastily and I made it too hastily)—you
are so comfortably and peacefully settled in your snug
little den that the very idea of travelling frightens you.
Well, so be it, but why did you wait till the trunks were
packed and everything was ready, to write of the difficult
position that Toots put you in . . . ?

It is too late not to go—you must think of some plan,
I see you want us to come to Geneva. Tell me how and

I will do it. The *only* difficulty is Liza (who remembers you and has a romantic affection for you). Are you really going to risk telling her straight away not only the whole secret history, but two secret histories?. . . And so I suggest that I should first come from Lyons by myself, and all the rest we will put off and settle later. I cannot guarantee that everything will be well at Prangius. Below the surface of peace there are sometimes very bad symptoms. One thing you might explain: why did you tell me that I was wrong, and that you really did want to come to Lausanne or anywhere else to see us all and to have a change from the monotony of your life that I find so trying? I would have arranged things accordingly. But there is no harm done. Now it is no use sacrificing yourself, for a sacrifice always makes itself felt. Believe me, I will manage it all, including the shock to Liza's feelings and the ridicule. I cannot endure ridicule (that is, being laughed at) as an insult, but everything else can be settled, and you can trust me to do all I can to make it right and not too conspicuous. Well, amen."

"MULHOUSE, *June* 30, 1868.

". . . We are going to Basle to-night. I expect I shall stay there till Tata[1] comes, or perhaps I shall go to Lucerne and wait there till the question of Prangius is settled. Lucerne is a beautiful place; I am quite ready to spend a month there.

But how I should like to settle down somewhere! though I see no prospect of it. . . . You have always preached immobility, and now you cannot walk; I, on the contrary, was always for movement—and here, at fifty-six, I am utterly homeless. . . . Liza is well, but Natalie[2] is convinced that she is ill and wants to ask Adolph Vogt's advice."

[1] Herzen's elder daughter Natalie, also called Natasha.
[2] Madame Ogaryov.—(*Translator's Notes*.)

"HOTEL BELLE VUE, LUCERNE.

"*July 7*, 1868. *Tuesday.*

". . . It is very nice here in the summer. The hotel
is expensive and the food is not up to much, but the view
from the windows—fields all round, gardens, and mountains . . . right in front is the lake, and mountains again.

Lucerne is infinitely more beautiful than Geneva, but
it probably begins to be cold here in October. . . . I
fancy Natalie, too, is tired of *vagabondage*, but as to where
are we to settle I must ask Tata's advice. I am not equal
to deciding it alone! You can't believe how tired I am.
Oh, for a house, a comfortable house, with a field adjoin-
ing—and then rest!"

"BERNERHOFF, No. 6, BERNE.

"*July 11*, 1868.

". . . Yesterday I spent a long day which I shall not
soon forget. It began wretchedly with Natalie's ill
humour; I set off *low-spirited*,[1] but all the way from
Olten I travelled with Lewes and his wife (you know,
who writes English novels): he cheered me up; he is
an extraordinarily intelligent and lively-minded man.
Among other things he asked me:' Est-ce que votre
"Golos" parait toujours?' for which he caught it
severely.

But to the tragedy. Dolgorukov is very bad, but his
strong constitution is like a fortress that will not surrender.
. . . He talks incoherently, his eyes are dim, he does not
know that the end is so near, but he fears it. The worst
of it is that there is a fearful conflict going on inside him.
His joy at seeing me was immense, but noiseless; he
keeps squeezing my hands and thanking me. There is
nobody in the world he trusts but me and my representative, Tchorszewski. In the morning he summoned
Tchorszewski and Vogt . . . then after all sorts of

---

[1] English in the original.—(*Translator's Note.*)

dreadful incidents, he sent Vogt to tell N . . . to go back at once.

Vogt carried out this commission. N . . . of course was furious. But Dolgorukov at once sent for him and begged his forgiveness. When I went up, he sent them all away, and taking both my hands, sat up and fixed his dim eyes on me.

'Herzen, Herzen! For God's sake, tell me, you are the only one I trust, the only one I respect—is it madness, is it nonsense?

'You see yourself,' I said, 'that it's madness. What reasons have you?

'Yes, yes, it's obvious, it's delirium—so you think it's delirium?' (And so on a dozen times over.) Then all at once, sinking back, he repeated slowly twice:

'No, but do you—for God's sake, do keep a watch on the way they are treating me,' and he signified that I was to say no more. After which he fell into a doze, and on waking asked us to have dinner with his son, which we did. The son was irritated at first, but after dinner, after two or three bottles of wine and some absinthe, he re-covered—he's a queer fellow. All this together affected my nerves, so that I did not sleep all night and my head aches.

Tell me what impression this letter makes on you?

Vogt says that there isn't a chance of saving him, and that if he is left like this, he'll pop off. I fancy there is a lot of strength in him yet. . . ."

"LUCERNE, BELLE-VUE.
"*July* 14 (1868).

"Well, at least I have escaped from the Dolgorukov nightmare. An awful agony, and what's more, he's actually better, he's eating incessantly, and so keeps himself up. Adolph Vogt quite worn out. The day before yesterday there was a hideous scene with N . . . in my presence; afterwards I made peace between them. He is persuaded that the fellow is only waiting to snatch his money and be off! . . . N . . . came in and protested against something. Dolgorukov shouted:

'Hold your tongue and be off to Petersburg!'

Then he sent Vogt to tell him not to come near him. And though I did bring him to reason a bit, yet next morning he told him to go away and let him die in peace or recover. Tchorszewski is the only one who is not moved to exasperation in this filthy slough, and though fearfully depressed behaves well."

". . . Vogt says I have a strong tendency to diabetes, and advises me to drink the waters at Lucerne, and not go to Berne again for a fortnight. Altogether I am better now, though still far from well. Tata has come with me. . . .

Auerbach and his wife are here; they have lately come from Russia, and have been in Vevey. Bakunin belongs heart and soul to Elpidin's party, and they are as thick as thieves.

Caro mio —it is time we retired and began on something else; writing a great work or settling down to old age. . . . Liza was very glad to see Tata, their meeting was delightful. I am very much pleased with Tata. . . . Tchorszewski has just arrived for a rest, and has brought the news that Dolgorukov is immensely better. See what medicine can do!"

"LUCERNE, BELLE VUE.
"*July* 23 (1868). *Thursday.*

". . . I posted you a letter at ten o'clock last night, enclosing one from Liza, who, *entfesselt* from town life, enjoys the woods and the fields so much that it is a pity

to take her away from here. She and Tata would have
got on well, but Liza's rude pranks (her only serious
defect) irritate Tata. Natalie in such cases does, of
course, everything to make matters worse. It's a bad
look-out.

In my letter of yesterday I wrote to you about striking
work—the millstone is turning more slowly; we labour
listlessly and in vain, surrounded by jeers and vile envy.
Russia is deaf. The seed has been sown, it is covered
with dung—there is nothing to do till autumn. It has
occurred to me to write to you an official letter suggesting
stoppage[1] —and I shall do so.

But how could you imagine that by retiring and rest
from the *Bell*. . . I meant empty inactivity, and how
could one set about it? For that, one must wait for
complete softening of the brain, hardening of the heart,
or terror over one's health. . . .

All I want after burying the *Bell* is external peace,
being able to keep calm, almost indifferent to the annoy-
ances all about me. But the *Bell* won't do that; there's
no managing it, it's a good thing you have got it—
make the most of it. Good-bye."

"St. GALLEN, *Aug.* 3,1868.

". . . Liza wants to write to you that we crossed the
Rhine under a waterfall. She is well, eats enough for
two, sleeps enough for three; and if one could persuade
Natalie not to spoil her, we could boast of her at Prangius.
But her temper and naughtiness are great defects."

[In September and October 1868 Herzen was at
Vichy first alone, then with his family, and had a quiet
and pleasant time there. It had been decided to go from
Vichy to Lyons and then to Zurich, but later the plan was
changed, and it was proposed to go to Lausanne.]

[1] English in the original. — (*Translator's Note.*)

"Lᴏʏᴏɴꜱ, Hᴏᴛᴇʟ ᴅᴇ ʟ'Eᴜʀᴏᴘᴇ.
"*Oct.* 23,1868.

"Well, here we are at Lyons. *Le chapitre* of water cure is over. What next?[1] In any case I shall come to Geneva. Our plans are all unsettled. Natalie wants to go to Nice—we are on the way to it here. I say that Liza's education ought to be our chief consideration. She is growing up mentally every day and quite naturally, *i.e.* it does not interfere with her health. Nice, of course, has no educational advantages except its climate. Even Lyons has plenty of the museums and other things that Liza needs. One winter can be sacrificed, but I won't agree to more."

"Mᴀʀꜱᴇɪʟʟᴇꜱ, *Dec.* 4,1868.
"Cafe at the railway station, 9 ᴀ.ᴍ.

'. . . Our last meeting was confused. I am somehow stunned and stupefied by such blows and shocks[2] and want to be alone. It is over now, and thank God, and in 1864 there was Lyola's[3] operation. You know, I have not till now had the courage to tell any one what happened then: 'It is wonderful what a man can endure.' Had Natalie understood that moment and my love now for Liza, she would not be constantly pulling at the strings, for fear of breaking them. I am ready to forgive, for, as Kukolnik puts it, 'only the strong can forgive.' But that's not all.

A propos, do you know I was expecting that Bakunin would send to inquire after Tata and so make peace. But he hasn't . . . *é rotta l' altissima colonna.*

It is summer here. All the windows are open. Sun is shining. No, we'll have to give up Zurich and Berne and Geneva. It would be better to live in the same town

---

[1] English in the original.
[2] The news that Tata had an attack of smallpox.
[3] Baby daughter who died. — (*Translator's Notes,*)

with you, but it is difficult. The irregularity of my position and (in a different way) of yours makes it hard. When Toots is sent to boarding-school, and you decide on some career for Henry, we will talk about it."

"After Lunch.
". . . As to Tata, it would have been too dreadful for me to lose her. Dear Natalie (my wife), you and she, in spite of her youth and crudity, understand me better than any one. But that menace is over. Natalie1 loves me, but she does not spare me. She never will be a *sister* (you remember her last letter), but Tata can be."

"LYONS, HOTEL DE L'EUROPE.
"Dec. 30, 1868.
". . . I am so sick of my irregular life that I keep thinking about the future, about 'a room of my own,' books, and a writing-table. . . . Ever since the end of 1864 I cannot settle down anywhere, and, of course, that is chiefly Natalie's fault. If something could be arranged in Geneva or here (anywhere between Nice and Genoa)! Florence does not attract me. However I shuffle the cards, nothing turns up. Well, that's an old story."

"NICE, *Feb.* 20,1869.
". . . Tata has had a long letter from Olga. There are hints and surmises in it so awful that I am afraid to comment on them. It is a systematic intrigue on the part of Meysenbug, who wants to estrange Olga from all of us, from me in particular—an intrigue that involves slander (I may have proofs of this). What is one to say to it! I have written to Sasha and am waiting for his answer."

¹ Natalya Alexyevna Tutchkov-Ogaryov. —(*Translator's Note.*)

"Paris, *Oct.* 28,1869.

". . . I have found temporary lodgings in a small but clean hotel in the Champs-Élysées, Avenue d'Antin, No. 33. Not expensive as prices are here. Then I have in view a very nice unfurnished flat right opposite the Luxembourg Gardens. I think that after knocking about all over the world one must at last fix somewhere a home for one's old age and settle the children and the grown-ups in it. If I venture to take a house for *three years*, I will offer you in a year's time to move to Paris too. For the present you had better stay in Geneva. . . . I can easily find a flat with two bedrooms, a sitting-room, and a kitchen somewhere near the Luxembourg Gardens. The worst of it is one needs the courage of a Suvorov to sign a contract for three years."

"Genoa, Hotel Feder.

"*Nov.* 14, 1869.

". . . I don't do anything at all, don't want to do anything, and don't read anything—this is why I write long letters.

S. P. Botkin is a terrible medical prophet. He said to me: 'All will go well if you have no violent shocks.' Here is a shock,[1] and apparently—thanks to your Providence, otherwise my stomach—all has gone off well . . . but no, Botkin is right. I shan't get off a visit to Vichy in the spring after all."

"Paris, 8 rue Rovigo.

"*Dec.* 23, 1869.

"Dr. Charcot came yesterday, stayed over half an hour. . . I did not even ask him about myself, I have no thoughts to spare on myself so far. I eat and drink well, but sleep badly. I drop off into a dead sleep when I go to bed in the evening, but wake up about four o'clock in terror that I shall not be able to sleep any more.

[1] Tata's nervous illness.—(*Translator's Note.*)

I have found a flat with full board, expensive but very good, quiet though quite central—172 rue Rivoli. By the end of two months I shall see whether we are going to stay in Paris and then find a permanent flat; as it is, I have to throw away 800 francs per month.

I very much dislike doing it, but large rooms and a certain amount of comfort are essential for the invalid.[1] We are saved all trouble and worries about housekeeping, etc."

"8 RUE ROVIGO, *Dec.* 29,1869.

"We are just going to move to Pavilion Rohan,172 rue Rivoli. It's a huge house let out in big and small flats, with or without board. We can rest there for a month, or even two, and see what happens. . . . I have earned this expensive rest by what I have been through during the last two months.

I cannot concentrate on anything, or settle down to any work, and I am doing nothing but reading.

. . . Best wishes for the New Year—from which I expect nothing new—and nothing good. All I ask is to keep what I have."

"PARIS,172 RUE RIVOLI.
"*Jan.* 4, 1870.

"Again I don't know what to write—everything is slow, dull, and not particularly smooth. Tata is getting better and better. All the rest hobbles on in the usual way. . . . I tell you candidly, it seems to me there is no chance of arranging a common life here. Everything hangs on a thread. With Tata alone we could manage things better, and that is how it will end."

[1] Tata.—(*Translator's Note.*)

ENDS AND BEGINNINGS

A YEAR ago, when I was writing 'Ends and Beginnings,' I did not expect to conclude them so abruptly. I wanted in two or three following letters to define the 'Beginnings' more closely; the 'Ends' seemed to me sufficiently clear of themselves. This I could not do. My outlook changed: events gave me neither peace nor leisure—they made their own commentaries and their own deductions. The tragedy is still developing before our eyes, and is more and more passing from an individual conflict into the prelude to a world struggle. Its prologue is complete; the plot is well constructed; all is in a tangle; neither men nor parties can be recognised. One cannot help recalling the image of Dante's wrestlers, in which the combatants' limbs were not only intertwined, but by some metamorphosis subsequently transformed into each other.

Everything youthful and enthusiastic, from the prayer before the Crucifix to the feat of reckless daring, from the woman dressed in black to the secret preserved by the whole people—everything that had faded away in the old world, from the mitre and the sword of chivalry to the Phrygian cap—has appeared once more in all its poetic brilliance in rebellious Poland, as though to deck with the flowers of youth the *elders of civilisation*, as they slowly move into the conflict that they dread.

On the other hand, the 'Beginnings' glimmer faintly through the smoke of burnt cities and villages. . . . What is happening here is the exact opposite. . . . All the surviving relics of the *old world* have risen up in defence of the rule of Petersburg, and are defending its ill-gotten gains with all the weapons bequeathed by the barbarous ages of military violence and the corrupt period of diplomatic intrigue. These range from the torture and murder of prisoners to false amnesties and sham declarations,

from the barbaric exile of whole sections of the population to newspaper articles and the filigree rhetoric of
Gortchakov's notes.

The storms of recent days have ruffled the still waters
of our pool. Much that has lain buried in silence
under the coffin-lid of past oppression has come to
the surface and revealed its utter putrefaction. Only
now we can measure the depth of the corruption which
the Imperial Government has developed in the cause
of Germanising us for a century and a half. The
German lymph has matured in the coarse Russian blood,
the healthy organism has given it fresh strength, and,
while infected by it, has lost nothing of its own vice.
The inhuman narrow ugliness of the German officer and
the petty vulgarity of the German official has long ago
blended in Russia with the features of the Mongol, the
savage and unrelenting cruelty of the oriental slave and
of the Byzantine eunuch. But we have not been used to
seeing this composite personality outside the army barracks
and the government offices; it has never appeared so
strikingly outside the Service: scantily educated, it not
only wrote little but even read little. Now our Mino-
taurs come to the surface not only in the palaces and
torture-chambers, but in society, in the universities, in
literature.

We thought that our literature was so lofty, that our
professors were such apostles; we were mistaken in them,
and how painful it is! we are revolted by it as by every
display of moral degradation. We cannot but protest
against the dreadful things that are being said and done;
we cannot but be repelled by the frenzy of violence, the
inhuman butchery and still more inhuman applause.
Perhaps it may be our lot to fold our hands and die in our
retreat before this delirium of 'cultured' Russia is over.
. . . But this storm will not uproot the seed that lies
hidden in the soil; it will not hurt it, and maybe it will

strengthen it. A new vital force is strengthened by everything—ill deeds and good alike. It alone can pass through blood, unstained, and say to the savage combatants: 'I know you not; you have worked for me, but it was not for my sake you worked.'

Look at the savage satrap in Lithuania: he strangles the Polish element, but the Russian autocracy will bear the marks of the struggle; he hunts down the Polish nobles, but it will be the Russian nobles who will flee.

Like house-porters, they know not for whom they are sweeping, for whom they are clearing a path, as little as the Roman she-wolf knew whom she was suckling, whom she was rearing. Not Romulus, but Remus, wronged in the past, will tread the bloodstained path: it is for him that Tsar and satraps are clearing a road.

But before he comes much blood yet will flow, and there will be a fearful collision of two worlds. Why must it flow? Why, indeed? There is no help for it, if men gain no more sense. Events move rapidly and the brain develops slowly. Under the influence of dark forces, of fantastic images, the peoples move as though sleep-walking through a succession of insoluble problems; after fighting together, and seeing nothing clearly, during all the fifteen hundred years from the fearful collapse of the Roman world, they reach the nineteenth century, which is no more civilised than the times of Germanicus and Alaric.

August 1,1863.

Letter 1

AND so, dear friend,[1] you will positively go no further, you want to rest amidst the rich autumn harvest, in shady parks, languidly ruffling their leaves

---

[1] Turgenev was the friend to whom these letters were addressed.— (*Translator's Note.*)

after the long, hot summer. You are not alarmed at the days growing shorter, at the mountain-tops turning white, and the cold, sinister wind that blows at times; you are more afraid of our spring floods, of the knee-deep mud, of the wild overflow of the rivers, of the bare earth showing under the snow, and, in fact, of our dreams of a future harvest from which we are separated by storms and hail, by drought and deluge, and all the hard work we have not yet accomplished. . . . Well, in God's name, let us part in love and concord like good fellow-travellers.

You have only a little way further to go, you have arrived, here is the brightly lighted house, the sparkling river and the garden, and leisure and books at hand, while I, like an old post hack, always in harness, shift from one task to another till I drop dead between two stations.

Believe me that I fully understand your dislike and dread of a life with no order nor beaten paths, and your affection for established civic and political forms, and, moreover, such as may become 'better,' but are so far the 'best' existing.

We men of European town civilisation can, as a rule, only exist under the established conventions. Town life accustoms us from early childhood to the fact that discordant forces are balanced and kept in check behind the scenes. When we are by chance thrown off the beaten track on which, from the day of our birth, it guides and carefully moves us, we are as completely at a loss as the theoretical savant, accustomed to museums and herbariums and to wild beasts in glass cases, is at a loss when confronted with the traces of a geological cataclysm, or with the dense population of the Mediterranean Sea.

I have chanced to see two or three desperate haters of Europe who have returned from beyond the ocean. They had gone thither, so revolted by the Reaction after 1848, so exasperated against everything European, that they had hastened on to Kansas or California, hardly willing to stop at New York. Three or four years later they reappeared in the familiar cafés and beer-shops of old Europe, ready to make any concession to avoid seeing the virginal forests of America and her untilled soil, to avoid being *tête-à-tête* with Nature and meeting wild animals, rattlesnakes, and men with revolvers. You must not imagine, however, that they were simply terrified by danger, material privations, or the necessity of work; here, too, men die of hunger if they do not work, and here, too, they work sixteen hours out of the twenty-four, while the police and the spies in the old continent are more dangerous than wild beasts and revolvers. They were, above all, terrified and depressed by Nature untouched by man, by the absence of that well-ordered organisation, that peace secured by the administration, that artistic and epicurean comfort which depend on permanent habitation, are protected by a strong wall of police, rest upon the ignorance of the masses, and are defended by the Church, the Law, and the Army. For the sake of this mess of pottage, *well served*, we sacrifice our share of human dignity, our share of sympathy for our neighbour, and give our *negative* support to the *régime* which is in reality hateful to us.

In France we have seen another example: the literary men who lived in rhetoric, the artists who lived in art for art's sake and for money's sake, were beside themselves at the disturbance caused by the Revolution of February. We have an acquaintance, a teacher of singing, who, to escape 1848, moved from Paris to London, to the home of sore throats, bronchitis, asthma, and speaking through the teeth—only to avoid hearing the alarm bell and the masses singing in chorus.

In the Russia of to-day the causes which led men to flee from Paris and from Arkansas are combined. In America what was most alarming was naked Nature, wild Nature with the dew of creation not yet dry upon its leaves, the Nature we love so ardently in pictures and poems. (The man with the revolver naively killing his neighbour is as much in place in the Pampas as the naive tiger with teeth an inch long.) In France Nature is not to be feared, it is swept and garnished, tigers do not walk about, and the vine flourishes; but, on the other hand, in 1848, passions broke loose again, and again the foundations of good order tottered. Among us in Russia, while Nature is untouched, men and institutions, culture and barbarism, the past that died an age ago, and the future which will be born in ages to come—all are in ferment and dissolution, being pulled down and built up, everywhere there are clouds of dust, posts and rafters. Indeed, if one adds to our primitive means of travel the highly developed means of making money in the Service, to the natural mud of our roads the filth of the life of our landowners, to our winter tempests the Winter Palace, together with the generals, the Cabinet Ministers, the refreshment bars, and the Filarets, 'the gendarme vanguard of civilisation' made in Germany, and the rearguard with axes in their belt, primeval in their force and their simplicity, one must have a great passion or a mighty madness to plunge of free will into that whirlpool, which redeems its chaos by the rainbow-lights of prophecy and the grand visions, for ever glimmering behind the fog and for ever unable to disperse it.

Passion and madness are talents of a sort, and do not come at will. One is irresistibly drawn into the whirlpool, another is repelled by its froth and uproar. The point is that to one man sleep is dearer than father and mother, and to another his dream. Which is better? I do not know: and, indeed, both may lead to the same delirium.

But we will not give way to these philosophic reflections; they commonly by one path or another conduct us to the unpleasant conclusion that whether you batten in a feather-bed or fret yourself in a squirrel's wheel, you will do no good one way or the other, except perhaps to enrich the soil when you are dead. Every life, as the students' song has it, begins with *Juvenes dum sumus,* and ends with *Nos habebit humus!*

We must not dwell on this mournful reduction of everything in the world to nullity, or you will call me a nihilist, and that is now the term of abuse which has replaced Hegelian, Byronist, and suchlike.

A living man thinks of what is living. The question between us is not whether a man has the right to withdraw into a peaceful retreat, to turn aside like an ancient philosopher from the Nazarene madness and the influx of barbarians. Of that, there can be no question. I only want to make clear to myself whether the ancient sanctuaries, built so solidly and overgrown with the moss of mediaeval Europe, are so peaceful and convenient, above all, so secure as they were; and, on the other hand, whether there is not a magic spell in the visions we see in the snowstorm and the ringing of the sledge-bells, and whether there is not some real force in that magic.

There was a time when you defended the ideas of Western Europe, and you did well; the only pity is that it was entirely unnecessary. The ideas of Western Europe, that is, scientific ideas, have long ago been recognised by all as the inalienable property of humanity. Science is entirely without latitude or longitude; it is like Goethe's 'Divan,' Western and Oriental.

Now you want to maintain that the actual forms of Western European life are also the heritage of mankind, and you believe that the manner of life of the European upper classes, as evolved in the historic past, is alone in harmony with the aesthetic needs of human development, that it alone furnishes the conditions essential for literary and artistic life; that in Western Europe art was born

and grew up, and to Western Europe it belongs; and
finally, that there is no other art at all. Let us pause first
at this point.

Pray do not imagine that I shall from the point of view
of civic austerity and Puritanism protest against the place
which you give to art in life. I am in agreement with
you on that point. Art—*c'est autant de pris*; together
with the summer lightnings of personal happiness, it is
our one indubitable blessing. In all the rest, we are
either toiling or drawing water in a sieve for humanity,
for our country, for fame, for our children, for money,
and at the same time are solving an endless problem. In
art we find enjoyment, in it the goal is attained; it, too,
is an 'End' in itself.

And so, giving to Diana of Ephesus what is due to
Diana, I ask you of what exactly you are speaking, of the
present or the past? Of the fact that art has developed
in Western Europe, that Dante and Michael Angelo,
Shakespeare and Rembrandt, Mozart and Goethe, were
by birth and opinion 'Westerners'? But no one disputes it. Or do you mean that a long historical life has
prepared both a better stage for art and a finer framework
for it, that museums are more sumptuous in Europe than
anywhere else, galleries and schools richer, students more
numerous, teachers more gifted, theatres better decorated,
and so on? And that, too, is true. Or nearly so, for
ever since the great opera has returned to its primitive
state of performers strolling from town to town, only
grand opera is *überall und nirgends*. In the whole of
America there is no such Campo Santo as in Pisa, but still
Campo Santo is a graveyard. It is quite natural, indeed,
that where there have been most corals there you find most
coral-reefs. . . . But in all this where is the new living
creative art, where is the artistic element in life itself?
To be continually calling up the dead, to be repeating
Beethoven, to be playing Phèdre and Athalie, is all very

well, but it says nothing for creativeness. In the dullest periods of Byzantium, Homer was read and Sophocles recited at the literary evenings; in Rome, the statues of Pheidias were preserved, and the best sculpture collected on the eve of the Generics and the Alarics. Where is the new art, where is the artistic initiative? Is it to be found in Wagner's 'music of the future'?

Art is not fastidious; it can depict anything, setting upon all the indelible imprint of the spirit of beauty, and impartially raising to the level of the madonnas and demigods every casual incident of life, every sound and every form, the slumbering pool under the tree, the fluttering bird, the horse at the drinking-trough, the sunburnt beggar-boy. From the sinister, savage fantasy of hell and the Day of Judgment to the Flemish tavern with the back view of a peasant, from Faust to Faublas, from the Requiem to the Kamarinsky, all lie within the domain of art. . . . But even art has its limit. There is a stumbling-block which neither the violinist's bow nor the painter's brush nor the sculptor's chisel can deal with; art to conceal its impotence mocks at it and turns it into caricature. That stumbling-block is petty-bourgeois vulgarity. The artist who excellently portrays a man completely naked, covered with rags, or so completely dressed that nothing is to be seen but armour or a monk's cassock, is reduced to despair before the bourgeois in a swallow-tail. Hence the necessity of flinging a Roman toga upon Robert Peel; hence a banker is stripped of his coat and his cravat, and his shirt is unbuttoned, so that if he could see his own bust after death he would be covered with blushes before his own wife. . . . Robert Macaire and Prudhomme are great caricatures. Sometimes caricatures are works of genius; in Dickens they are tragically true to life, but still they are caricatures. Beyond Hogarth that style cannot go. The Vandyke and Rembrandt of petty bourgeoisie are Punch and Charivari,

they are its portrait gallery and pillory; they are the
family records and the whipping-post.

The fact is that the whole petty-bourgeois character,
both in its good qualities and its bad qualities, is opposed
to art and cramping to it; art withers in it like a green
leaf in chlorine, and only the passions common to all
humanity can| at times, by breaking into bourgeois life,
or, even better, breaking out of its decorum, raise it to
artistic significance.

Decorum, that is the real word. The petty bourgeois,
like Moltchalin,[1] has two talents, and he has the same
ones, Prudence and Punctuality. The life of the middle
class is full of petty defects and petty virtues; it is self-
restrained, often niggardly, and shuns what is extreme,
what is superfluous. The park is transformed into the
kitchen garden, the thatched cottage into the little town
house with an escutcheon painted on the shutters, but
every day they drink tea in it, and every day they eat
meat. It is an *immense step* in advance, but not at all
artistic. Art is more at home with poverty and luxury
than with crude prosperity, with comfort when it is an
end in itself; if it comes to that, it is more at home with
the harlot selling herself than with the respectable woman
selling at three times the cost the work of the starving
seamstress. Art is not at ease in the stiff, over-neat, careful house of the petty bourgeois, and his house is bound
to be such; art feels instinctively that in that life it is
reduced to the level of external decoration such as wall-
paper and furniture, to the level of a hurdy-gurdy; if
the hurdy-gurdy man is in the way he is kicked out, if
they want to listen they give him a halfpenny and with
that have done with him. . . . Art which is pre-
eminently elegance of proportion cannot endure the yard-
measure; a life self-satisfied with its narrow mediocrity
is defiled for art by the worst of blots—vulgarity.

[1] A character in the play *Woe from Wit.—(Translator's Note.)*

But that does not in the least prevent the whole cultured world from passing into petty bourgeoisie, and the vanguard has arrived there already. Petty bourgeoisie is the ideal to which Europe is everywhere striving and ascending. It is the 'hen in the soup,' of which Henry the Fourth dreamt. A little house, with little windows looking into the street, a school for the boy, a dress for the girl, a servant for the hard work—all that makes up indeed a haven of refuge—Havre de Grace! The man turned off the soil which he had tilled for ages for his master, the descendant of the villager, crushed in the struggle, the homeless workman, doomed to everlasting toil and hunger, the day-labourer, born a beggar and dying a beggar, can only wipe the sweat from their brows and look without horror at their children by becoming property owners, masters, bourgeois; their sons will not be kept in lifelong bondage for a crust of bread, their daughters will not be condemned to the factory or the brothel. How should they not strive to be bourgeois? The bright image of the shopkeeper—who has replaced the knight and the priest for the middle classes—hovers as the ideal before the eyes of the casual labourer, until his tired and horny hands drop on his sunken chest, or until he looks at life with that Irish tranquillity of despair which precludes every hope, every expectation, except the hope of a whole bottle of whisky next Sunday.

Bourgeoisie, the last word of civilisation, founded on the absolute despotism of property, is the 'democratisation' of aristocracy, the 'aristocratisation' of democracy. In this order Almaviva is the equal of Figaro—everything below is straining up into bourgeoisie, everything above sinking down into it through the impossibility of maintaining itself. The United States present the spectacle of one class—the middle class—with nothing below it and nothing above it, and the petty bourgeois manners and morals are retained. The German peasant is the

petty bourgeois of agriculture; the workman of every
country is the petty bourgeois of the future. Italy, the
most poetical land in Europe, was not able to hold out,
but at once forsook her fanatical lover, Mazzini, and
betrayed her husband, the Hercules Garibaldi, as soon
as Cavour, the petty bourgeois of genius, the little fat man
in spectacles, offered to keep her as his mistress.

With the coming of bourgeoisie, individual characters
are effaced, but these effaced persons are better fed;
clothes are made by the dozen, not to measure or to order,
but there are more people who wear them. With the
coming of bourgeoisie, the beauty of the race is effaced,
but its prosperity increases, the statuesque beggar from
Transteverino is employed for rough work by the puny
shopkeeper of the Via del Corso. The crowds of holiday-
makers in the Champs-Élysées or Kensington Gardens,
or the audiences in churches or theatres, depress one with
their vulgar faces, their dull expressions; but the holiday-
makers in the Champs-Élysées, the audiences listening
to the sermons of Lacordaire or the songs of Levasseur,[1]
are not concerned at that, they do not notice it. But
what is very important to them and very striking is that
their fathers and elder brothers were not in a position to
go holiday-making or to the theatre as they are; that their
elders sometimes drove on the box of carriages, but they
drive about in cabs, and very often too.

It is for this reason that bourgeoisie is triumphing and
is bound to triumph. It is useless to tell a hungry man,
'It suits you much better to be hungry; don't look for
food.' The sway of bourgeoisie is the answer to emancipation without land, to the freeing of men from bondage
while the soil is left in bondage to a few of the elect. The
masses that have earned their halfpence have come to

[1] A famous singer who made his début in *La Caravane* in 1813.
He is frequently mentioned in French memoirs of the period.—
(*Translator's Note.*)

the top and are enjoying themselves in their own way and possessing the world. They have no need of strongly marked characters, of original minds. Science cannot help stumbling upon the discoveries that lie closest at hand. Photography — that barrel-organ version of painting — replaces the artist; if a creative artist does appear he is welcome, but there is no desperate need of him. Beauty, talent, are altogether out of the normal; they are the exceptions, the luxury of Nature, its highest limit or the result of great effort, of whole generations. The voice of Mario, the points of the winner of the Derby, are rarities. But a good lodging and a dinner are necessities. There is a great deal that is bourgeois in Nature herself, one may say; she very often stops short in the middle, half-way, and evidently has not the spirit to go further. Who has told you that Europe will have it?

Europe has been through a bad quarter of an hour. The bourgeois were all but losing the fruits of a long lifetime, of prolonged efforts, of hard work. A vague but terrible protest has arisen in the conscience of humanity. The petty bourgeois have been reminded of their wars for their rights, their heroic age and biblical traditions. Abel, Remus, Thomas of Münster have been slain once more, and long will the grass grow upon their tombs as a warning how the all-powerful bourgeoisie punishes its enemies. Since then all has returned to its normal routine, which seems secure, which is based on reason, which is strong and growing, but has no artistic plan, no aesthetic chord: it does not seek to have them; it is too practical; it agrees with Catherine 11. that it is not becoming for a serious man to play the piano well; the Empress, too, regarded men from the practical point of view. The gardens are too heavily manured for flowers to grow; flowers are too unprofitable for the petty bourgeois' garden; if he does sometimes grow them, it is for sale.

In the spring of 1850 I was looking for lodgings in Paris. By that time I had lived so long in Europe that I had grown to hate the crowding and crush of civilisation, which at first we Russians like so much. I looked with horror mixed with disgust at the continually moving, swarming crowd, foreseeing how it would rob me of half my seat at the theatre and in the diligence, how it would dash like a wild beast into the railway carriages, how it would heat and pervade the air—and for that reason I was looking for a flat, not in a crowded place, and to some extent free from the vulgarity and deadly sameness of the lodgings *à trots chambres à coucher de maître.*[1]

Some one suggested to me the lodge of a big old house on the further side of the Seine in the Faubourg St. Germain, or close by. I went there. The old wife of the concierge took the keys and led me by the yard. The house and the lodge stood behind a fence; within the courtyard behind the house, there were green trees. The lodge was neglected and deserted-looking, probably no one had been living there for many years. The somewhat old-fashioned furniture was of the period of the First Empire, with Roman straight lines and blackened gilt. The lodge was by no means large or sumptuous, but the furniture and the arrangement of the rooms all pointed to a different idea of the conveniences of life. Near the little drawing-room to one side, next the bedroom, was a tiny study with cupboards for books and a big writing-table. I walked through the rooms, and it seemed to me that after long wanderings I had come again upon a dwelling for a man, *un chez soi*, not a hotel room nor a human stall.

[1] A very intelligent man, Count Oscar Reichenbach, said to me once, speaking of the better-class houses in London: 'Tell me the rent and the storey, and I will undertake to go on a dark night without a candle and fetch a clock, a vase, decanters . . . whatever you like of the things that are invariably standing in every middle class dwelling.'—(*Author's Note.*)

Everything—the theatre, holiday-making, books, pictures, clothes—everything has gone down in quality and gone up terribly in numbers. The crowd of which I was speaking is the best proof of success, of strength, of growth; it is bursting through all the dams, overflowing and flooding everything; it is content with anything, and can never have enough. London is crowded, Paris is cramped. A hundred railway carriages linked on are insufficient; there are forty theatres and not a seat free; a play has to be running for three months for the London public to be able to see it.

'Why are your cigars so inferior?' I asked one of the leading London tobacconists.

'It is hard to get them, and, indeed, it is not worth the trouble; there are few connoisseurs and still fewer well-to-do ones.'

'Not worth while? You charge eightpence each for them.'

'That brings us hardly any profit. While you and a dozen like you will buy them, is there much gain in that? In one day I sell more twopenny and threepenny cigars than I do of these in a year. I am not going to order any more of them.'

Here was a man who had grasped the spirit of the age. All trade, especially in England, is based now on quantity and cheapness, and not at all on quality, as old-fashioned Russians imagine when they reverently buy Tula penknives with an English trademark on them. Everything has a wholesale, ready-made, conventional character, everything is within the reach of almost every one, but does not allow of aesthetic distinction or personal taste. Everywhere the hundred-thousand-headed hydra lies in wait close at hand round a corner, ready to listen to everything, to look at everything indiscriminately, to be dressed in anything, to be fed on anything—this is the all-powerful crowd of 'conglomerated mediocrity' (to use Stuart

Mill's expression) which purchases everything, and so dominates everything. The crowd is without ignorance, but also without culture. To please it art screams, gesticulates, falsifies, and exaggerates, or in despair turns away from men and paints animal portraits and pictures of cattle, like Landseer and Rosa Bonheur.

Have you seen in the last fifteen years in Europe an actor, a single actor, who is not a clown, a buffoon of senti-mentality, or a buffoon of burlesque? Name him!

Many blessings have been vouchsafed to the epoch of which the last expression is to be found in the notes of Verdi, but the artistic vocation was certainly not among them. Its own creation—the *café chantant* —an amphi-bious product, half-way between the beer-cellar and the boulevard theatre, is precisely on its level. I have nothing against *cafés chantants*, but I cannot give them serious artistic value; they satisfy the 'average customer,' as the English say, the average purchaser, the average bidder, the hundred-headed hydra of the middle class, and there is nothing more to be said.

The way out from this position is far off. Behind the multitude now ruling stands an even greater multitude of candidates eager to enter it, to whom the manners, ideas, and habits of life of the middle class appear as the one goal to strive for. There are enough to multiply their numbers ten times over. A world without land, a world predominated by town life, with the rights of property carried to the extreme point, has no other way of salvation, and it will all pass through petty bourgeoisie, which in our eyes has not reached a high level, but in the eyes of the agricultural population and the proletariat stands for culture and progress. Those who are in advance live in tiny cliques like secular monasteries, taking no interest in what is being done by the world outside their walls.

The same thing has happened before, but on a smaller

scale and less consciously; moreover, in the past there were ideals, convictions, words which set both the simple heart of the poor citizen and the heart of the haughty knight beating; they had holy things in common, to which all men did homage as before the sacrament. Where is there a hymn nowadays which could be sung with faith and conviction in every storey of the house from the cellar to the garret? Where is our 'Ein feste Burg ist unser Gott' or our 'Marseillaise'?

When Ivanov was in London he used to say with despair that he was looking for a new religious type, and could find it nowhere in the world about him. A pure artist, dreading falsehood in his painting like blasphemy, understanding rather by imagination than by analysis, he asked us to show him where were the picturesque features in which a new Atonement would shine forth. We could not show them. 'Perhaps Mazzini will,' he thought.

Mazzini would have pointed him to the unity of Italy, perhaps to Garibaldi in 1861, to that *last of the great men* as to a *forerunner*.

Ivanov died knocking in vain, the door was not opened to him.

Isle of Wight.   *June* 10, 1862.

Letter 2

APROPOS of Mazzini. A few months ago the first volume of his collected works appeared. Instead of a preface or notes, Mazzini connected the articles written by him at various times, by means of a series of amplifications; there is a mass of the most living interest in these explanatory pages. The poem of his monastic life dedicated to one god and one service is unintentionally revealed in these disconnected jottings, possibly more fully than he meant.

An enthusiast, a fanatic with Ligurian blood in his veins, Mazzini was from youth up irrevocably devoted to the great cause of the freedom of Italy, and to that cause he remains faithful for ever—*ora e sempre*, as his motto says: he finds his youth, love, family, faith, duty, all in that. Espoused to one wife, he has not betrayed her, and grey-headed, emaciated, sick, he holds off death, he refuses to die before Rome is the capital of United Italy and the lion of Saint Mark tears to tatters the black-and-yellow rag which flies above him.

The testimony of such a man, one, too, who attacked scepticism, socialism, and materialism, a man who lived in every heart-throb of European life for forty years, is extremely important.

After the first schoolboy enthusiasm of every revolutionary career, after the romance of conspiracies, mysterious passwords, meetings at night, vows over bloodless daggers, the young man reconsiders things.

In spite of the fascination for a youthful Latin soul of the setting and ritual, the earnest and ascetic Mazzini soon discerned that there was in Carbonarism far more ceremony and empty form than action, far more meeting and preparing than doing. We, too, perceived long ago that the political liturgy of the priests of conspiracy, like the church liturgy, is only a dramatic performance; however much feeling and sincerity the priests sometimes bring to the service, still the Lamb is slain in bread and bleeds in wine. Mazzini noticed that thirty-five years ago.

Having reached that point, it was hard for the young Carbonaro to stop. Watching recent events in the crumbling Empire, an eye-witness of monarchical restorations, revolutions, constitutional attempts and republican failures, Mazzini reached the conclusion that contemporary European life had, as he expressed it, 'no initiative of any sort,' that the conservative idea and the revolutionary idea have only negative significance: one destroys, not knowing to what end, the other preserves, not knowing to what end; that in everything that was going on (and the revolution of 1830 was going on at that time) there was nothing inaugurating a new order of things.

In these words of the future rival of the Pope there are echoes of the funeral knell struck by the Pope's friend, Maistre.

The void of which Mazzini was sensible may well be understood.

The flood-tide of the revolutionary sea rose triumphantly in 1789 and, untroubled by any doubts, drowned the old world. But when everything was covered by its waves, and when mitres, plumed hats, and heads without bodies (among them one wearing a crown) had bobbed up for a moment and sunk again to the bottom, then for the first time a fearful freedom and emptiness was felt. The forces set free attacked one another, then stopped, exhausted; they had nothing to do, they waited for the events of the day as casual labourers wait for work. Those standing armies of the Revolution boiled with martial energy, but there was no war to fight; above all, there was no clear aim to fight for. And when there is no aim, anything may become the aim. Napoleon assured them that he was the aim, that war was the aim, and set blood flowing faster than the revolutionary tide had flooded the world with ideas.

Mazzini saw that, and, before uttering his final verdict, he looked beyond the political walls. There he was met by the colossal egotism of Goethe, his serene callousness, his interest as of a naturalist in human affairs; there he was met by the self-consuming colossal egotism of Byron; the poetry of scorn beside the poetry of contemplation; lamentation, laughter, proud flight, and revulsion from the modern world beside the haughty satisfaction in it. The heroes of Byron impress Mazzini; he tries to discover the origin of these strange hermits with no religion and no monastery, these egoists, concentrated on themselves, useless, unhappy, without work, without fatherland, without interests, these ascetics, ready for sacrifices which they know not how to make, ready to despise themselves as human beings. And again Mazzini stumbles upon the same cause. Byron's heroes are lacking in faith, in an objective ideal; the poet's vision, turning aside from his barren, repellent surroundings, was reduced to the lyrical expression of states of feeling, to the impulses of activity turned inwards, to morbid nerves, to the spiritual abysses where madness and sense, vice and virtue, lose their limits and turn to phantoms, to gnawing remorse and, at the same time, morbid ecstasy.

Mazzini's active spirit could not stop at this analysis of the malady. At all costs he longed to find motive for action, the word of a new faith,—and he found them.

Now the lever is in his hands. He will turn the world upside-down, he will re-create Europe, he will exchange the coffin for the cradle, will turn the demolishers into architects, will solve the problem of society and the individual, of freedom and authority, will give faith to the heart without robbing the mind of reason . . .. What, you may wonder, is this *magnum* ignotum? *The unity and freedom of Italy with ancient Rome for its centre.*

In all this, of course, there is no place for analysis nor for criticism. Was it not because Mazzini had found a new revelation, a new redemption of the world, and an Italian *resorgimiento*, that he failed to foresee one thing —Cavour? He must have hated Cavour more than Antonelli. Cavour was the prose translation of his poem, he fulfilled the prosaic part of Mazzini's programme, *à la longue* Rome and Venice will follow suit. Cavour is the Italian Martha, thwarting the all-absorbing dream of the Italian Mary with household trivialities; and while Mary, with tender ecstasy, saw the redemption of the world in liberated Italy, Martha was cutting out a Belgian dress for Italy, and the country, pleased that the new garment did not pinch her, went along the beaten European track, the great trade route, though there is no reaching a regeneration of the world without risking a more perilous path.

The fanatic Mazzini was mistaken; the immensity of his error made Cavour and United Italy possible. But for us it matters little how Mazzini solved the question; what is of interest to us is that as soon as a Western European stands on his own feet and shakes off ready-made formulas, as soon as he begins to look at the state of contemporary Europe, he is conscious of something amiss, he feels that things are not going the right way, that progress has taken the wrong turning. Revolutionaries and conservatives can easily cheat this feeling by replacing what they lack with the principle of nationalism, especially if, luckily for them, their native country is under foreign rule. But what comes next? What are they to do when they have established the independence of their people? Or what are they to do if it is already independent?

Mazzini, conscious of the emptiness of the democratic idea, points to the emancipation of Italy from the 'Tedeschi.' Stuart Mill sees that everything around him is growing vulgar and petty; he looks with despair at the overwhelming myriads of petty bourgeois massed together like pressed caviare, with no initiative, no understanding, but in England they have no Austrian yoke, no Pope, no Neapolitan Bourbon. What is to be done there?

I foresee the wrath of our bond-slaves of the factories of learning and the foundries of scholasticism; I can see how malignantly in the light of day they will look at me with their night-owls' eyes and say: 'What nonsense is he talking? As though historical development could turn aside, as though it did not move according to its laws, like the planets which never turn aside, and never break away from their orbits.'

To this last contention it may be said that anything may happen, and that there is no reason why a planet should not sometimes break away from its orbit. Saturn's ring has been preserved and revolves with it, while Jupiter's necklace has broken into separate beads, and the earth has one moon like a cataract in the eye. But one has but to glance into a hospital instead of an observatory to see how the living *go off the track*, develop in their abnormality and carry it to comparative perfection, distorting and sometimes destroying the whole organism. The delicate equilibrium of every living creature is uncertain and to some extent adapts itself to abnormalities: but one step too far in that direction, and the overstrained knot is broken and the elements released form into new combinations.

The general laws, of course, remain the same, but they may vary in their particular applications, till they appear absolutely opposite in their manifestations. Fluff flies and lead falls in obedience to the same law.

In the absence of a set plan and fixed date, of a yard-measure and a clock, development in nature and in history, far from not being able to turn aside, is bound to be continually turning aside, in accordance with every influence and by virtue of its irresponsible passivity and lack of definite aim. In the individual organism the deviation reveals itself by pain, and the warning of pain often comes too late. Complex, composite organisms fly off at a tangent and are carried downhill, unconscious of the road or the danger, owing to the constant change of generations. There is very little possibility of stopping the deviation, arresting the downward flight or overtaking it, and there is little desire to do so; such a desire would in every case presuppose consciousness and aim.

Consciousness is a very different thing from practical application. Pain does not cure, but calls for treatment. The diagnosis may be correct, but the treatment may be bad; one may have no knowledge of medicine, yet clearly perceive the disease. To demand a cure from a man who points out some evil is exceedingly rash. The Christians who wept over the sins of this world, the socialists who exposed the sores of the social order, and we, dissatisfied, ungrateful children of civilisation, we are not the physicians, we are the pain; what will come of our moaning and groaning we do not know; but the pain is recorded.

We are confronted with a civilisation which has developed consistently on the basis of a landless proletariat and the unlimited right of the owner over his property. What Sieyès prophesied has come to pass: the middle class has become all-important because it possesses property. Whether we know how to emerge from petty-bourgeois rule to the rule of the people or not, we have the right to regard bourgeois rule as a one-sided development, a monstrosity.

By the word monstrosity, disease, we commonly understand something unnatural, exceptional, not reflecting that abnormality and disease are more *natural* than the normal, which is merely the algebraical formula of the organism, an abstraction, a generalisation, an ideal formed from different particulars by the exclusion of what is accidental. The deviation and the abnormality follow the same law as the organisms; if they were not subjected to it, the organism would die. But, in addition to that, they rest on their peculiar rights, they have their private laws, the consequences of which we have again the right to deduce, apart from any ability to correct them. Seeing that the forepart of the giraffe has acquired a one-sided development, we could surmise that this development was at theexpense of the hind part, and that in consequence there would infallibly be a series of defects in his organism corresponding with his one-sided development, but for him natural and comparatively normal.

Bourgeoisie makes up the forepart of the European camelopard; that might be disputed, if the fact were not so obvious; but, once that is accepted, we cannot overlook all the consequences of this supremacy of the shop and trade. It is clear that the man at the helm of this world will be the tradesman, and that he will set his trademark on all its manifestations. The ineptitude of an aristocracy by birth and the misery of a prole-tariat by birth are equally helpless against him. The government must die of hunger or become his menial; its comrades in unproductivity, the guardians of the human race in its immaturity, the lawyers, notaries, judges and such, are equally under his yoke. Together with his supremacy, the whole of moral life is degraded, and Stuart Mill, for instance, did not exaggerate when he talked of the narrowing of men's minds and energies, the filing down of individuality, life continually becoming more shallow, and wide human interests being continually more excluded from it by its being confined to the interests of the counting-house and bourgeois prosperity. Mill says plainly that, going by that road, England will become a second China; to which we would add, and not England alone.

Perhaps some crisis will save us from the Chinese decay. But whence and how will it come, and will the aged body survive it? That I cannot tell, nor can Stuart Mill. Experience has taught us; more cautious than Mazzini, we humbly adhere to the point of view of the dissector. We know of no remedies and have little faith in surgery.

I have been particularly fortunate, I have lived next door to the hospital and have had a first-rate seat in the anatomical theatre; I had not to look in the atlas, nor to attend lectures on parliamentary therapeutics, nor theoretical pathology; disease, death, and dissolution were taking place before my eyes.

The death agony of the July monarchy, the fever of the Papacy, the premature birth of the Republic and her death, the June days following on the February twilight, all Europe in a fit of somnambulism falling from the roof of the Pantheon into the muddy pond of the police! And then ten years in the spacious museum of pathological anatomy, the London Exhibition of specimens of all the progressive parties in Europe, side by side with the indigenous specimens of every form of conservatism from the times of the Judæan high priests to the Puritans of Scotland.

Ten years!

I had leisure to look deeply into that life, into what was going on around me; but my opinion has not changed since in 1848 I ventured, not without horror, to decipher on the brow of those men the *Vixerunt* of Cicero!

With every year I struggle more and more against the lack of comprehension of men here, their indifference to every interest, to every truth, the trivial frivolity of their senile intellects, the impossibility of persuading them that routine is not the infallible criterion, and that habit proves nothing. Sometimes I stop short, I fancy that the worst time is over, I try to be inconsistent: I fancy, for instance, that suppressed speech in France is growing into thought. . . . I expect, I hope. . . . Exceptions do happen sometimes. . . . Something seems to be dawning. . . . No, nothing!

And no one feels this. . . . People look at you with a sort of pity as at one deranged. . . . But I have happened to meet with old, old men who shake their heads very mournfully. Evidently these old men are ill at ease with the strangers of their household, that is, with their sons and grandsons. . . .

Yes, *caro mio*, there is still in the life of to-day a great type for a poet, a type altogether untouched. . . . The artist who would look intently at the grandfathers and grandsons, at the fathers and children, and fearlessly, mercilessly embody them in a gloomy, terrible poem, would be the laureate at the graveside of this world.

That type—the type of the Don Quixote of the Revolution, the old man of 1789, living out his old age on the bread of his grandsons, French petty bourgeois grown rich—has more than once moved me to horror and depression. Think of him a little and your hair will stand on end.

Isle of Wight, Cowes.   *July* 20, 1862.

Letter 3

· · · PHEW, what a disgusting summer! Cold, darkness, sleet, continual winds, constant irritation of the nerves and also of the membrane of the nose; and all that has been going on for three months, and there were seven months before that on this side of the Sign of the Ram.

At last the sun has come out in a cloudless sky. The sea is smooth and sparkling. I am sitting at my window in a tiny farm; I cannot take my eyes off it; it is so long since I saw the sun and the distance. To-day it is actually warm. I am simply delighted, seeing that Nature is not played out yet. The rejoicing is endless: bees and birds are flying, buzzing, singing, droning; in the little yard of the farm the cock, dry at last, is crowing his loudest; and the old dog, oblivious of his age and social position, lies on his back like a puppy, with his legs in the air, rolling from side to side with an unconscious epicurean growl. There are no people to be seen from my window, but fields, trees, and gardens without end; in spite of the sea on one side, this view reminds one of our great Russian landscapes, and there is the scent of grass and trees, too.

It was more than time for the weather to improve, for I had really begun to be afraid not of a social, but of a geological catastrophe; I had begun to expect that after ten months of bad weather Europe would crack, and by volcanic means cut the Gordian knot of contemporary problems and *impasses*, bidding those who will to begin, not from their ABC, but from a second Adam.

You, as a poet and idealist, probably don't believe in such nonsense, but Lamé,[1] as one of the greatest mathematicians of our age, is not of that opinion. He fancies that the equilibrium of the crowded continents is very insecure, and that, taking also into account their rapid movement in one direction, and certain facts of the shifting of contours in Iceland, the earthly globe may crack in Europe at any moment. He has even drawn up a series of formulas and made a series of calculations. . . . But there is no need to frighten you; the crack won't reach as far as the province of Orel.

We had better, taking advantage of the phenomenally fine weather, return to our discussion of 'Ends and Beginnings,' and if the earthquake comes it will settle things.

The Don Quixote of the Revolution sticks in my head. That austere, tragic type is vanishing, vanishing like the aurochs of the White Russian forest, like the Red Indian, and there is no artist to record his old clear-cut features, marked with the traces of every sorrow, every grief that comes from general principles and faith in humanity and reason. Soon these features will perish, still unyielding,

---

[1] Lamé, Gabriel, born 1795, was a French mathematician who for many years held an important post in the Transport Department of the Russian Government. He published *Leçons sur la Théorie Mathématique de l'Élasticité,* and many other works.—(*Translator's Note.*)

still wearing an expression of proud and reproachful disdain, then their image will be effaced and the memory of man will lose one of its noblest and loftiest types.

These are the peaks in which the mountain range of the eighteenth century ends; with them it reaches the limit; with them a series of ascending efforts breaks off. There is no reaching a higher level through volcanic action.

Titans, left after the struggle, after defeat, representatives of unsatisfied ambitions, for all their Titanic effort turn from great men into melancholy Don Quixotes. History rises and falls between the prophets and the Knights of the Grievous Countenance. Roman patricians, republicans, stoics of the early ages, hermits fleeing into the wilderness from a Christianity vulgarised into the official religion, Puritans who passed a whole century gnashing their teeth over failure to attain their tedious ideal—all these, left by the retreating tide, obstinately struggling forward and sticking in the mud, unsupported by the wave, all are Don Quixotes, but Don Quixotes who have found their Cervantes. For the champions of the early church, there are volumes of legends, there are ikons and paintings, there are mosaics and sculpture. The type of Puritanism is firmly fixed in English literature and in Dutch painting, but the type of the Don Quixote of the Revolution is fading before our eyes, growing rarer and rarer, and no one thinks of even photographing it.

Fanatics of earthly religion, dreamers not of the Kingdom of Heaven, but of the Kingdom of Man, they are left the last sentinels of the ideal, long ago deserted by the army; in gloomy solitude they stand for half a century, incapable of changing, still expecting the coming of the republic on earth. The ground sinks lower and lower; they refuse to see it. I still come upon some of these apostles of the 'nineties; their clear-cut, melancholy, striking figures, standing out above two generations, seem to me like austere, immovable Memnons, falling into ruins stone by stone in the Egyptian desert. . . . While at their feet tiny men and little camels swarm, bustle, drag their goods, hardly visible through the whirling sand.

Death gives more and more warning of his approach; the aged, lustreless eye is sterner, grows weary with the effort of seeking a successor, looking for one to whom to yield place and honour. Son?—the old man frowns. Grandson?—he waves his hand in despair. Poor King Lear in democracy, whenever he turns his dimming eyes upon those of his own household, everywhere he is met by lack of understanding, lack of sympathy, dis-approval, half-concealed reproach, petty considerations and petty interests. They are afraid, before strangers, of his Jacobin words; they beg pardon for him, pointing to his scanty grey hair. His daughter-in-law worries him to be reconciled with the Church, and a Jesuit *abbé* flits in at times, like a passing crow, to see what strength and consciousness is left, so as to catch him for God in his deathbed delirium. Well it is for Citoyen Lear if there is somewhere in his neighbourhood a Citoyen Kent who finds that 'he is every inch' a hero of 1794, some obscure comrade of Santerre,[1] a soldier of the army of Marceau and Hoche, Citoyen Spartacus Brutus junior, childishly faithful to his tradition, and proudly keeping shop with the hand which held a lance crowned with the Phrygian cap. Lear will visit him sometimes to relieve his heart, to shake his head, and to recall old days, with their immense hopes, with their great events, to abuse Tallien[2] . . . and Barras[2] . . . the Restoration, with its *cafards*, the shopkeeper king, and *ce traître de Lamartine*. Both *know* that the hour of revolution will strike, that the people

---

[1] A brewer who was in command of the 'Garde Nationale' in 1793.

[2] Members of the 'Convention' of 1792.—(*Translator's Notes.*)

will awaken like a lion and again hoist the Phrygian cap, and one of them will fall asleep in these dreams.

Scowling Lear will follow the coffin of Spartacus Brutus junior, or Spartacus Brutus junior, not concealing his profound loathing of all the kindred of the deceased, will follow the coffin of Lear, and of the two majestic figures one only will be left, and that one absolutely superfluous.

'He, too, is no more; he, too, has not lived to see it,' thinks the old man who is left, as he comes back from the funeral. Can superstition and monarchy, the party of Pitt and of Coburg, have triumphed for good and all? Can all our long lifetime, our efforts, our sacrifices? . . . No, that cannot be; the truth is on our side, and the victory will be with us. . . . Reason and justice will triumph, in France first of all, of course, and then in all humanity, and 'Vive la République Une et Indivisible'! The old man at eighty prays with his aged lips, just as another old man, giving up his soul in peace to his Maker, murmurs 'Thy Kingdom come,' and both tranquilly close their eyes and do not see that neither the Kingdom of Heaven on earth nor the sole and indivisible Republic in France is coming at all, and do not see it, because not the Lord but their decaying body has received their soul in peace.

Holy Don Quixotes, the earth rest lightly upon you!

This fanatical conviction of the possibility of bringing about harmonious order and the common weal, of the possibility of realising the truth because it is the truth, this renunciation of everything private and personal, this devotion which survives every ordeal, every blow, is the topmost peak. . . . The mountain ends there; higher, beyond, is icy air, darkness, nothing. We must go down again. Why cannot we go on? Why does not Mont Blanc stand on Chimborazo and one of the Himalayas continue them? That would be a mountain!

But no—every geological cataclysm has its romance, its mountain poem, its individual peaks of granite and of basalt, whose mass towers above the lower slopes. Monuments of the revolutions of the planets, they have long ago been overgrown with forest and moss, bearing witness to thousands of years of immobility. Our pioneers of the Revolution have left their Alps in history; the traces of their titanic efforts have not passed away, and it will be long before they pass. What more would you have?

Yes, that is enough for history. It has its own wholesale, ruthless valuation; in it, as in the description of battles, we have the movement of companies, the action of artillery, the attack of the left flank, the retreat of the right; it has its leading figures, the '30th Light Cavalry and afterwards the 45th.' The bulletin goes no further; it is satisfied with the sum total of the dead, but the 'fifth act' of every soldier goes further, and it has a purely civilian interest.

What was not endured by these men of the latest floodtide, left stranded in the slime and mud by its ebb! What did not these fathers endure—more solitary in their own families than monks in their cells! What terrible conflicts every hour, every day! . . . What moments of weariness and despair?

Is it not strange that in the long series of 'Misérables' brought before us by Victor Hugo there are old men . . . but *the* miserable old man *par excellence* is thrust into the background, neglected? Hugo scarcely noticed that side by side with the agonising sense of guilt there is another anguish, the agonising sense of one's useless rectitude, the recognition of one's fruitless superiority over the feebleness of every young creature near that has survived. . . . The great rhetorician and poet, while dealing with the sorrowful lives in modern France, scarcely touches upon the greatest sorrow in the world—that of the old man, young in soul, surrounded by a generation growing more and more shallow.

Beside them what are the poignant but useless and purely subjective sufferings of Jean Valjean described with such wearisome minuteness in Hugo's omnibus of a novel? Of course, one may feel compassion for every form of unhappiness, but one cannot feel deep sympathy for all. The pain of a broken leg and the pain of a broken life stir a different kind of sympathy.

We are not sufficiently Frenchmen to understand such ideals as Jean Valjean, and to sympathise with such heroes of the police as Javert. To us Javert is simply loathsome. Probably Hugo had no idea, when he drew this typically national figure of the jackal of Law and Order, how he was branding his 'charming France.' In Jean Valjean all we can understand is his external struggle of the good-luckless wild beast, baited by a whole pack of hunting dogs. His inner conflict does not touch us; this man, so strong in will and muscles, is in reality a singularly weak man. A saintly convict, an Ilya Muromets[1] from the galleys of Toulon, an acrobat at fifty, and a lovesick boy at almost sixty, he is a mass of superstition. He believes in the brand on his shoulder, he believes in his sentence, he believes that he is an outcast, because thirty years ago he stole a loaf, and that not for himself. His virtue is morbid remorse, his love is senile jealousy. His strained existence is raised to truly tragic significance only at the end of the book by the heartless narrow-mindedness of Cosette's husband and the boundless ingratitude of herself. And here Jean Valjean really has something in common with our old men — the remorse of the one and the rectitude of the others blend in burning suffering. The mercury frozen in the thermometer scalds like the molten lead of the bullet. The consciousness of rectitude, consuming half the heart, half the existence, is as painful as

---

[1] A traditional hero of Russian legend. — (*Translator's Note.*)

the gnawings of conscience, and worse indeed. In the latter case there is the relief of confession, the prospect of reward; in the former there is nothing. Between the old man of the 'nineties—fanatic, dreamer, idealist—and the son, older than he in prudence, good sense, and disillusionment, the son so extremely well satisfied with things on a lower plane, and the grandson who, swaggering in his uniform of *Guide Impérial*, dreams of how to get a berth as a *sous-préfet pour exploiter sa position*, the natural relation is violated, the balance is destroyed, and the normal succession of generations is distorted.

Jean Valjean in his aged virginity, in his lyrical personal concentration, did not himself know what he wanted from the younger generation. What did he really want from Cosette? Could she have been a friend to him? In the inexperienced innocence of his heart, he went beyond the love of a father. . . . He wanted to love her exclusively for his own sake, and a father's love is not like that. Moreover, though he has mentally been draping himself all his life in the jacket of a convict, he is crushed under the burden of repulsion evinced for him by the very narrow-minded young man—the typical representative of a generation sinking into vulgarity.

I don't know what Hugo meant to make of his Marius, but to me he is as much a type of his generation as Javert is of his. In the instincts of the young man there is still a glimmer of the virtues of another period—warm and generous impulses, with no reflection, no roots, almost no significance, springing from tradition and example. There is in him no trace of the leaven of the eighteenth century, that restless itch for analysis and criticism, that menacing summons of everything in the world to the test of the intellect; he has no intellect, but he is still a good comrade; he goes to the barricades, not knowing what is to come afterwards; he lives by routine, and, knowing *à code ouvert* what is good and what is evil, troubles his head as little about it as a man who knows for certain that it is sinful to eat meat in Lent. With this generation, the revolutionary epoch comes finally to a standstill and begins its descent; another generation, and there will be no more generous impulses; everything will fall into its commonplace routine, personality will be effaced, and the succession of individual specimens will be scarcely perceptible in the daily routine of life.

I imagine that there must have been something of the sort in the development of animals. The species in course of formation stirring towards what is above its strength, while failing to make the most of its powers, has gradually gained equilibrium and proportion, and lost its anatomical eccentricities and physiological excesses while gaining fertility, and beginning from generation to generation, from age to age, to repeat its distinct form and its individuality in the image and semblance of the first forefather who adopted steady habits.

When the species is evolved development almost stops; at any rate, it is slower and on a humbler scale, as it is with our planet. Having reached a certain stage of cooling, it changes its crust very slowly; there are floods, but there are no world-wide deluges; there are earthquakes here and there, there is no universal cataclysm. Species become stationary, and are consolidated in various forms more or less one-sided in one direction or another, and are satisfied with them; they are scarcely able to escape from them, and if they did, or if they do, the result would be just as one-sided. The mollusc does not try to become a crab, the crab a trout, or Holland Sweden. . . . If we could presuppose ideals in animals, the ideal of a crab would still be a crab, but with a more perfect equipment. The nearer a country is to its final condition, the more it regards itself as the centre of all civilisation and of every perfection, like China, which stands unrivalled; like England and France, which in their antagonism, in their rivalry, in their mutual hatred, never doubt each that she is the foremost country in the world. Some species are at rest in the position they have attained; development continues in the unfinished species, beside the finished which have completed their cycles.

Everywhere where human swarms and ant-heaps have attained comparative prosperity and equilibrium, progress becomes slower and slower, imagination and ideals are dimmed. The satisfaction of the rich and the strong suppresses the efforts of the poor and the weak. Religion appears as the comforter of all the heavy laden. Everything that gnaws at the heart, that makes men suffer, every craving left unsatisfied on earth, all are set right and satisfied in the eternal realm of Ormuzd, loftier than the Himalayas at the foot of Jehovah's throne. And the more unrepiningly men endure the temporary sorrows of earthly life, the fuller the heavenly consolation, and that for no brief period, but for ever and ever. It is a pity that we know little of the inner story of the Asiatic peoples who have dropped out of history, know little of those uneventful periods which preceded the violent inroads of savage races who devastated everything, or the predatory civilisation which uprooted or reconstructed everything. It would show us in simple and elementary form, in those plastic biblical images which only the East creates, the transition of the people from historical upheavals into a peaceful *status quo* of life, persisting in the accepted, untroubled sequence of generations, like winter into spring, spring into summer. . . .

With slow, untroubled steps England is advancing to that repose, to that unruffled stagnation of forms, ideas, convictions. The other day *The Times* congratulated her on the lack of interest in parliamentary debates, on the unrepining submission with which workmen starve to death, 'while so lately their fathers, the contemporaries of O'Connor,' agitated the country with their menacing murmurs. As firmly as an aged oak stands the English Church, its roots deep in the soil, graciously tolerating all forms of Dissent, and convinced that they will not move far away.

Swaggering and resisting, as is her wont, France is shoved backwards while making a show of progress. Behind these giants will come in two columns others, once prophetically united under one sceptre . . . on the one hand, the thin, austere, ascetic type of the Spaniard, brooding without thought, enthusiastic without an object, anxious without cause, taking everything to heart, unable to improve anything, in short, a type of a true Don Quixote de la Mancha; on the other, the sturdy Dutchman, content when he has had a good meal, reminiscent of Sancho Panza.

Is not the reason that the children of to-day are older than their fathers, older than their grandfathers, and able *à la* Dumas junior to talk of their 'prodigal fathers,' that senility is the leading characteristic of the present age? At any rate, wherever I look I see grey hairs, wrinkles, bent backs, last wills and testaments, balanced accounts, funerals, *ends*, and I am always seeking and seeking beginnings. They are only to be found in theories and abstractions.

August 10, 1862.

Letter 4

L AST summer a friend, a Saratov landowner, and a great Fourierist, came to see me in Devonshire.

Please don't be angry with me (it was not the landowner who said that to me, but I who say it to you) for so continually wandering from the point. Parentheses are my joy and my misfortune. A French literary man of the days of the Restoration, a classic and a purist, more than once said to me, taking a pinch of snuff in the prolonged academic fashion which will soon have passed away altogether: '*Notre ami abuse de la parenthèse avec intempérance!*' It is for the sake of digressions and parentheses that I prefer writing in the form of letters, especially letters to friends; one can write without check whatever comes into one's head.

Well, so my Saratov Fourierist came to Devonshire and said to me: 'Do you know what is odd? I have just been for the first time in Paris. Well—of course . . . it is all very fine, but, seriously speaking, Paris is a dull place—really dull!'

'What next?' I said to him.

'Upon my soul, it is.'

'But why did you expect it to be amusing?'

'Upon my word, after the wilds of Saratov!'

'Perhaps it is just owing to that. But were not you bored in Paris because it's so excessively gay there?'

'You are just as silly as you always were.'

'Not at all. London, looking like a permanent autumn, is more to our taste; though the boredom here, too, is awful.'

'Where is it better, then? It seems the old proverb is right. It is where we are not!'

'I don't know: but it must be supposed that it is not very nice there either.'

This conversation, though it is apparently not very long, nor particularly important, stirred in me a whole series of old notions concerning the absence of a sort of fish-glue in the brain of the modern man; that is why his mind is cloudy and thick with sediment—new theories, old habits, new habits, old theories.

And what logic! I say it is dull in Paris and London, and he answers, 'Where is it better, then?' Not noticing that this was the line of argument employed by our house-serfs of the old style: in reply to the observation,

'I fancy you are drunk, my boy,' they answered, 'Well, did you stand treat?' What grounds are there for the idea that men are happy anywhere? that they can or ought to be happy? And what men? And happy in what? Let us assume that men do have a better life in one place than another. Why are Paris and London the pinnacles of this better life?

Is it from Reichardt's guidebook?

Paris and London are closing a volume of world-history —a volume in which few pages remain uncut. People, trying with all their might to turn them as quickly as possible, are surprised that as they approach the end there is more in the past than in the present, and are vexed that the two fullest representatives of Western Europe are setting together with it. The audacity and recklessness in general conversations which float, as once the Spirit of God, over the waters, are terrific, but as soon as it comes to action, or even to a critical appreciation of events, all is forgotten, and the old weights and measures are hauled out of the grandmother's storeroom. Worn-out forms can only be restored by a complete rebirth: Western Europe must rise up like the Phoenix in a baptism of fire.

'Oh, well, in God's name, into the flames with it.'

What if it does not rise up again, but singes its beautiful feathers, or maybe is burnt to ashes?

In that case continue to baptize it with water, and don't be bored in Paris. Take my father, for example: he spent eight years in Paris and was never bored there. Thirty years afterwards he was fond of describing the fêtes given by the marshals and by Napoleon himself, the suppers at the Palais Royal in company with actresses and opera dancers, decked in diamonds that had been wrenched out of conquered royal crowns, of the Yussupovs, the Tyufyakins and other *princes russes* who lost there more souls of peasants than were laid low at Borodino. With various changes and *un pen plus canaille* the same thing exists even now. The generals of finance give banquets as good as those of the generals of the army. The suppers have moved from the Rue St. Honoré to the Champs-Élysées and the Bois de Boulogne. But you are a serious person; you prefer to look behind the scenes of world-history rather than behind the scenes of the Opera. . . . Here you have a parliament, even two. What more do you want? . . . With what envy and heartache I used to listen to people who had come home from Europe in the 'thirties, as though they had robbed me of everything they had seen and I had not seen. They, too, had not been bored, but had great hopes, some of Odilon Barrot, some of Cobden. You, too, must learn not to be bored; and in any case be a little consistent; and if you still feel dull, try to find the cause. You may find that your demands are fantastic, then you must try to get over it; that it is the boredom of idleness, of emptiness, of not knowing how to adapt yourself. And perhaps you will find something else: that you are bored because Paris and London have no answer to make to the yearnings that are growing stronger and stronger in the heart of the man of to-day—which does not prevent their standing for the highest culture and most brilliant result of the past, and being rich endings of a rich period.

I have said this a dozen times. But it is impossible to avoid repetitions. Persons of experience are well aware of it. I spoke to Proudhon of the fact that articles which are almost identical, with only slight variations, often appeared in his journal.

'And do you imagine,' Proudhon answered, 'that once a thing has been said, it is enough? That a new idea will be accepted straight off? You are mistaken. It has to be repeated, it has to be dinned into people, repeated over and over again, so that the mind is no longer surprised by it, so that it is not merely understood, but is assimilated, and obtains real rights of citizenship in the brain.'

Proudhon was perfectly right. There are two or three ideas which are particularly precious to me; I have been repeating them for about fifteen years; fact upon fact confirms them with unnecessary abundance. Part of what I anticipated has come to pass, the other part is coming to pass before our eyes, yet these ideas seem as wild, as unaccepted, as they were.

And what is most mortifying, people seem to understand you; they agree, but your ideas remain like aliens in their heads, always irrelevant, never passing into that integral part of consciousness and the moral being, which as a rule forms the undisputed foundation of our acts and opinions.

It is owing to this inconsistency that people apparently highly cultured are continually being startled by the unexpected, caught unawares, indignant with the inevitable, struggle with the insurmountable, pass by what is springing into life, and apply all sorts of remedies to those who are at their last gasp. They know that their watch was properly set, but, like the late 'unlamented' Kleinmihel, cannot grasp that the meridian is not the same.

Pedantry and scholasticism prevent men from grasping things with simple lively understanding more than do superstition and ignorance. With the latter the instincts are left, hardly conscious, but trustworthy; moreover, ignorance does not exclude passionate enthusiasm, and superstition does not exclude inconsistency, while pedantry is always true to itself.

At the time of the Italian war a simple-hearted, worthy professor lectured on the great triumphs of 'international law,' describing how the principles of Hugo Grotius had developed and entered into the conscience of nations and governments, how questions which had in old times been decided by rivers of blood and the miseries of entire provinces, of whole generations, were now settled, like civil disputes between private persons, on the principles of national right.

Who, apart from some old professional condottiere, would not agree with the professor that this is one of the greatest victories of humanity and culture over brute violence? The trouble is not that the lecturer's judgment is wrong, but that humanity is very far from having gained this victory.

While the professor in eloquent words was inspiring his young audience to the contemplation of these triumphs of peace, very different commentaries on international law were taking place on the fields of Magenta and Solferino. It would not have been easy for any international court to avert the Italian war, since there was no international cause for it, for there was no subject in dispute. Napoleon waged this war as a remedial measure to pacify the French by the gymnastics of liberation and the galvanic shocks of victory. What Grotius or Vattel[1] could have solved such a problem? How was it possible to avert a war which was essential for domestic interests? If it had not been Austria the French would have had to beat somebody else. One can only rejoice that the Austrians presented themselves.

Then, India, Pekin—war waged by democrats to maintain the slavery of the blacks, war waged by republicans to obtain the slavery of political unity. And the professor goes on lecturing; his audience are touched; they fancy that they have heard the last creak of the gates of the temple of Janus, that the warriors have laid down their weapons, put on crowns of myrtle and taken up the distaff, that the demobilised armies are tilling the fields. . . . And all this at the very moment when England is covered with volunteers, when at every step you meet a uniform, when every shopkeeper has a gun, when the

[1] Vattel (1714-1767), a Swiss writer, author of *Traité du Droit des Gens.*—(*Translator's Note.*)

French and Austrian armies stand with lighted matches, and even a prince—I think it was of Hesse Cassel—put on a military footing and armed with revolvers the two hussars who had from the time of the Congress of Vienna ridden peacefully without weapons behind his carriage.

If war breaks out again—and that depends on thousands of chances, on one casual shot—in Rome or on the borders of Lombardy, a sea of blood would flow from Warsaw to London. The professor would be surprised, the professor would be pained. But one would have thought he should not be surprised nor pained. The trend of history is plain for all to see! The misfortune of the doctrinaires is that they, like our Diderot, shut their eyes when arguing, that they may not see that their opponent wants to retort; and their opponent is nature itself, history itself.

To complete the absurdity we ought not to lose sight of the fact that in abstract logic the professor is right, and that if not a hundred but a hundred million men had grasped the principles of Grotius and Vattel, they would not slaughter each other either for the sake of exercise or for the sake of a bit of land. But the misfortune is that under the present political *régime* only a hundred and not a hundred million men can understand the principles of Grotius and Vattel.

That is why neither lectures nor sermons have any effect, that is why neither the learned fathers nor the spiritual fathers can bring us any relief; the monks of knowledge, like the monks of ignorance, know nothing outside the walls of their monasteries, do not test their theories by facts, their deductions by events, and, while men are perishing from the eruption of the volcano, they are blissfully beating time, listening to the music of the heavenly spheres and marvelling at its harmony.

Lord Bacon long ago divided the learned into the spiders and the bees. There are periods in which the spiders are distinctly in the ascendancy, and then masses of spiders' webs are spun, but little honey is gathered. There are conditions of life which are particularly favourable to spiders. Lime trees, thickets, and flowering meadows, above all, wings and a social conception of life, are necessary for the production of honey. A quiet corner, untroubled leisure, plenty of dust, and lack of interest in anything outside the inner process, is all that is needed for producing spiders' webs.

At ordinary times it is even possible to saunter along the dusty, smooth highroad without breaking the spiders' webs, but as soon as it comes to crossing rough ground and hillocks there is trouble.

There was a really good, quiet period of European history beginning with Waterloo and lasting till the year 1848. There was no war then, but plenty of international law and standing armies.

The governments openly encouraged 'true enlightenment' and quietly suppressed the *false*; there was not much freedom, but there was not much slavery; even the despotic rulers were all good-natured in the style of the patriarchal Francis 11., the pious Friedrich Wilhelm, and Alexander the friend of Araktcheyev. The King of Naples and Nicholas came by way of dessert. Manufactures flourished, trade flourished even more, factories worked, masses of books were written; it was the golden age for all the spiders; in academic retreats and in the libraries of the learned endless spiders' webs were spun! . . .

History, criminal and civil law, international law, and religion itself, were all brought into the region of pure science and thence dropped in lacy fringes of spider's web. The spiders swung at their own sweet will in their meshes, never touching the earth. Which was very fortunate, however, since the earth was covered with other crawling insects, who stood for the idea of the state *armed for self-defence*, and clapped over-bold spiders into Spandau and other fortresses. The doctrinaires understood everything most perfectly *à vol d'araignée*. The progress of humanity was as certain in those days as the route mapped out for the Most High when he travelled incognito—from stage to stage with horses ready at the stations. And then came—February the 24th, June the 24th, the 25th, the 26th, and December the 2nd.

These flies were too big for a spider's web.

Even the comparatively slight shock of the July revolution gave the final death-blow to such giants as Niebuhr and Hegel. But its triumph was still to the advantage of the doctrinaires; the journalists, the Collège de France, the political economists sat on the top steps of the throne beside the Orleans dynasty, those who remained alive recovered and adapted themselves somehow to 1830; they would have probably got on all right even with the republic of the troubadour, Lamartine.

But how could they compromise with the days of June?

How could they live with the 2nd of December?

Of course, Gervinus teaches us that an epoch of centralisation and despotism necessarily follows a democratic revolution, but yet something seemed amiss. Some began asking whether we should not go back to the Middle Ages, others simply urged a return to Catholicism. The fakirs of the Revolution pointed out with undeviating finger along the whole railway line of time to the year 1793; the doctrinaires went on lecturing regardless of facts, in the expectation that mankind will have had its fling and return to Solomon's temple of wisdom.

Ten years have passed.

Nothing of all that has come off. England has not become Catholic, as Donoso-Cortès desired; the nineteenth century has not become the thirteenth, as some of the Germans desired; the peoples resolutely refuse French fraternity (or death!), international law after the pattern of the Peace Society, honourable poverty after Proudhon, and a Kirghiz diet of milk and honey.

While the Catholics . . .

The mediaevalists . . .

The fakirs of 1793 . . .

And all the doctrinaires go on preaching. . . .

Where is humanity going since it despises such authorities?

Perhaps it does not know.

But we ought to know for it.

Apparently not where we expected it to go. And, indeed, it is hard to tell where one will get to, travelling on a globe which a few months ago only just missed a comet, and may any day crack, as I informed you in my last letter.

September 1, 1862.

Letter 5

IN the early days of my youth I was struck by a French novel which I have not met since; it was called *Arminius*. Possibly it has no great merits, but at the time it had a great influence on me, and I remember the chief incidents to this day.

We all know something of the meeting and conflict between two different worlds; the one, the classical world of culture, corrupt and effete; the other, savage as a wild beast of the forest, but full of slumbering forces and chaotic impulses. But we only, for the most part, know the official public side of this contact, not that side concerned with details and the privacy of home life. We know the events in the rough, but not individual fortunes; not the dramas in which lives were silently broken and perished in personal struggle, in which blood was replaced by bitter tears, and devastated towns by ruined families and forgotten graves.

The author of *Arminius* tried to reproduce these two worlds—the one moving from the jungle to history, the other from history into the grave—as they met at the domestic hearth. In this, world history is reduced to personal gossip, is brought nearer to us, more within our grasp and comprehension.[1]

It never entered my head then that I should find myself in a similar conflict, that a similar conflict would come into my own life with all its ruinous force, and that my hearth would be devastated and shattered at the meeting of two historic worlds.

In our attitude to the Europeans, in spite of all the points of difference, which I understand quite well, there are points of resemblance to the attitude of the Germans to the Romans. In spite of our exterior, we are still barbarians. Our civilisation is skin-deep, our corruption is crude, our coarse hair bristles through the powder on our heads, and our sunburn shows through the powder on our cheeks. We have plenty of the cunning of savages and the evasiveness of slaves. We are ready to give blows indiscriminately and to fall at a man's feet, when we are guiltless, but I obstinately repeat we are very far behind the corrosive hereditary subtleties of West European corruption.

Among us, intellectual development serves as a purification and a guarantee—at least it has done so hitherto;[2] exceptions are exceedingly rare, culture among us is a barrier which much that is infamous never crosses; and it is owing to this that all through the reign of Nicholas the government could not succeed in establishing a secret

I was so interested by *Arminius* that I began writing a series of similar scenes, and the chief police-master, Tsinsky, made a critical analysis of them in my presence at the committee in 1834.

[2] This was written in 1855.—(*Author's Notes.*)

police nor a literature in the pay of the police, like the French.

In Western Europe this is not so, and that is how it is that Russian dreamers who have made their way into freedom readily surrender to any man who touches with sympathy on their holy things, who understands their cherished thoughts, forgetting that for him these holy things have long ago passed into a commonplace, into a convention, that, for the most part, they repeat them possibly even sincerely, but in the way in which a priest, thinking of something else, blesses any one he meets. We forget how many other elements are tangled in the complex, exhausted, morbidly struggling soul of the Western European, how utterly he is exhausted, worn out with envy, penury, vanity and *amour-propre*, and into what a terrible epicureanism of the higher morbidly nervous kind the humiliation, poverty, and struggle of competition have developed.

We find out all this when the blow has fallen; it stuns us. We feel ourselves made fools of, and want to revenge ourselves. Looking at this I sometimes think that much blood will flow from the 'conflict of these two different forms of culture. . . .' These lines were written some years ago.

I am still of the same opinion despite the fact that in Europe Russians enjoy the reputation of a most depraved people. This is due to the lack of polish in our conduct and the rustic habits of our landowners. We have convinced the whole world of our viciousness, just as the English have convinced it of their domestic virtue. As a matter of fact, neither the vice nor the virtue goes very deep. Russians abroad not only lead a disorderly life, but boast of their savage and dissolute habits. Unfortunately, being brought into contact as soon as they pass the frontier with the clumsy and servile country of *kellners* and *hofraths*, the Russians, like half-educated people in

general, cease to stand on ceremony, and let themselves
go further and further, and in this reckless mood arrive
in Paris and London. It has happened to me many times
to observe how conspicuous Russians make themselves by
absolute trifles, and they keep up the first impression by
the sort of defiant *nargue* with which they refuse to obey
the received conventions (though they are models of
submissiveness and correctness at home!). A man is
recognised as a Russian in the big hotels, because he
shouts in the public room, guffaws loudly, and invariably
protests at smoking being forbidden in the dining-room.
All this aggressiveness of an upper servant outside his
master's house shows far more immaturity and unfamiliar-
ity with freedom than deep depravity; bragging always
goes with this moral 'unripeness.' Like boys of fourteen,
we not only want to drink too much, but to show off to all
the world: 'Look how I have been going it!' But all
the world judges differently. Looking at what the
Russians lay bare, it thinks, shaking its head, 'What must
they have concealed?' And all the while there is
nothing there, just as there is nothing in the soldier's
haversack on parade, though it looks as though it were
stuffed.

Ages of civilisation, passing from generation to generation, acquire a special bouquet which one does not catch
at once; in this the fate of man is similar to the fate of
Rhine wine. There is nothing particularly attractive
about the propriety that is gained, though it is pleasanter
to go by its rules, as it is to go along a well-swept path.
We, it must be admitted, are badly swept, and there are
a good many hard stones and plenty of mud on our path.

Our breaking-in to culture is fresh in our memory: it
was accomplished by rough-and-ready means, just as a
peasant taken into the master's house is shaved like a
German and turned into a servant. Renouncing at the
command of the Most High the whole structure of the

national life, the nobility have obstinately retained all its bad qualities; flinging overboard together with its prejudices the severe decorum and propriety of the national manners, they have retained all the coarse habits of the master and the Tatar lack of respect for self and for others. The oppressive traditional morality of old days has been replaced neither by the aristocratic conception of honour nor the citizen's conception of public duty and independence; it has been replaced much more simply by German barrack discipline *in the army*, mean servility and cringing dependence *in the public service*, and nothing at all *outside it*.

Outside the government service, the nobleman was transformed from the servant who is beaten to a Peter the Great who is beating; in the country he had full scope: there he became at once corporal, emperor, grand gentleman, and father of his domain. This life of both wolf and enlightener produced colossal monstrosities, from torturers like Bühren and Potyomkins on the grand scale to the hangmen and Potyomkins on a microscopic scale; from Izmailov flogging police captains to Nozdryov with one whisker torn off; from the 'Araktcheyev of all the Russias' to the minor Araktcheyevs of battalions and companies who flogged the soldier into his grave; from the bribe-takers of the first three grades to the hungry swarms of clerks who scribbled the poor peasants into their graves; with endless variations of drunken officers, bullies, cardsharpers, heroes of fairs, dog-fanciers, brawlers, devotees of flogging, and seraglio-keepers. Here and there among them is a landowner who has turned a foreigner in order to remain a human being, or a 'noble soul,' a Manilov,[1] a turtle-dove of a nobleman, cooing in his mansion beside the stable where chastisement was administered.

One might wonder what good thing could arise, grow,

[1] A character in Gogol's *Dead Souls.—(Translator's Note.)*

and flourish in this soil between the Araktcheyevs and the Manilovs? What could be reared by these mothers who sent men for soldiers, cut off women's hair, and beat their servants, by these fathers who fawned on all above them and were savage tyrants to all below them? Yet it was among them that the men of the 14th of December arose, a phalanx of heroes, suckled like Romulus and Remus on the milk of a wild beast. . . . Finely they throve on it! They were heroes, wrought out of pure steel from head to foot, martyr warriors who went forth consciously to inevitable ruin to awaken the younger generation to new life and to purify the children, born in the midst of brutality and slavishness. But who cleansed their souls with the fire of purification, what virgin force renounced in them its filth and its corruption, and made them the martyrs of the future?

It was in them; that is enough for me for the present. I make a note of it and return to what I was saying: there is a sort of unstable, unbalanced ferment and frenzy in the pothouse debauchery of our vice; it is the delirium of intoxication which has taken hold of an entire class, that has strayed off the path with no serious plan and aim. But it has not that deeply penetrating, deeply rooted, subtle, nervous, intelligent, fatal depravity from which the educated classes of Western Europe are suffering, dying, and decaying.

But how has it come to pass, what moral simoom has blown on the civilised world? . . . There has always been progress and more progress, there are free institutions, railways, reforms, and telegraphs.

Much that is good is being accomplished, much that is good is being accumulated, but the simoom still blows and blows like a *memento mori*, continually increasing, and sweeping everything in the world before it. To be wroth at this is as useless as to be wroth with the squirrels for losing their fur, at the sea because after full tide, as though to mock us at its very best moment, it begins to ebb. It is high time that we accepted this fluctuation, this rhythm of all creation, this alternation of night and day.

The period of 'moulting' in which we have found Western Europe is the hardest; the new fur is scarcely showing while the old skin has grown stiff, like that of the rhinoceros; here is a crack, there is a crack, but *en gros* it holds fast. This position between two skins is extremely disagreeable. Everything strong suffers, everything weak that struggles to the surface is ruined; the process of renewal is inextricably connected with the process of decay, and there is no telling which will get the upper hand.

Let me explain my thought further in the next letter. Perhaps I shall succeed in proving to you that this is not a *manière de dire*, not subjective indignation (indeed, it is difficult to have a personal quarrel with world history), but a few facts noted by eyes free from the myopia of scholastic pedantry and the blindness of mysticism.

Letter 6

WE stopped at the reflection that we must not be angry with squirrels for losing their fur, nor at the winter for following the summer every year. To recognise the inevitable is a source of strength. It is only by knowing the currents of the sea and the continually shifting equatorial winds, apart from any desire to correct them, that one can navigate the ocean.

Look how things are done as a rule in Nature. In every species, in the shaping of every form, development goes on the principles by which the germ was determined.

It grows, is defined, and acquires a more or less unalterable character from the mutual interaction of the elements and environment. New factors may arise, new conditions may alter the direction of growth, may arrest what has begun, and change it into something quite different; but if the development does not lose its individuality, if it continues, the form will inevitably progress on the same lines, with its own special characteristic, and will develop its one-sidedness, that is, its individual case. This does not in the least hinder its neighbours, either in space or time, from developing all sorts of variations on the same theme with various complements and differences, with their own one-sidedness in accordance with other conditions and another environment. Only at the beginning of the development of forms there is an undefined and characterless epoch, an epoch of, so to speak, the pre-zoological stage in the egg and the embryo.

Of the transmutation of animal species we know very little. Their whole history has taken place behind man's back and covers whole periods of time in which there has been no witness. We are confronted now with finished, settled types, so far removed from each other that any interchange between them is impossible. Behind every animal there glimmers a long history—of efforts, of progress, of *avortements*, and of reaching the equilibrium, in which its forms have come to rest at last, not reaching its vague ideal, but coming to a standstill at the possible, at what will just do.

Needless to say, there are no sharp limits nor irrevocable decisions in any natural phenomena. The creative process that has come to a standstill, that has been reduced to mere repetition, may always be re-awakened; in some cases it has passed from the influence of the stars under the influence of man; by his cultivation he has developed vegetable and animal species which would not have developed of themselves.

All this casts an immense light on the question we are considering.

History presents us with a formation, caught in the very act, not yet settled but settling, and preserving in its memory the leading phases of its development and their ebbs and flows. Some sections of the human race have attained consistent forms and have conquered their history, so to speak; others in the heat of struggle and activity are creating it; while others, like the bottom of a sea that has only recently dried up, are ready for any sort of seeds, any sort of sowings, and give an unexhausted rich soil for everything.

As it is impossible looking at a calm sea to say that it will not within an hour be ruffled into a storm, so we cannot positively assert that China, for instance, or Japan, will for ages and ages maintain their aloof, cramped, stagnant form of existence. How can we tell that some word will not fall like a drop of yeast among those sleepy millions, and rouse them to a new life? But if we have no right to form a final, unconditional conclusion, it does not follow that after careful observation we have not the right to draw some conclusions. The fisherman, looking at a cloudless sky, and noting that there is no wind, will almost certainly be right if he concludes there will not be a storm for an hour.

This is all I ask in my scrutiny of modern history. To me it is evident that Western Europe has developed up to certain limits . . . and at the last moment has not the spirit either to cross them, or to be satisfied with what it has gained. The difficulty of the position to-day rests on the fact that at this moment the active minority does not feel itself capable, either of creating forms of existence consistent with modern thought, or renouncing its old ideals, or frankly accepting the petty-bourgeois state that has been built up incidentally, as a form of life suitable for the Germanic Latin people just as the Chinese civilisation is for China.

This agonising state of hesitation and uncertainty makes

the life of Europe unendurable. Whether it will come to rest by casting off the prejudices of the past and the hopes of the future, or the restless spirit of the Western European heights and depths will wash away the new dams, I do not know; but in any case I consider the present condition a period of agony and exhaustion. Life is impossible between two ideals.

History provides us with one example in full detail.

The long process of the decline of the ancient world and the rise of the Christian world presents us with every form of historical death, transmigration of souls and re-birth. Whole States stood still, remained outside the movement, did not come into the Christian formation, grew decrepit, and fell into ruins. Savage races, as yet hardly gathered into orderly herds, developed at their side into new and powerful State-organisations. . . . While Rome, pre-eminently the classical city, was transformed into a city pre-eminently Catholic.

Those who deny the inner inevitability of the death of ancient Rome, and hold that it was slain by violence, forget one thing, that every death is violent. Death does not enter into our conception of the living organism; it is outside it, beyond its limit. Old age and disease protest against death in their sufferings, and do not invoke it, and, if they could find strength in themselves, or means outside themselves, they would conquer death.

The barbarians are all very well, but we must not assume that the whole sickness of the ancient world was due to their onslaughts. From the days of Tacitus, its thought had unmistakably become gloomy and despondent. The depression, the misery, reached the pitch of suicide; such a pitch, in fact, that all the world almost went out of its mind and really became unhinged, believing in the most incredible theodicy and the most unnatural salvation, taking despair for consolation and the religion of death for a new life. Men who could not go out of their minds withdrew from the general saturnalia of death, the funerals in wreaths of roses, with amphoras of wine, the funerals in crowns of thorns, with lamentations over the sins of this world, and withdrew through the two narrow gates of stoicism and scepticism.

Beside the men who disdained death, beside the men who disbelieved in life, beside the fanatics who went forth to destroy the ancient world to the last stone, and the fanatics who expected the old world to rise up again with all the virtues of the days before the Punic Wars, there was a pinchbeck mediocre class, a crowd of those who were neither blind nor seeing, a crowd of the myopic who saw nothing, neither Catiline nor death behind the bustle of their daily cares, the news of war, the affairs of the senate, the gossip of the Court, the puzzles of scholasticism and the endless problems of household management, who shrugged their shoulders, listening to the ravings of the Christian Jacobins, despised the barbarians and laughed at their uncouthness, never guessing that these forest Hottentots, with their long hair and flaxen eyebrows, were coming to take their place in history.

The barbarians, too, have played their part, their duty is over; an immensely rich and ample period was developed by them, but they have reached the limits of their formation; they must reject their fundamental principles or come to a standstill in them.

It is very hard for the modern civilised world to come to terms with the new principles which are harassing it. What could be improved has been improved, what could be overturned has been overturned; it has next to preserve what it has gained, or to move out of the *onesidedness*, the individual variation which constitutes its personality. The last word of Catholicism was uttered by the Reformation and the Revolution; they revealed its mystery; the mystic redemption was solved by the political emancipation. The Nicene Creed founded on the remission of

sin to the Christian was expressed in the recognition of
the rights of every man in the Creed of the last œcu-
menical council, that is, the Convention of 1792. The
morality of the Judean proletarian, Matthew the Evan-
gelist, is the same as that professed by the Geneva proletarian and deist, Jean Jacques Rousseau. It came in
as faith, hope, and charity, and goes out as liberty, fraternity, and equality.

The Germanic Latin world reached its climax in the
storms and the hurricanes that followed the triumphal
year 1789. The upheaval of the French Revolution
went on by summits and abysses, the great and the terrible,
victories and the Terror, partial landslides and earthquakes, till 1848; then came *Amen, Ne plus ultra*. The
cataclysm that had begun with the Renaissance and the
Reformation was over.

The work goes on inwardly: the weaving of the microscopic web, the slow growth of drift from wind and water,
the scurrying to and fro of history, the volcanic labours
underground, the impenetrable passing of last year's
autumn into this year's spring. Overhead are terrible
apparitions, dead men in old armour and old tiaras, and
fantastic figures, incredibly radiant shapes, agonisings,
sufferings, frantic hopes, the bitter consciousness of weakness and the impotence of reason. Below is the bottom-
less pit of elemental passions, of primeval slumber, of
childish dreams, of cyclopean molelike labour. The
voice of man does not reach to these depths, as the wind
does not reach to the bottom of the sea; only at times
the trumpet-blasts and drum-beats of war are heard
there, calling to blood, promising slaughter and dealing
destruction.

Between the fantastic dreamers at the top and the
savages beneath hovers the middle class, having neither
the strength proudly to utter its: I am king! nor the
self-sacrifice to join the Jesuits or the Socialists.

Hesitating between two moralities, they furnish precisely by this hesitation the material for developing that
corruption of which I am speaking.

But how is it between two moralities? What does it
mean, 'between two moralities'? And are there two
moralities? Is there not one eternal morality, *une et
indivisible*?

Absolute morality is bound to share the fate of everything absolute; it has no existence at all outside theory,
outside abstract thought. There are several moralities,
and they are all very relative, that is, historical.

The first Christians stated this very directly, very boldly,
without beating about the bush, and, having announced
that the new Adam brought a new morality, that the
heathen virtues were for the Christian but brilliant vices,
they closed Plato, closed Cicero, and proceeded to drag
from their pedestals golden-haired Aphrodite, ox-eyed
Hera, and the other sinful saints of the old morality.

Pliny looked upon them as fools, Trajan despised them,
Lucian laughed at them, but they ushered in a new
world and a new morality. Their new morality has
grown old in its turn. And that is just what we are
talking about.

The Revolution secularised what it could out of the
catechism, but the Revolution, like the Reformation,
took its stand in the precincts of the Church. Egmont
and Alva, Calvin and Guise, Louis xvi. and Robespierre,
had the same general convictions; they differed, like
Dissenters, in shades only of opinion. Voltaire, who
arrived wrapped up in a fur cloak, in a carriage, to see the
sunrise, and who fell on his trembling knees with a
prayer on his lips, Voltaire, who blessed Franklin's grandson 'in the name of God and liberty,' is as religious as
St. Basil the Great and Gregory of Nazianzus, only of a
different sect. The cold moonlight of Catholicism has
passed through all the vicissitudes of revolution, and at its

last gasp has unfurled a new standard inscribed *Deo et Popolo!*

Somewhere on the heights the dawn of a new day is struggling with the moonlight, revealing the glaring incompatibility of faith and knowledge, of church and science, of law and conscience; but of that they know nothing in the plains below—that is for the small band of the elect.

The union of science and religion is impossible, but there *is* an irregular union, from which one can draw one's conclusion as to the morality which rests on such a union. The fact is that Reason, fearing a scandal, conceals the truth she knows; Science conceals that she is with child, not by Jehovah but by Pan, and will bear a new redeemer; and both are keeping it quiet, whispering, talking in cypher or simply lying, leaving men in an utter chaos of confused ideas, in which prayers for rain are mixed up with barometers, chemistry with miracles, telegraphs with rosaries. And all this is somehow through routine, through habit; you may believe or not, so long as you maintain certain forms of propriety. Who is deceived? What is it all for? One obligatory rule has remained, strong and accepted. Think what you please, but lie like the rest.

Prophets may guide the people by visions and passionate words, but they cannot guide them if they conceal the gift of prophecy or bow down to Baal.

Is it any wonder that life grows emptier with terrible rapidity, driving men by lack of understanding and by deadly dullness to every kind of frenzy, from gambling on the Exchange to playing at turning tables?

Apparently everything is going in the usual way; respectable people are occupied with their daily cares and business, with practical objects, they hate every sort of Utopia and all far-reaching ideals; but in reality this is not so, and the most respectable people as well as their forefathers have won everything good that they have won by constantly running after the rainbow and accomplishing impossibilities, such as Catholicism, the Reformation, the Revolution. These rainbow visions are no more, or, at any rate, the optical illusion deceives no more.

All the old ideals are dead, every one of them, from the Crucifixion to the Phrygian cap.

Do you remember that awful picture after the style of Jean Paul Richter's inspired rhapsody, in which he depicts, apropos of what I forget, all the penitent nations on the dread Day of Judgment fleeing terrified to the Cross, praying for salvation and the good offices of the Son of God? Christ answers briefly: 'I have no father!'

A similar answer is heard now from all the crosses, to which the yearning peoples, worn out with struggle, weary and heavy laden, appeal. From every Golgotha the answer comes more and more loudly: 'I have no liberty!' 'I have no equality!' 'I have no fraternity!' And one hope after another grows dim, casting its last dying light on the melancholy figures of the Don Quixotes, who obstinately refuse to hear the voices from Golgotha . . . they beckon to men to follow them more quickly, and one after another vanish in the dark night of winter.

And that is not all; with redoubled horror men have begun to discern that the Revolution not only has no father, but no son.

The terrible fruitless days of June 1848 were the protest of despair; they did not create, they destroyed . . . but what they attacked turned out to be the strongest. With the taking of the last barricade, with the deportation of the last batch of untried exiles, came the era of order. The Utopia of the democratic republic proved to be as evanescent as the Utopia of the kingdom of heaven on earth. Emancipation has turned out to be as much a failure as redemption.

But the social ferment has not calmed down sufficiently

to allow people to be occupied with their own affairs; they must occupy their minds, and without Utopias, without epidemics of enthusiasm for ideals, they are badly off. It would not be so bad if the masses of the people, disappointed in their expectations, would simply rot and mildew in the Irish manner, like stagnant water; but, as it is, they may rise up in exasperation and test their Samson-like muscles, and see how strong are the pillars of the social edifice in which they are fettered!

Where are we to find ideals that are free from danger? No need to look far—in the soul of man are many mansions. The classification of man by nationalities becomes more and more the wretched ideal of this world which has buried the revolution.

Political parties have dissolved into national parties: that is not merely a backsliding from the Revolution, it is a backsliding from Christianity. The human ideals of Catholicism and the Revolution have given place to a heathen patriotism; and the honour of the flag is the one honour of the peoples that has remained inviolate.

When I recall how twelve years ago the rake and buffoon Romieu[1] used to preach in the Paris salons to all who would listen that the revolutionary forces that had been roused should be turned from their path to national, maybe dynastic, questions, I cannot help blushing with shame at the memory.

There must be fighting whatever it is for, or a Chinese slumber will fall upon the people in this stagnation, and it will be long before there is an awakening. But is there any need of an awakening? That is just the question.

The last of the Mohicans of the eighteenth century,

[1] Auguste Romieu, celebrated in Paris for his wit and droll adventures, began by writing vaudevilles (1822-1834). The Government of July turned him into *un homme politique*, appointing him prefect of several places in succession, and in 1849 he wrote *De l'Administration sous le Régime républicain.*—(*Translator's Note.*)

the Don Quixotes of the Revolution, the Socialists, some of the literary men, the poets, and the eccentric folk of all sort, sare not sleepy, and, as far as they can, they prevent the masses from sleeping.

The taciturn bourgeois is ashamed to confess that he is sleepy and, half-asleep, goes on muttering incoherent phrases about progress and liberty. . . .

He needs war to awaken him. And is there in all the arsenal of the past a standard, a banner, a word, an idea for which men would go out to fight, which they have not seen put to shame and trampled in the mud? . . . Universal suffrage, perhaps? . . .

No; no man of our day will go out to fight for a deposed idol with the radiant self-sacrifice with which his forefather went to the stake for the right to sing psalms, with the proud self-confidence with which his father faced the guillotine for the sake of the one and indivisible republic. To be sure, he knows that neither psalms sung in German nor the emancipation of the people *à la française* will lead to anything.

And no one can die for a god of whom he knows nothing, and who keeps hidden behind a wall. Let him first speak out who he is, let him own himself for a god, and with the impertinence of St. Augustine declare in the face of the old world that 'its virtues are vices, its truths falsehood and absurdity.'

Well, that will not be to-day nor to-morrow.

The sensible man of our age is like Frederick 11., an *esprit fort* in his study and an *esprit accommodant* in the market-place. When he entered his study from which his lackeys were dismissed, the king became a philosopher; but when he came out of it, the philosopher became a king.

 . . . Here, too, 'the bulls stand before the mountain.' And yet it cannot be denied that the light of reason is more and more widely dissipating the darkness of prejudice.

. . . What is most annoying is that people have no time and die early—a man is only beginning to grow sensible when in a trice he is carried to the cemetery. One cannot help recalling the celebrated horse whose master trained it to eat nothing, but death interfered with his plans.

In the Alpine glaciers every summer a crust of ice melts, but its mass is so great that the autumn always catches the work of the sunbeams half-way, and the crust begins to freeze again, though sometimes it does not attain its former thickness. The meteorologists have reckoned many times how many ages and ages the summer will need to beat the winter at its work and melt all the ice. Many doubt whether the sun itself will last long enough to do all the work: possibly a volcanic eruption will help.

A similar calculation has not yet been worked out in history.

October 20, 1862.

Letter 7

SIX days for labour and the seventh for rest. Moses and Proudhon were right to defend the Sabbath day. Monotonous work is terribly exhausting. A man must have periodical pauses, in which, after washing his hands and putting on clean clothes, he can go out, not to work but for a walk, have a look at his fellow-creatures and at Nature, possess his soul, breathe freely, be [1] 'resurrected.'[2]

[1] The Russian word for Sunday means Resurrection.—(*Translator's Note.*)

[2] Sie feiern die Auferstehung des Herrn,
      Denn Sie sind selber auferstanden
      Aus niedrigern Häuser dumpfen Gemächer.—*Faust*.
                    —(*Author's Note.*)

Here I, too, have made of my periodical chatter about 'Ends and Beginnings' my Sunday rest, and in it I withdraw from the daily discords, the journalistic rascalities and the workaday wrangles, in which the hours and days of the month change, but opinions and the expression of them remain the same. . . . I withdraw as into some remote cell from the windows of which many details are unseen, many sounds unheard, though the silent outlines of mountains, far and near, are clearly visible, and the murmur of the sea comes in distinctly.

Perhaps you will think that I am not spending my holiday very gaily; remember that I am in England, where of all the dull days Sunday is the dullest.

Well, there is no help for it. You must be bored once more, while, for my part, I will try to tell you as amusingly as I can about the melancholy matters which we discuss.

But are they really melancholy? And if it really is so, is it not high time we were resigned to them? We really should not talk for ever about things which it is not in our power to change. Would it not be better, like a sensible man, to make up the account-books we have inherited, and, forgetting our inordinate expenses and irreparable losses, accept the total in meekness of spirit as a new starting-point. Grieve as you will, you will not mend things; there are plenty of ways of using inherited capital; there are plenty of dreams men cherish when they receive it. We have had such dreams too.

. . . The *symphonia heroica* is over, practical life is beginning. The wine has gone flat, let us drink the dry *tisane de champagne*. It is not so nice, but they say it is more wholesome. Part of the cultured world pines, with the old maid's yearning for happiness which she has not lost but has never had, and, instead of firmly making up her mind to widowhood without marriage, laments that the *ideal* of her youth has not carried her off. . . . Well, what is to be done? It has not, and now it is too late.

People are vexed at not having wings, and so will not trouble to be well shod. The painfulness of European life in its more cultured classes is directly due to their false position between dreams of what is not and contempt for what is.

Side by side with the ideals of seraphic wings which are retreating more and more into the darkness of the past and the ideals of other wings that are vanishing into the future, there is a whole independent world at which the dreamers are incensed, because it has achieved what it could and not what the dreamers expected, that is, not wings. So long as the authority and power of this world is not recognised, so long will the feverish ferment, the perpetual falsity in life, the involuntary faithlessness both to its ideal and to practical life, which is revealed in the continual contradiction of words and deeds, phrases and conduct, continue. That world is not nimble in words and not eloquent, although it has created a great lever, comparable with steam and electricity, the lever of advertisement, of proclamation, of *réclame*.

With all that, it cannot stand at its full height in all its breadth and say aloud to the people: 'I am the alpha and omega of your development; come to me and I will comfort you, I will give what can be given; but leave off knocking at all the doors which are not opened to you, some because there is no one to open them, others because they lead nowhere. Remember at last that you have no other god but me, and cease to bow down to all sorts of idols and desire all sorts of wings. Understand that you cannot preach at the same time Christian poverty and political economy, socialist theories and the unlimited right of property. So far my power exists as a fact, but not as the recognised foundation of morality, not even as a flag, and, what is worse, I am denounced, I am insulted in churches, in academies, in aristocratic halls and clubs, in speeches and in sermons, in novels and in newspapers.

. . . I am sick of playing the part of a provincial relation from whom city fops take money and domestic supplies, but about whom they keep quiet or speak with a blush. I want not only to rule, but to wear the purple.'

Yes, my dear friend, it is time to come to recognising with all meekness and humility that bourgeoisie is the final form of Western European civilisation, its coming of age—*état adulte*; this closes the long series of its visions; with this the epic of its growth, the romance of its youth, everything that has brought so much poetry and calamity into the life of the nations, ends. After all men's dreams and efforts . . . this offers them modest repose and a less troubled life and a comfort within their capacity, not beyond the reach of any one, though insufficient for the majority. By hard work the nations of the West have won their winter quarters. Let others show their mettle. From time to time, of course, men of a different leaven, of heroic times, of other formations— monks, knights, Quakers, Jacobins—will be seen again, but their transient appearance will not be able to affect the prevailing tone.

The mighty elemental hurricanes, that tossed up the whole surface of the European sea, have sunk into a quiet sea-breeze, not perilous for ships, but helping them to sail along the coast. Christianity has grown shallow and quietened down into the calm stony haven of the Reformation; the Revolution, too, has grown shallow and sunk into the calm sandy haven of liberalism. Protestantism, a religion austere in trifles, has found the secret of reconciling the Church which despises earthly goods, with the supremacy of commerce and profit. Liberalism, austere in political trifles, has learned even more artfully to unite a continual protest against the government with a continual submission to it.

With so indulgent a Church, with so docile a Revolution, Western Europe has begun to settle down, to find its equilibrium: everything that hindered it has been drawn gradually into the solidifying waves, like insects caught in amber. Byron, unable to breathe, let out a scream of anger and fled, one of the first, anywhere . . . to Greece.[1] Stoically remaining in Frankfort, Schopenhauer slowly expired, noticing, like Seneca when his veins had been opened, the progress of death and welcoming it as his deliverer. . . . This did not in the least hinder the tendency of all European life towards stillness and crystallisation; on the contrary, this tendency grew more and more distinct. Individuality was effaced, the racial type concealed everything strikingly original, restless, or eccentric. Men, like goods, were turned into something wholesale, ready-made, cheaper, and commoner, individually, but stronger and more numerous in the mass. Individual characteristics were lost, like the drops of a cataract in the general flood, without even the poor consolation of

'Gleaming bright in the rainbow's passing streak.'

Hence their hateful but natural indifference to the life of their neighbours and the fate of individuals; it is the type, the race, the work that matters, not the person. To-day one hundred men are buried in a coal-mine, to-morrow fifty more will be buried; to-day ten men are killed on one railway, and to-morrow five more will be; and every one looks on this as individual misfortune. Society suggests insurance . . . What more can it do? . . . There can be no shortage in the transport of stock because somebody's son or father has been killed; there can be no shortage in the living apparatus for coal-mining either. A horse is needed, a workman is needed, and whether it is a bay, or whether it is Tom or Harry, is

[1] The intensity with which cultivated people felt their isolation at that time, and tried to devise a life, pursuits, and so on for themselves, you can see clearly in Trelawney's *Recollections of the Last Days of Shelley and Byron,*—(*Author's Note.*)

absolutely no matter. In this *no matter* lies the whole secret of persons being replaced by masses, of individuals being swallowed up by the race.

A storm seemed about to arise, threatening to awaken every one and hinder the bourgeois crystallisation, to bring down belfries and towers and frontiers and customs-houses, but it was turned aside in time by the lightning conductors, and had not a chance. It is easier to picture Europe returning to the Catholicism of the times of Gregory Hildebrandt at the summons of Donoso Cortès and Count Montalembert, than turning into a socialist republic of Fourier's or Cabet's pattern. But who speaks seriously of socialism nowadays? The European world may rest easy on that score; the shutters are put up, there are no lightnings on the horizon, the storm is far away . . . the bourgeois can quietly tuck himself up in his quilt, tie his kerchief round his head, and put out his candle.

> 'Gute Nacht, gute Nacht,
> Liebe Mutter Dorothee!'

But poor Mother Dorothy, like Gretchen, has a brother a soldier, and like all soldiers he is fond of noise and fighting and will not let her sleep. She would have got rid of him long ago, but she has some valuable belongings, so she must have a guard in case of hungry neighbours. Well, it is not enough for her brother to be her guard; he is ambitious. 'I am a knight,' he says,' I thirst for heroic deeds and promotion.'

Yes, if the army could be reduced to the defenders of property, the bodyguard of capital, everything would quickly reach its stable final order. But there is nothing perfect in this world, and the hereditary knightly spirit keeps up the ferment and prevents life from settling down. However tempting is plunder and however natural is blood-thirstiness to men in general, the dash of a hussar, the aggressiveness of a Suvorov, are not compatible with maturity, with quiet unruffled culture. The dislike for everything military in China is much more comprehensible in a mature people than the passion of a Nicholas for 'braid and epaulettes and buttonholes.'

That is just the trouble. What is to be done with the great people which boasts of being a military people, which is all made up of Zouaves, *pioupious*, and Frenchmen, who are also soldiers?

Peuple de France, peuple de braves!

It is absurd to talk about quiet nights, moonlight walks, free trade, political freedom, or freedom of any sort, while five hundred thousand bayonets, bored and idle, are clamouring for their 'right to work.'

The Gallic cock sees to it that no turkey, duck, or goose in Europe can sleep in peace.

As a matter of fact, if France would abandon the army and enter the Civil Service (she cannotexist withoutbeing an official of some sort) everything would go swimmingly. England would fling the useless guns bought for her riflemen into the sea, my grocer Johnson (and Son) would be the first to exchange his weapon for a fishing-rod, and go fishing in the Thames. Cobden would weaken everything that Palmerston had strengthened, and the Duke of Cambridge would be elected President of the Peace Society.

But France does not dream of leaving military service—and, indeed, how could she? Who would look after Mexico, the Pope, and the *almost* united Italy? The honour of the flag is involved, there is no help for it!

Peuple de France, peuple de braves!

What is to be done?

Allow me to break off here and to describe another meeting with an old friend: he from his 'crazy' standpoint has found a bolder solution of these questions than I have.

Some two years ago I was walking along the Strand,

when I saw busily engaged in the doorway of a big shop of travelling requisites a fat, nimble little figure, startlingly out of place in London, and in various ways suggestive of Italy, wearing a light grey hat, and a thin yellow overcoat, and adorned with an immense black beard: I fancied I had seen this figure before somewhere. . . . I looked more closely . . . it was he, it really was he, my vigorous, jolly medical student, with teeth like a wolf's and the good humour of a good digestion, the demonstrator with whom in old days I had 'cut up cats and dogs,' as he expressed it, and not in Italy, but in the anatomical theatre of the Moscow University.

This time I said to my Russian-Italian, 'You can't claim to be the first to recognise an old friend.'

'*Eccolo!* How charming! Upon my soul!' and he impetuously kissed me, so intimately had he come to know me during his absence.

'If you often fling up both hands like that,' I observed to him, 'you certainly will have your travelling wallet stolen.'

'I know, I know. It is the traditional home of thieving. . . . Do you remember Don Juan, at the end of the poem, when he goes back to London?'

'I remember. Well, and is your eccentric friend with you?'

'To be sure. He is expecting me at the hotel; he did put his nose out into the street, but went back at once. He said it was so crowded and stuffy that he was afraid he would be sea-sick. So he sent me to buy a few things for the journey. To-morrow we are setting out for Texas.'

'Where?'

'To Texas, you know, in America.'

'What for?'

'What we lived in Calabria for. My Telemachus has not changed one bit, only he discourses with more assurance than ever. You remember how he used to explain to you that the terrestrial globe was sick, and that it was high time for men to be cured of civilisation, so now he is convinced that the cure is progressing too slowly in Europe, so he is going off to Texas or somewhere. I am used to him; we spend the whole day, as we always did, in arguing, and it is wonderful what a tie that is. Oh, well, we 'll have a look at America!'

'And how did you get on in Calabria?'

'At first he liked it there, though to my thinking the humblest district town in the province of Saratov, say, is superior to the whole of Calabria. You can get billiards there, anyway, and, maybe, some little widow, or at any rate a soldier's wife in a neighbouring village, but we found none but brigands, shepherds, and priests, and there was no telling which was a brigand, which was a shepherd, and which was a priest. We took a tumbledown ruin of a Radcliffe castle; lizards, the beasts, ran over the floor in broad daylight, while at night the bats flew about the drawing-room, *flop, flop,* against the wall. But I did go away several times to Naples and to Palermo. . . . And what do you think of Garibaldi? Now he is a man! you can depend upon him! . . . But our friend stayed on in his castle; he only once left it to go to Rome. Rome suited him, as though the choir had just left off singing, "May he rest in peace with the Saints." He is a Hamlet, a grave-digger!'

'Well, will your Hamlet show himself?'

'Not a doubt. He has mentioned you several times; you are still astray at times, but are on the right path, he says. Ha, ha, ha!'

'I am glad to hear it. Let us go to him.'

'Delighted.'

I found Yevgeny Nikolayevitch greatly aged. His face, much calmer, had gained a shade of a sort of clerical pensiveness: the dry, even pallor of his face gave it a lifeless appearance; the dark rings round his eyes, which were more sunk than ever, gave a sinister look to their old melancholy expression.

'You are fleeing from us across the ocean, Yevgeny Nikolayevitch,' I said to him.

'And I advise you to do the same.'

'Why so?'

'It is very wearisome here.'

'Well, you knew that in the past. You told me so eight years ago.'

'That is true. But I confess I thought there would be war.'

'What war?'

'War!' and he waved his hand.

'Have you grown so bloodthirsty in Calabria?'

'It does not matter to me personally, but it is painful to be the witness of it; I am sorry for the young generation.'

'But what do you want war for? To help the young generation?'

'I can't help it. That is what it has come to.'

'I frankly confess I do not clearly understand what you mean.'

'You have hit on a knotty point!' put in Filipp Danilovitch.

'That is because you both doubt and believe. That is the trouble. It is clear that tables do not turn, but when the question arises: but what if tables really do turn, then it is not clear. Filipp Danilovitch here is quite a different matter; he is orthodox; he knows that there is progress, and that everything is for the best. But however I look at it, I see that men have kicked over the traces and are plunging deeper and deeper into the morass.'

'The horse has kicked over the trace, so off with his leg, amputate it at once. Drastic treatment!' observed Filipp Danilovitch.

'Find a remedy and amputation will not be necessary. But since there is none, would you leave the invalid alone? The nations of West Europe are tired out, and they have reason to be; they want to rest, to live for their own pleasure; they are sick of perpetually remodelling and reconstructing, and knocking down each other's houses. They have everything they need—capital and experience and order and moderation . . . what hinders them? They had difficult problems, they had cherished dreams: all that is over. Even the problem of the proletariat has subsided. The hungry have become zealous admirers of other men's property in the hope of obtaining their own; they have become the quiet lazzaroni of industry, whose murmuring and indignation have been stifled, together with all their faculties, and that is undoubtedly one of the greatest debts we owe the factory system. . . . But still there is no peace, no peace . . . armies are kept up, fleets are kept up, all that is gained is wasted on defence—and what can put an end to armaments except war?'

'That is knocking out one nail with another in the homeopathic way,' observed Filipp Danilovitch.

'Is it possible,' my queer friend continued, 'to work in one's own little garden, with a light heart, knowing that there is a gang of bandits, pandours, janissaries, in a cave close by?'

'Allow me one word,' Filipp Danilovitch interrupted. 'I bet you a bottle of Burgundy that you don't know who these brakes on the wheels of progress and enlightenment, these pandours and janissaries, are!'

'Austria and Russia, I suppose.'

'Ha, ha, ha! I knew I should win it. Pay up with a bottle of Chambertin; it is the only wine I care for.'

'Upon my word,' Yevgeny Nikolayevitch observed reproachfully, 'what can Austria do? The country is exerting every effort to keep alive, straining every muscle

to hold its parts together. How could she be a menace
to any one? She is like a man holding his leg with one
hand for fear it should walk off without him, and his head
with the other for fear it should drop off his shoulders,
and then people talk of her rushing into a quarrel. It is
high time after the last campaign to strike Russia, too, off
the list of bogeys: far: from any one's being afraid of her,
no one even builds any hopes on her now, neither Serbs
nor Bulgars, nor any of the Slav patriots who have been
trying ever since the fourth century to discover their
fatherland and their independence. And a good thing
too! Let Russia "look for the life of the world to come,"
while in the present she is teaching her officials not to steal
and her landowners not to use their fists. In Europe there
are systems of oppression better organised which prevent
the lungs from breathing and the heart from being at rest.'

'So it is England and France whom you honour in this
way?'

'Of course, one might put up with England still, though
she is stealthily, indirectly, negatively oppressive, on the
one hand supporting what is decayed, on the other
oppressing what is young, so that it cannot grow: she
tells the hungry man when she meets him: "Go your
way and God bless you, you are a free man, I won't keep
you." While France . . . oh, well—it is one battalion:
all France will follow the drum and fife wherever you like
—to Kazan or Ryazan, while she would make a dash at
England even without a drum if only to play the master
of the house in the docks and in the City, as she does in
the Palace of Pekin. Who can hope that these two sworn
foes will go on calmly gazing at each other with a hatred
which centuries, education, and commercial interests
have been unable to overcome, while they move closer
and closer together, so that already it is only ten hours'
journey between Paris and London? On the one side
of the Channel the *légion d'honneur*, on the other the

Habeas Corpus, and they put up with each other! Do
you understand what it means to cherish that passionate
hatred, and not to have the spirit to fight? It makes me
decide to go to Texas.'

'It is difficult to understand, that's true, but it is not
altogether a bad thing that it is so. You know, when your
war does come and the French cross the Channel to
emancipate England, then I shall start for Texas too.'

'*À la bonne heure!*' exclaimed Filipp Danilovitch,
delighted.

'It is drainage; war is a system of drainage for the
purification of the soil and the air. How could they
remain in London? Moscow is not London, and even
the Russians picked up Germans on the way, and invaded
Paris.'

'Have you got a Louis XIX. up your sleeve?'

'He won't be wanted.'

'Yevgeny Nikolayevitch,' I said, after a pause, 'and
all this is simply in order to reach a Dutch stagnation, and
for this mess of pottage to part with the finest dreams, the
most sacred aims.'

'And what is wrong,' observed Filipp Danilovitch,
showing his white teeth again, 'with eating herrings and
pancakes, with a clear conscience and a clean table-napkin
in a house which has just been scrubbed, with a wife of
Rubens contours, and a ring of little toddlers about you!
Schiedam, faro, and curaçao, they are the only things
Dutch I know. Ha, ha, ha! What were all your
Fouriers and Owens struggling to find?'

'Not only they: the Catholics and the Protestants, the
Encyclopaedists and the Revolutionists . . . what were
they all struggling for . . . and their toil, their faith,
their doom, does it all count for nothing? Do you expect
the City of God and the *Feste Burg* and the Phalanstery
and the Jacobin Republic all to be realised in fact? I
remember . . .' he paused, and then, with some inner

emotion, asked me: 'Have you ever experienced what a man feels when he imparts his outlook to another and sees how it grows up in him?'

'That is all very well, saving your presence,' the pupil of Hippocrates interrupted, 'but what is the use of idle talk, what is the use of bothering?'

'*Ech*, Filipp Danilovitch, what is the use of you or me bothering? we have not succeeded in finding a remedy for death, and you know the peace of death is worse than Dutch stagnation. But there, God will forgive you; you are orthodox. But you, now, how can you make such a blunder?' he added, turning to me, and shaking his head mournfully.

And then suddenly breaking into his nervous, mirthless laugh, he said: 'I have just remembered a German book in which the laborious existence of the mole is described —it is very funny. The little beast, with big paws and little chinks instead of eyes, tunnels in the dark, underground, in the damp, tunnels day and night, without weariness, without recreation, with passionate persistence. It barely stops to eat some little grains and worms and sets to work again, but the hole is ready for the children, and the mole dies in peace, while the children begin boring holes in all directions for their children. What is the price paid for the lifetime of toil underground? What correspondence is there between effort and attainment? Ha, ha, ha! The funniest thing about it is that after making his splendid corridors and passages which cost him the labour of a lifetime, he cannot see them, poor mole!'

With this moral drawn by my crazy friend, I will conclude the first part of my 'Ends and Beginnings,' and the last month of 1862. Within two days we shall have the New Year, and I wish you a happy one; in it we must gather up fresh strength for our mole-like labour; my paws are itching to begin.

December 29, 1862.

Letter 8

Be a man, stop and make answer?

'*HALTE-LÀ!* Stop!' was said to me this time, not by a lunatic, but, quite the contrary, by a very sane gentleman who walked into my room with a number of the *Bell.* in his hand. 'I have come,' he said, 'to have it out with you. Your "Ends and Beginnings" have passed every limit; it is high time to take leave and put an end to them, with regrets for having begun them.'

'Has it really come to that?'

'It has. You know I love you, I respect your talent . . .'

'Well,' I thought, 'it's a bad look-out; it is clear that he means to abuse me in earnest, or he wouldn't have attacked me with such a flattering introduction.'

'Here is my heart,' I said; 'strike.'

My resignation, together with the classical allusion, had a happy effect on my irritated friend, and with a more good-natured air he said: 'Listen to me quietly, laying aside the vanity of the author and the narrow exclusiveness of the exile: with what object are you writing all this?'

'There are many reasons for it; in the first place, I believe what I write to be the truth, and every man who is not indifferent to the truth has a weakness for spreading it abroad. Secondly . . . but I imagine the first reason is sufficient.'

'No. You ought to know the public whom you are addressing, the stage of development it has reached, and the circumstances in which it is placed. I'll tell you plainly: you have the most fatal influence on our young people, who are learning from you to despise Europe and her civilisation, and consequently do not care to study it seriously, but are satisfied with a smattering of the newest ideas and think that the breadth of their own nature is enough.'

'Ough! how elderly you have grown since I saw you last! you abuse the young and want to rear them on falsehoods, like nurses who tell children that the mid-wife brings the babies, and the difference between the boy and the girl is the cut of their clothes. You had better consider for how many centuries men have been lying shamelessly with a moral object, and morality has been none the better. Why not try speaking the truth? If the truth turns out to be bad, the example would be good. As to my bad influence on the young—I've long been resigned to that, remembering how all who have been of any use to the younger generation have n invariably been accused of corrupting it, from Socrates to Voltaire, from Voltaire to Shelley and Byelinsky. Besides, I am comforted by the fact that it is very difficult to corrupt our young Russians. Brought up on the estates of slave-owners by Nicholas' officials and officers, completing their studies in army barracks, government offices, or the houses of the gentry, they are either incapable of being corrupted, or their corruption is already so complete that it would be hard to add to it by any bitter truth about Western Europe.'

'Truth! . . . But allow me to ask you whether your truth really is the truth?'

'I can't answer for that. You may rely on one thing, that I say conscientiously what I think. If I am mistaken, unaware of it, what can I do? It is more your job to open my eyes.'

'There's no convincing you—and you know why; it's because you are partly right; you are a good dis-sector, as you say yourself, and a bad accoucheur.'

'But you know I am not living in a maternity hospital, but in a clinic and an anatomical theatre.'

'And you are writing for nursery-schools. Children must be taught that they may not snatch each other's porridge and pull each other's hair. But you regale them with the subtleties of your pathological anatomy, and keep on telling them besides: Look here, how nasty the entrails of these old Europeans are! What is more, you use two different measures and two different standards. If you do take up the scalpel, you should be fair in your dissection.'

'What, am I dissecting the living too? How awful! And children too! You do make me out a Herod!'

'You may joke as you like, you won't put me off with that. With great insight you diagnose the malady of modern man, but when you have analysed every symptom of chronic disease, you say that it is all due to the patient's being French or German. And our people at home actually imagine that they have youth and a future. Everything that is precious to us in the traditions, the civilisation, and the history of the Western nations you cut open relentlessly and unsparingly, exposing horrible sores, and in that you are performing your task as a demonstrator. But you are sick of messing about for ever with corpses. And so, abandoning every ideal in the world, you are setting up for yourself a new idol, not a golden calf, but a woolly sheepskin, and you set to bowing down to it and glorifying it as "The Absolute Sheepskin, the Sheepskin of the Future, the Sheepskin of Communism, of Socialism!" You who have made for yourself a duty and a profession of scepticism, expect from a people, which has done nothing so far, a new and original form of society in the future and every other blessing; and, in the excess of your fanatical ecstasy, you stuff up your ears and close your eyes that you may not see that your god is as crude and hideous as any Japanese idol, with its threefold belly and flattened nose and moustaches like the King of Sardinia. Whatever you are told, whatever facts are brought forward, you talk in "ardent ecstasy" of the freshness of spring, of rising crops, of beneficent tempests, of rainbows full of promise! It is no wonder that our young people, after drinking deep of your still fermenting brew of Slavophil socialism, are staggering, drunk and dizzy, till they break their necks or knock their noses against our *real* reality. Of course, it is as hard to sober them as it is to sober you—history, philology, statistics, incontestable facts, go for nothing with both of you.'

'But excuse me, I, too, must tell you to call a halt. What are these incontestable facts?'

'There are masses of them.'

'Such as?'

'Such as the fact that we Russians belong both by race and language to the European family, *genus europaeum*, and consequently by the most inevitable laws of physiology we are bound to follow the same line of development. I have never heard of a duck belonging to the genus of ducks breathing with gills. . . .'

'Only fancy, I haven't either.'

I pause at this agreeable moment of complete agreement with my opponent to turn to you again and submit to your judgment such attacks on the honour and virtue of my epistles.

My whole sin lies in avoiding dogmatic statement and perhaps relying too much on my readers; this has led many into temptation and given my *practical* opponents a weapon against me—not always of the same quality and equal purity. I will try to condense into a series of aphorisms the grounds of the theory on the basis of which I thought myself entitled to draw the conclusions, which I have passed on like apples without mentioning the ladder which I had put up to the tree, nor the pruner with which I picked them. But before I proceed to do this, I want to show you by one example that my stern judges cannot be said to be on very firm ground. The learned friend who came to trouble the peace of my retreat takes it as you see for an incontestable fact, for an invariable physiological law, that if the Russians belong to the European family the same line of development awaits them as that followed by the Latin and Germanic peoples. But there is no such paragraph in the laws of physiology. It reminds me of the typically Moscow invention of all sorts of institutions and regulations in which every one believes, which every one repeats, and which have never existed. One friend of mine and of yours used to call them the laws of the English Club.

The general plan of development admits of endless unforeseen deviations, such as the trunk of the elephant and the hump of the camel. There are any number of variations on the same theme: dogs, wolves, foxes, harriers, wolf-hounds, water-spaniels, and pugs. . . . A common origin by no means implies a similar biography. Cain and Abel, Romulus and Remus, were brothers, but what different careers they had! It is the same in all spiritual societies or communities. Every form of Christianity has similarities in the organisation of the family, of the Church, and so on, but it cannot be said that the history of the English Protestants has been very similar to that of the Abyssinian Christians, or that the most Catholic Austrian Army has much in common with the extremely orthodox monks of Mount Athos. That the duck does not breathe through gills is true; it is even truer that quartz does not fly like a humming-bird. You certainly know, however, though my learned friend does not, that there was a moment's hesitation in the duck's life when its aorta had not taken its downward turn, but branched out with pretensions to gills; but having a physiological tradition, the habit and possibility of development in the duck did not stop short at the inferior form of breathing, but passed on to lungs.

It only comes to this, that the fish has become adapted to the conditions of aquatic life and does not advance beyond gills, while the duck does. But why the fish's breathing should blow out my theory, I do not understand. It seems to me, on the contrary, to illustrate it. In the *genus europaeum* there are peoples that have grown old without fully developing a bourgeoisie (the Celts, some parts of Spain, of Southern Italy, and so on), while there are others whom the bourgeois system suits as water suits gills. So why should not there be a nation for whom the bourgeois system will be a transitory and unsatisfactory condition, like gills for a duck?

Why is it a wicked heresy, a desertion of my own principles, and a contradiction of the absolute laws of creation and rules and doctrines, human and divine, that I do not regard the bourgeois system as the final form of Russian society, the organisation towards which Russia is striving and to attain which she will probably pass through a bourgeois period? Possibly the European peoples will themselves pass to another order of life, perhaps Russia will not develop at all; but just as that is possible, there are other possibilities too. Especially as the order in which problems arise, the accidents of time and place and development, the conditions and habits of life and the permanent traits of character, may give endlessly varied direction to development.

The Russian people, covering such wide spaces between Europe and Asia, and standing to the general family of European peoples somewhat in the relationship of a cousin, has taken scarcely any part in the family history of Western Europe. Developing late and with difficulty, it must either show a complete incapacity for progress, or must produce something of its own under the influence of the past and of its neighbours' examples and its own point of view.

Hitherto Russia has developed nothing of its own, but

has preserved something; like a river, she has reflected things truly but superficially. The Byzantine influence has perhaps been the deepest; all the rest has passed like Peter's innovations: beards have been shaved, heads have been cropped, the skirts of kaftans have been cut off, the people have been silent and given way, while the minority changed their costumes and went into the Service, while the State, after receiving the general European outline, grew and grew. . . . It is the usual history of childhood. It is over, that no one doubts, neither the Winter Palace nor Young Russia. It is time to stand on our own feet: why must we take to wooden legs because they are of foreign make? Why should we put on a European blouse, when we have our own shirt with the collar buttoning on one side?

We are vexed at the feebleness, at the narrow outlook of the Government, which in its impotence tries to improve our life by putting on the tricolor *camisole de force* cut on the Parisian pattern, instead of the yellow and black *Zwangsjacke*, which it wore for a hundred and fifty years. But here we have not the Government, but the mandarins of literature, the senators of journalism, the university professors preaching to us that such is the inevitable law of physiology, that we belong to the *genus europaeum*, and must therefore cut all the old capers to a new tune, that we must stumble like sheep over the same ditch, fall into the same pit, and afterwards settle down as an everlasting shopkeeper selling greens to other sheep. A plague on their physiological law! And why is it Europe has been luckier, why has no one made her play the part of Greece and Rome over again? There are in life and nature no monopolies, no measures for preventing and suppressing new biological forms, new historical destinies and political systems—they are only limited by practical possibility. The future is a variation improvised on a theme of the past. Not only the phases of development and the forms of life vary, but new nations are created, new nationalities whose destinies are on other lines. Before our eyes, so to speak, a new race has been formed, a variety European by free choice and elemental com-position. The manners, morals, and habits of the Americans have developed a peculiar character of their own; the Anglo-Saxon and the Celtic physical types have so changed beyond the Atlantic that you can scarcely ever mistake an American. If a fresh soil is enough to make an individual characteristic nation out of old peoples, why should a nation that has developed in its own way under completely different conditions from those of the West European States, with different elements in its life, live through the European past, and that, too, when it knows perfectly well what that past leads to? Yes, but what are those elements?

I have said what they are many times, and not once have I heard a serious objection, but every time I receive again the same answers, and not from foreigners only, but from Russians. . . . There is no help for it; we must repeat our arguments again, too.

January 15, 1863.

ANOTHER VARIATION ON AN
OLD THEME

A Letter to X

NO, dear friend, I am not going to keep the promise I made you to write an article in explanation of what I said of Western Europe and what I said of Russia.

After you had gone, under the influence of your criticisms and the criticisms made by our common friends, I looked through part of what I had written and found I had nothing to add. I had said all that was in my heart, what I understood, and how I understood it. If I have not succeeded in making my outlook clear in whole books, in a series of articles, and a series of letters, how can I succeed in doing so in a few pages? Even if my view were really simply morbid, partial, and personal when I wrote 'From the Other Side' eight years ago, time has so terribly confirmed it that it has become a more settled conviction, and has merely cooled without being changed in anything essential, I refuse to repeat coldly what I said then with warmth, and I write now rather to show you that I listened to you attentively and took our friends' criticisms sincerely to heart. The chief points of their censure may be reduced to two: first, that my attitude to Western Europe weakens convictions which are still essential in Russia; secondly, that my attitude to Russia approximates to that of the Slavophils. These criticisms are themselves the proof that your feud with the Moscow Old Believers has not subsided; that is a pity.

Carried away by your polemics, you do not notice how tedious and boring your disputes have become. Your quarrel with the Slavophils has lost all interest, especially since the death of Nicholas. It is high time to apply the manifesto of August 26, 1856, to all these wretched wrangles, and to consign them to oblivion with the other transgressions of Nicholas' reign.

A new life is unmistakably surging up in Russia; even the Government is carried away by it. Questions, each more pressing than the last, are arising on all sides; hopes crushed to the earth are reviving; one wants to know what is being thought in Russia about the Emancipation of the Serfs, about the abolition of spiritual and corporal punishment — the censorship and the stick — about the restraint of official plundering and the irresponsible tyranny of the police, and one reads instead scholastic controversies about the precedence of races and the nationality of truth. I have never denied that the Slavophils have a true sense of the *living soul* in the people, that they 'look for the world to come,' but unhappily I must repeat that their instinct is clearer than their understanding, clearer, indeed, than their conscience. I have read with horror and repulsion some articles in Slavophil reviews; they stink of the torture chamber, of slit nostrils, penances, and the Solovetsky monastery. If power came into the hands of these gentry, they would be worse than the 'Third Section,' and am I supposed to be like these savages in sympathy and opinion and language? Why, then, did one of them not so long ago, under the protection of the irresponsible police, fling at me a handful of patriotic mud with the insolence of a flunkey protected from the stick by his safe perch behind the carriage, diffusing such a national stench of the servants' hall, and such a flavour of orthodox lenten oil, that for several minutes I fancied myself in one of the remote quarters of Moscow?

But your controversy with them is of no use; leave them alone or beat them on their own ground. They do not know the real Russia, they are change-lings and corpses; not one of them will take up your challenge; they have distorted their understanding by a false show of orthodoxy and a pretence of nationalism.

It would be difficult to confute them by holding up Western Europe as an example (here I am answering another criticism) when a single copy of any newspaper you like is enough to show the terrible malady from which Europe is suffering. To ignore her wounds and to preach reverence not only for the ideas which she has worked out and which are inconsistent with her life of to-day, but for her herself, is as impossible as to persuade us that the fanatically crazy lucubrations of the followers of Buddha, or the Carpathian Dissenters, are of more value and significance than all the problems that occupy us.

You love European ideas—I love them too; they are the ideas of all history, they are the monument on which is inscribed what has been bequeathed not only by the men of yesterday, but by Egypt and India, Greece and Rome, Catholicism and Protestantism, the Latin peoples and the Germanic peoples. Without them we should sink into Asiatic quietism or African blankness of mind. With those ideas, and only with them, can Russia be brought into possession of that great part of the heritage which comes to her share. About that we are completely in agreement. But you are unwilling to recognise that contemporary life in Europe is not in harmony with her ideas. You are alarmed for them; ideas which fail to find their realisation at home seem to you unrealisable anywhere. Historical embryology scarcely warrants such a conclusion. From the fact that the new social ideas are not applied in the contemporary life of the European peoples (even if this were completely proved) you cannot deduce that they are impossible of realisation, that they cannot be applied in practice anywhere. Has not the European ideal in one form, to wit, the Anglo-Saxon, found complete expression on the other side of the Atlantic Ocean?

The ways of development are very hard, and far from simple in nature and in history; they make use of a terrible number of forces and forms. That is not very obvious to us, because we are always confronted with the complete result, with what has been accomplished and successful. Numbers of unsuccessful forms were evolved by the way, did not attain a full life (in comparison with those that follow), and were replaced by others of which we know nothing. They were not sacrificed, for they lived for themselves, but when they passed away they handed on their heritage not to their own offspring, but to strangers, the mammoths and ichthyosaurians to the elephants and crocodiles, Egypt and India to Greece and Rome. It may very well be that the whole creative ability of the Western European peoples has been spent and is exhausted in evolving their social ideal, their science, in striving towards it, and in realising separate partial phases of it with all the passion and fervour of the struggle, in which men are ready to die because at every step they fancy they are attaining the whole of their ideal.

Will the down-trodden masses wrest out of the hands of the monopolists the powers evolved by science, and all the accumulation of technical improvements, and make of them the common weal? Or will the propertied classes, resting on the force of government and the ignorance of people, keep the masses down? In either case the ideas are saved, and that is what is of first importance for you. Science, independent of political systems and nationality, remains as the grand achievement of European life, ready to transform men's hard existence of the past everywhere where it meets a suitable soil, understanding and, together with understanding, strength and freedom. The question of the future of Europe I do not regard as finally settled; but, looking at it conscientiously with the humble desire to see the truth and with prejudices rather in favour of Western Europe than opposed to it,

studying it for ten years, not in theories and books, but in
clubs and in market-places, in the centre of its political
and social life, I am bound to say that I see neither a
speedy nor a happy solution. Looking on the one hand
at the feverish, one-sided development of industry, at the
concentration of all riches, moral and material, in the
hands of the minority of the middle class, at the way in
which that minority has taken hold of the Church and
the Government, the machines and the schools, at the
fact that the army obeys it, that the judges interpret the
law in its favour, and, looking on the other hand at the
undeveloped state of the masses, the immaturity and
instability of the revolutionary party, I cannot predict
the speedy downfall of the bourgeoisie and the reform of
the old political order without a most terrible and bloody
struggle.

It is of no use to dream now of the ordinary revolutions of the past, made half in jest, with a song of Béranger
and a cigar in the mouth; now there is no Charles x.
ready to flee at the sight of danger, no Louis Philippe
who would not bombard Paris; now there is no silly
Austrian Emperor who would give a Constitution at the
first musket-shot. Though the Prussian King is the
same, he would not now take the cap off his drunken
head at the sight of murdered revolutionaries; even
Pius ix. has grown wiser. The June days of 1848 and
Cavaignac have shown the world what massacres of St.
Bartholomew, what September days, await the future
conflict. Whether Europe will emerge rejuvenated
from this ordeal, or be drowned like Seneca in her own
blood, I do not know; but I fancy neither you nor I will
live to see the day. Your hair is grey, while I am
forty-four.

Is it not natural under these circumstances for an
enlightened man to enlarge his horizon, to look about him,
to enquire how other lands, not drawn into the death-

struggle of Europe, stand in regard to the future, what can be expected from them, whither they are tending, and whether there is no inconspicuous preliminary work being done there. But outside Europe there are only two progressive countries, America and Russia, with possibly Australia just beginning. All the rest lie in unbroken slumber or struggle in convulsions which are alien to us and outside our comprehension, like the Chinese rebellion, with its piles of corpses and revolting butchery.

America is Europe colonised, the same race (predominantly Anglo-Saxon), but living under different conditions. Wave after wave carries the overflow to her shores further and further. Just as in Cromwell's days England sailed across the ocean and was scattered over the northern plains and forests, so now crowds of European fugitives sail thither to escape from hunger, from the stifling atmosphere, from persecution, 'from the future,' foreseeing troubles at home. It is the continuation of the age-long movements to the West. Three millions of Irishmen have settled there since the days of Robert Peel; the German monarchs who, in the eighteenth century, traded in herds of their subjects for making war against independence, for settling Pennsylvania, and so on, pause when they see how the population is flowing away. The movement goes on in America itself: the newcomers make their way through the settled population, sometimes draw it with them, and keep pressing, crowding, and hurrying to the South; to-day to the equator, where there will be a new meeting and a new combination of the Anglo-Saxon element with the Latin-Spanish.

We see that all this is but the clearing of the ground, the marking out of the arena, and that no power can prevent the North Americans with their overflowing strength, plasticity, and untiring energy from reaching

Central America and Cuba. While in Europe Venice is falling into ruins, Rome is reduced to beggary, the little towns of Italy and Spain are declining from lack of capital and labour, from indolence and lack of energy, in California, in Honduras and Nicaragua, deserts are in a few years being transformed into cultivated fields and clearings into towns, the plains are lined with railways, capital is abundant, and the restless vigour of the Republic absorbs more and more. What is growing is young.

The growth of Russia has been vigorous too, and it can hardly be over yet, it can hardly have reached its natural limits; that is evident, not only from its geographical physiology, but also from the unceasing aggression of the Government, from the perpetual striving to get hold of every morsel of land. But Russia is extending by a different law from America; because in its present state it is not a colony, not an overflow, not a migration, but an independent world advancing in all directions, yet sitting tight on its own soil. The United States, like an avalanche torn away from its mountain, carries everything before it; every step gained by it is a step lost by the American Indians. Russia saturates all about it like water, surrounds races on all sides, then covers them with the uniform layer of the ice of autocracy—and under it makes of the worshippers of the Grand Llama defenders of orthodoxy, of Germans uncompromising Russian patriots. There is the same youthful plasticity here. Why did Joseph ii. laugh at laying the foundation of Ekaterinoslavl, saying that the Empress had laid the first stone of the city, and he the last? It was not a city that was founded then, but a State. The Novorossisk region is the best proof of the plastic power of Russia. And all Siberia? And the settlements on the banks of the Amur, where to-morrow the Stars and Stripes of the American Republics will be fluttering? And indeed the Eastern Provinces of European Russia themselves.

Reading the chronicle of the Bagrov family,[1] I was struck by the resemblance of the old man who migrated into the Province of Ufa to the settlers who migrate from New York to Wisconsin or Illinois. It is a completely new clearing of uninhabited places, and the turning of them to agriculture and civilised life. When Bagrov summons the people from all parts to dig the dam for the mill, when the neighbours come singing and bring the earth, and he triumphantly crosses the conquered river at their head, one fancies one is reading Fenimore Cooper or Washington Irving. And all that happened only a hundred years ago; it was the same thing in the Saratov province and in Perm. In Vyatka, in my day, it was hard to keep the peasants from migrating into the forests and there making new clearings; the land was still in their eyes common property, the *res nullius* to which every man has a right.

America presents no new elements; it is a further development of Protestant Europe, set free from its historic past, and put under different conditions of life. The grand idea developed by the Northern States is purely Anglo-Saxon, the idea of self-government, that is of a strong people with a weak government, the home rule of every tract of land without centralisation, without bureaucracy, held together by an inner moral unity. What attitude America will take up to socialism is hard to say; the spirit of comradeship, of association, of enterprise in common is highly developed in her, but it has not common ownership nor our *artel*, nor the village community; the individual combines with others only for a definite task, apart from which he jealously guards his complete independence.

Russia, on the contrary, is a quite special world, with her own natural habit of life, with her own physio-

---

[1] *A Family Chronicle*, by Aksakov. There is an excellent translation by Mr. Duff.—(*Translator's Note*.)

logical character—not European, not Asiatic, but Slav. Site takes her share in the destinies of Europe, though she has not its historical traditions and is free from its obligations to the past. 'What good fortune for a Russian lawgiver,' said Bentham to Alexander 1., when the latter was in London after the Napoleonic Wars, 'that he has not to contend with Roman law at every step!' And we add, nor with feudalism, nor with Catholicism, nor with Protestantism. The Book of Church Law and the Civil Code do not cover every aspect of life, do not govern every action; other institutions have been introduced by force and are maintained by force. We have nowhere those hard-and-fast prejudices which, like a paralysis, deprive the Western European of the use of half his limbs. The village commune lies at the basis of our national life with the re-division of fields, with the common ownership of land, with an elective control, with the equality of duties laid on each workman (the *tyagla*). All this is in an oppressed, distorted state, but it is all living, and has outlived its worst period.

If there is any truth in all this, one need not be a Russian to turn special attention to Russia in these black days for Europe. And, as a matter of fact, many vigorous minds are occupied with Russia. I have myself chanced to speak of Russia with serious men like Proudhon and Mazzini . . . and I assure you that the attitude of hatred and fear, fully deserved by the thirty years' reign of Nicholas, is being replaced by hesitation and a desire to gain a closer knowledge of this newcomer, whose rights and power for the future they are neither able nor willing to deny.

Russia could not really be understood by Western Europeans so long as the latter had faith in themselves, and were advancing; but they are convinced of the impossibility of progressing by way of revolutions, having lost at one blow all the fruits of them, except the lesson of failure. 'The equality of slavery' has let them look more closely at each other, and this is why it is in England that there is least understanding of Russia; the English have not taken an equal share in the Continental revolutions, nor in the general downfall that has followed. Free after their own fashion, they look with indifference at the land of slavery and despotism. But other nations in their fetters feel instinctively that, though a temporary necessity may yesterday have forced the discipline of the barracks on a peaceful agricultural people and turned all Russia into military settlements, another necessity may to-morrow do away with all that, just as Alexander 11. has done away with Araktcheyev's settlements; the period of military despotism will pass, leaving behind a political unity indissolubly welded together and forces hardened in a harsh and bitter school. The stumbling-blocks over which Europe has tripped scarcely exist for us. In the natural simplicity of our peasant life, in our uncertain and unsettled economic and judicial conceptions, in our vague sense of property, in our lack of a strong middle class, and in our extraordinary capacity for assimilating foreign ideas, we have an advantage over nations that are fully organised and exhausted. The Russian State has been firmly established by terrible means; by slavery, the knout, and executions, the Russian people have been driven into making a vast empire, through torture they have moved to the achievement of their destinies. It is idle to waste anger on the past; it is the task of the living to take advantage of all forces alike, whether they have been won by good means or ill, by bloodshed or by the ways of peace. The military settlements, as I have said, are passing away, but the villages remain. In our shifting primitive soil there is nothing conservative but the village commune; that is, nothing but what ought to be preserved.

I have read your discussions about the commune; they are very interesting, but less to the point than appears on the surface. Whether the village commune is racial in origin or the work of the Government, whether the land belonged in the past to the commune, to the landowners, or to the princes, whether the institution of serfdom strengthened the commune or not, all that ought to be investigated; but what is most important for us is the present position of affairs. The fact, whether distorted or not, whether right or wrong, forces itself upon us. The Government and the institution of serfdom have, in their own fashion, maintained our native commune; the stable, permanent principle left in it from patriarchal days is not lost. The common ownership of land, the *mir*, and the village elections form a groundwork upon which a new social order may easily grow up, a groundwork which, like our black earth, scarcely exists in Europe.

That is why, dear friend, in the midst of the gloomy, heartrending requiem, in the midst of the dark night which is falling upon the sick and weary West, I turn away from the death agony of the mighty warrior whom I honour, but whom I cannot aid, and look with faith and hope to our native East, inwardly rejoicing that I am Russian.

The period upon which Russia is now entering is extraordinarily important; instead of small political reforms for which we are too old, not in experience, but in intelligence, we are confronted with a vast economic revolution, the emancipation of the peasants. And that is not all: our problems are so set that they can be solved by social and political measures without violent upheavals. We are called to overhaul the rights of land ownership and the relations of the workman to the means of production. Is this, perhaps, our solemn entry upon our future growth? The whole new programme of our historical activity is so simple that there is no need of genius for it, but merely eyes to see what to do. It is only the timidity, the clumsiness and bewilderment of the Government that hinder it from seeing the way, and it is letting the marvellous chance slip by. Good Lord! What might not be done in this spring sunshine after the winter of Nicholas! The blood is thawed in the veins and the oppressed heart beats more freely, and what profit might be made of it!

Few feelings are more painful and oppressive than the sense that one might make a dash forward now at once, that everything is in readiness, and that the only thing lacking is understanding and courage on the part of the leaders. The machine is stoked up and ready, the fuel is burning for nothing, energy is being wasted, and all because there is no bold hand to turn the key without fear of an explosion. Our leaders should know that nations pardon a great deal—the barbarism of Peter and the dissoluteness of Catherine; they pardon violence and wickedness, if only they are aware of strength and boldness of mind. But however good the heart may be, lack of understanding, colourless vacillation, incapacity to take hold of circumstances and turn them to account, in a ruler whose power is unlimited, is never forgiven, either by the people or by history.

My passionate impatience in this case is in no way a contradiction of my resigned acceptance of the tragic fate of Europe. In Russia I see the chance at hand. I feel I can touch it; there is no such possibility in Western Europe, at any rate, at this moment. If I were not a Russian, I should long ago have gone away to America. You know that I am not a fatalist, and do not believe in anything ordained beforehand, not even in the famous 'Perfectibility of Humanity.'

Nature and history plod along from day to day and from age to age, stepping aside, making new ways, stumbling upon old ones, amazing us now by their swiftness, now by their slowness, now by their sense, now by their folly, pressing in all directions, but advancing only where the gates are open. When I talk of possible development I am not talking of its inevitability; what part of all that is possible will be accomplished I do not know, because very much in the life of nations depends on persons and will. I feel in my heart and in my mind that history is knocking at our door; if we have not the strength to open it, and those who have are unwilling or incapable, progress will find fitter means in America or in Australia, where political life is being formed on quite a different basis. Perhaps even Europe herself will be renewed, will rise up, will take up her bed and walk on her Holy Land, under which so many martyrs are buried, and on which so much sweat and blood has been spent. Perhaps!

But is it really possible that after setting one foot on the beaten track we shall sink back into the swamp, giving the world the spectacle of immense strength and complete incapacity to use it? Something forbids the heart to accept that!

How bitter are these doubts, how bitter this loss of time and strength! . . . When will the scales fall from their eyes? And why are they afraid to answer the loud summons of the future? 'A new period has come for Russia,' we said, when we heard of the death of Nicholas; now all the Russian journals are saying it, the Tsar himself is saying it in other words. Well, then let it be new.

Everything that is being done shows our unhappy passion for prefaces and introductions at which we love to stop short complacently. As though it were enough to decide to do something, for the thing to be done.

The Petersburg Government has but few traditions, yet those are like fetters on the legs of Alexander 11. How slowly and indirectly he advances along the path of reform, of which he has himself said so much! In what shallow waters the boat of his autocracy floats! At this rate it will take us over two hundred years to catch up the

Prussia of to-day. And it is all due to the Nicholas tradition, the Nicholas policy, and, what is perhaps worst of all, the Nicholas men.

It is high time to give up this stupid fear of free speech and daylight through dread of some phantom revolution, for which there are no elements ready. It is high time to abandon the futile meddling in every European squabble, always in support of despotism, of brute force, and of flagrant injustice. To the devil with this diplomatic influence which makes all the nations hate us. It is not the Russian, but the Holstein policy of Nicholas. Nicholas turned the sentimental Holy Alliance into a police compact. Why does Alexander go on playing the same part? The Russian Tsardom is not bound up in any way with the fate of the decrepit European thrones, so why will he needlessly share all their abominations and bring upon himself all the hatreds gained by them?

With the partition of Poland the attitude of the new Empire to old Europe was transformed. But the memory of that crime ought not to lead to mere dread of losing the ill-gotten gains, but to pangs of conscience and to repentance. What has Alexander 11. done to show repentance? All that remains in our memory is the refrain of the song with which he concluded his speech at Warsaw — *Pas de rêveries! Pas de rêveries!*

Pas de rhétorique! Pas de rhétorique! we say in our turn. We have no dreams! Crushed by authority, by injustice, by bribery, by the suppression of free speech and the contempt for personal freedom, we want to speak out fearlessly, to exchange ideas with each other and to unmask the abuses of which even the Government is ashamed and which it will never check without publicity. We want the peasants to be freed from the power of the landowners and all subject Russia to be freed from the stick; of course, that is not *rêverie*, but is something very practical and extremely little. Yes, it is very little, but it is just our youthfulness and our strength which makes us need so little in order to push ahead boldly and rapidly. We ask no help from the Government; all we ask of it is not to meddle. Western Europe, on the contrary, having so much, cannot make use of its riches; they have cost it so much that it is miserly over them; it is conservative, like every property-owner. We have nothing to preserve. Of course, poverty is not of itself a claim to a different future, nor are years of slavery a claim to freedom, but here, starting from the opposite principles to opposite ends, I meet not the Slavophils but some of their ideas.

I believe in the capacity of the Russian people; I see from the seedling crop what the harvest may be; I see in their life, poor and oppressed as it is, an unconscious fitness for the social ideal which European thought has consciously reached.

So that, dear friend, is why it is that you have found a similar strain in my views and in those—worse than false—mischievous and dangerous views of the Moscow literary Old Believers, those orthodox Jesuits who reduce every one to despondency. And that is why, warmly accepting the new social religion that is arising on the blood-soaked fields of reformation and revolution, repeating with throbbing heart the great legends of those days, I turn away from contemporary Europe and have little sympathy with the pitiful heirs of mighty fathers.

Do not let us dispute about methods, our aim is the same. Let us devote all our efforts, each according to his strength at his own post, to throw down every barrier that hinders the free development of the abilities of our people and maintains the present worthless *régime*, let us stir the minds of the people and the Government alike. And so I conclude my long letter to you with the words: to work, to toil, to toil for the Russian people, which has toiled enough for us!

LONDON, *February* 3, 1857.

THE SUPERFLUOUS AND THE
EMBITTERED

*The Onyegins[1] and the Petchorins[2] were perfectly true to life,
they expressed the real misery and dislocation of the Russian life of the
period. The melancholy type of the superfluous man, lost merely because he had developed into a man, was to be seen in those days not
only in poems and novels but in the streets and the villages, in the
hotels and the towns. . . . But the days of the Onyegins and the
Petchorins are over. There are no superfluous men now in Russia:
on the contr ary, now there are not hands enough to till the vast fields
that need ploughing. One who does not find work now has no one else
to blame for it. He must be really a frivolous person, a wastrel or a
sluggard.* —'The Bell,' 1859, p. 44.

THESE two classes of superfluous men, between
whom Nature herself raised up a high mound of
Oblomovs,[3] and History, marking out its boundaries, dug
out a ditch—the one in which Nicholas is buried—are
continually confounded. And so we want, with a
partiality like that of Cato for the cause of the vanquished,
to champion the older generation. Superfluous men
were in those days as essential, as it is now essential that
there should be none.

Nothing is more lamentable than, in the midst of the
growing activity as yet unorganised and awkward, but
full of enterprise and initiative, to meet the flustered,
nervously overwrought lads who lose their heads before
the toughness of practical work, and hope and expect
to arrive without effort at a solution of difficulties, and to
find answers to problems, which they can never state
clearly.

We will lay aside these voluntary superfluous men, and
just as the French only recognise as real grenadiers *les
vieux de la vieille*, so we will recognise as honourably

[1] Onyegin, hero of Pushkin's poem.

[2] Petchorin, hero of Lermontov's novel, *A Hero of Our Time.*

[3] Oblomov, hero of Goncharov's novel of that name.—(*Trant-
lator's Notes.*)

and truly superfluous men only these of the reign of Nicholas. We ourselves belong to that unhappy generation, and, grasping very many years ago that we were superfluous on the banks of the Neva, very practically took our departure as soon as the rope was loosened.

There is no need for us to defend ourselves, but we are sorry for our former comrades and want to distinguish them from the batch of invalids that followed them from the hospital of Nicholas.

One cannot but share the healthy realistic attitude of one of the best Russian magazines, in attacking the effete moral point of view which in the French style seeks personal responsibility for public events. Historical formations can no more be judged by a criminal court than geological ones. And men who say that one ought not to direct one's thunders and lightnings against bribe-takers and embezzlers of Government funds, but at the environment which makes bribes a characteristic symptom of a whole tribe, such as the whole race of *beardless* Russians for instance, are perfectly right. All we desire is that the superfluous men of Nicholas's reign should have the rights of bribe-takers and enjoy the privileges granted to the embezzlers of public funds. They deserve it the more, since they are not only superfluous, but almost all dead; while the bribe-takers and embezzlers are alive, and not only prosperous, but historically justified.

Whom have we here to attack, whom have we here to ridicule? On the one hand, men who have fallen from exhaustion; on the other, men crushed by the machine; to blame them for it is as ungenerous as to blame scrofulous and lymphatic children for the poorness of their parents' blood.

There can be but one serious question about them: were these morbid phenomena really due to the conditions of their environment, to their circumstances? . . .

I think it can hardly be doubted.

There is no need to repeat how cramped, how painful, was the development of Russia.

We were kept in ignorance by the knout and the Tatars: we were civilised by the axe and by Germans: and in both cases our nostrils were slit and we were branded with irons. Peter the Great drove civilisation into us with such a wedge that Russia could not stand the shock and split into two layers. We are only just beginning now, after a hundred and fifty years, to understand how this split was made: there was nothing in common between the two parts; on the one hand, robbery and contempt; on the other, suffering and mistrust: on the one hand, the liveried lackey, proud of his social position and haughtily displaying it; on the other, the plundered peasant, hating him and concealing his hatred. Never did Turk, slaughtering men and carrying off women to his harem, oppress so systematically, nor disdain the Frank and the Greek so insolently, as did the Russia of the privileged class despise the Russia of the peasant. There is no instance in history of a caste of the same race getting the upper hand so thoroughly and becoming so completely alien as our military nobility.

A renegade always goes to the extreme, to the absurd and the revolting, to the point at last of clapping a literary man in prison for wearing the Russian dress, refusing to let him enter a restaurant because he is wearing a kaftan and has a sash tied round his waist. It is colossal, and reminds one of Indian Asia.

On the margins of these savagely opposed worlds strange figures appeared, whose very distortion points to latent forces, cramped and seeking something different. The Raskolniks and Decembrists stand foremost among them, and they are followed by all the Westerners and Easterners, the Onyegins and the Lenskys, superfluous and disillusioned people. All of them, like Old Testament prophets, were at once a protest and a hope. By them Russia was striving to escape from the Petersburg period, or to transform it to her real body and her healthy flesh. These pathological formations called forth by the conditions of the life of the period invariably pass away when the conditions are changed, just as superfluous people have passed away now; but it does not follow that they deserved judgment and condemnation unless from their younger comrades in the Service. And this is on the same principle on which one of the inmates of Bedlam pointed with indignation at another inmate who called himself the Apostle Paul, while he who was Christ himself knew that the other was not the Apostle Paul, but simply a shopkeeper from Fleet Street.

Let us recall how superfluous people were evolved.

The hangings of the 13th of July 1826 on the Kronverg Courtyard could not at once check the current of ideas, and as a fact the traditions of the reign of Alexander and the Decembrists persisted through the first half of Nicholas's reign, though disappearing from sight and turning inwards. Children still at school dared to hold their heads erect, they did not yet know that they were the prisoners of education.

They were the same when they left school.

These were far different from the serene, self-confident, enthusiastic lads, open to every impression, that Pushkin and Pushtchin[1] were when they were leaving the Lyceum. They have neither the proud, unbending, overwhelming daring of a Lunin,[2] nor the dissipated recklessness of a Polezhaev,[3] nor the melancholy serenity of Venevitinov.[4] But yet they preserved the faith inherited from their

[1] Ivan Ivanovitch Pushtchin was a great friend of the poet Pushkin.

[2] One of the Decembrists.

[3] See vol. i. page 193.

[4] A young poet of the greatest promise who died in 1827 at the age of twenty-two. — (*Translator's Notes.*)

fathers and elder brothers, the faith that 'It is coming—
the dawn of radiant happiness,' the faith in Western
liberalism in which all—Lafayette, Godefroi Cavaignac,
Börne, and Heine—believed. Frightened and disconso-
late, they dreamed of escaping from their false and unhappy position. This was like that last hope which every
one of us has felt before the death of one we love. Only
doctrinaires (whether red or parti-coloured, makes no
difference) readily accept the most terrible deductions,
because they really accept them *in effigy*, on paper.

Meanwhile every event, every year, confirmed for them
the dreadful truth that not only the Government was
against them, with gallows and spies, with the irons with
which the torturer compressed Pestel's head, and with
Nicholas putting those irons on all Russia, but that the
people, too, were not with them, or at least were completely alien. If the people were discontented, the
objects of their discontent were different. Together
with this crushing recognition they suffered, on the other
hand, from growing doubt of the most fundamental
principles of the Western European outlook. The
ground was giving way under their feet; and in this perplexity they were forced either to enter the Service or to
fold their hands and become superfluous, idle. We
venture to assert that this is one of the most tragic positions
in the world. Now these superfluous people are an
anachronism, but, of course, Royer Collard or Benjamin
Constant would be an anachronism now, too. But they
cannot be blamed for that.

While men's minds were kept in misery and painful
hesitation, not knowing where to find an outlet, how to
move, Nicholas went his way with dull elemental obstinacy, trampling down the tilled fields and every sign of
growth. A master in his work, he began from the year
1831 his war upon children; he grasped that he must
beat out everything human in the years of childhood, in

order to make faithful subjects in his own image and semblance. The training of which he dreamed was organised. A simple word, a simple gesture was reckoned as much an insolence and a crime as an open neck, as an unbuttoned collar. And this torture of the souls of children went on for thirty years!

Nicholas—reflected in every inspector, every school director, every tutor—confronted the boy at school, in the street, in church, even to some extent in the parental home, stood and stared at him with pewtery unloving eyes, and the child's heart ached and grew faint with fear that those eyes might detect some budding of free thought, some human feeling.

And who knows what chemical change in the composition of a child's blood and nervous system is caused by intimidation, by the checking of speech, by the concealment of thought, by the repression of feeling?

The terrified parents helped Nicholas in his task; to save their children by ignorance, they concealed from them their one noble memory. The younger generation grew up without traditions, without a future, except a career in the Service. The Government office and the barracks gradually conquered the drawing-room and society, aristocrats turned gendarmes, Kleinmihels turned aristocrats; the stupid character of Nicholas was gradually imprinted on everything, vulgarising everything and giving everything a formal red-tape aspect.

Of course, in all this misery, not everything perished. No plague, not even the Thirty Years' War, exterminated every one. Man is a tough creature. The craving for humane culture, the striving for independent initiative, survived, and most of all in the two Macedonian phalanxes of our culture, the Moscow University and the Tsarskoe Syelo Lyceum. On their youthful shoulders they carried across the whole kingdom of dead souls the

Ark in which lay the Russia of the future, her living thought, her living faith in what was to come.

History will not forget them.

But in this conflict they lost, for the most part, the youthfulness of their early years: they were overstrained, grew up prematurely. Old age reached them before their legal coming of age. These were not idle, not superfluous people; these were embittered people, sick in body and soul, people who had been wrecked by the insults they had endured, who looked at everything askance, and were unable to shake off the bitterness and venom accumulated more than five years before. They unmistakably stand for a step in advance, but still it is a morbid step; it is no longer a heavy, chronic lethargy, but an acute suffering which must be followed by recovery or death.

The superfluous people have made their exit from the stage, and the embittered, who are more angry with the superfluous than any, will follow them. Indeed, they will be gone very soon. They are too forbidding, and they get too much on one's nerves to last long. The world, in spite of eighteen centuries of Christian austerities, is in a very heathen fashion devoted to epicureanism and *à la longue* cannot put up with the depressing faces of Nevsky Daniels, who gloomily reproach them for dining without gnashing their teeth, and for enjoying pictures or music without remembering the troubles of this life.

Others are coming to take their place; already we see men of quite a different stamp, with untried powers and stalwart muscles, coming from remote universities, from the sturdy Ukraine, from the sturdy North-east, and perhaps we old folks may yet have the luck to hold out a hand across a sickly generation to the newcomers, who will briefly bid us farewell and go on their wide road.

We have studied the type of embittered people, not on the spot, and not from books, we have studied it from specimens who have crossed the Nieman and sometimes even the Rhine since 1850.

The first thing that struck us in them was the ease with which they despaired of everything, the vindictive pleasure of their denial, and their terrible ruthlessness. After the events of 1848 they saw themselves at once in a superior position, from which they looked down on the defeat of the Republic and the Revolution, on the decay of civilisation, on the defilement of banners, and could feel no compassion for those who still struggled on. Where we stopped short, tried to restore animation, and looked to see if there were no spark of life, they went further into the desert of logical deduction, and easily arrived at those final, violent, abrupt conclusions, which are alarming in their radical audacity, but which, like the spirits of the dead, are but the essence gone out of life, not life itself. In these deductions the Russian enjoys a terrible advantage over the European; he has no traditions, no habits, nothing akin to him to lose. The man who has no wealth of his own or of others goes most safely along dangerous roads.

This emancipation from everything traditional fell to the lot not of healthy youthful characters, but of men whose heart and soul had been strained in every fibre. After 1848 there was no living in Petersburg. The autocracy had reached the Hercules' Pillars of absurdity; they had reached the instructions issued to teachers at the military academies, Buterlin's scheme for closing universities, the signature of the censor Yelagin on patterns for stencils. Can one wonder that the young men who broke out of this dungeon were nervous wrecks and invalids?

So they faded without ever blossoming, knowing nothing of space and freedom, nothing of frank speech. They bore on their countenances deep traces of a soul roughly handled and wounded. Every one of them had some special neurosis, and apart from that special neurosis they all had one in common, a sort of devouring, irritable, and distorted vanity. The denial of every right, the insults, the humiliations they had endured developed a secret craving for admiration; these undeveloped prodigies, these unsuccessful geniuses, concealed themselves under a mask of humility and modesty. All of them were hypochondriacs and physically ill, did not drink wine, and were afraid of open windows; all looked with studied despair at the present, and reminded one of monks who from love for their neighbour came to hating all humanity, and cursed everything in the world from desire to bless something.

One half of them were continually remorseful, the other half continually damning and denouncing.

Yes, the iron had entered deeply into their souls. The Petersburg world in which they had lived was imprinted on themselves; it was thence they took their restless tone, their language—*saccadé*, yet suddenly passing into bureaucratic vapidity—their elusive meekness and haughty fault-finding, their intentional frigidity and readiness on any occasion to break out into abuse, the insulting way in which they scorned to justify themselves, and the uneasy intolerance of the director of a department.

This tone of a director's reprimand, uttered contemptuously with eyes screwed up, is more hateful to us than the husky shout of the general, like the deep bark of an old dog, who growls in deference to his social position rather than from spite.

Tone is not a matter of no importance.

Das war innen—das ist draussen!

Extremely kind at heart and noble in theory, they, I mean our embittered people, may drive an angel to fighting and a saint to cursing by their tone. Moreover, they exaggerate everything in the world with such *aplomb*—and not to amuse but to wound—that there is simply no bearing it. To every criticism, to every censure, they are always ready to add gloomier details. 'Why do you defend these sluggards (an embittered friend, *sehr ausgezeichnet in seinem Fache*, said to us lately), drones, cumberers of the earth, white-handed laggards *à la Onyegin*? . . . They were formed differently, if you please, and the world surrounding them was too dirty for them, not polished enough; they will dirty their hands, they will dirty their feet. It was much nicer to go on moaning over their miserable position, at the same time eating and drinking in comfort.'

We put in a word for our classification of the super-fluous people into those of the Old Dispensation and those of the New. But our Daniel would not hear of a distinc-tion: he would have nothing to say to the Oblomovs nor to the fact that Nicholas cast in bronze had been gathered to his fathers, and just for that reason had been cast in bronze. On the contrary, he attacked us for our defence and, shrugging his shoulders, said that he looked upon us as on the fine skeleton of a mammoth, as at an interesting bone that had been dug up and belonged to a different world with a different sun and different trees.

'Allow me on that ground and in the character of a *Homo Benkendorfii testis* to defend our contemporaries. Surely you do not really imagine that these men did nothing, or did something silly of their own choice?'

'Most certainly; they were romantics and aristocrats; they hated work, they would have thought themselves degraded if they had taken up an axe or an awl, and it is true they would not have known how to use them.'

'In that case I will quote names: for instance, Tchaa-dayev. He did not know how to use an axe, but he knew how to write an article which thrilled all Russia, and was a turning-point in our understanding of ourselves. That article was his first step in the literary career. You know what came of it. The German Vigel took offence

on behalf of Russia, the Protestant and future Catholic
Benkendorf took offence on behalf of orthodoxy, and, by
the falsehood of the Most High, Tchaadayev was declared mad and forced to sign an undertaking not to
write. Nadyezhdin, who published the article in the
Telescope, was sent to Ust Sysolsk; the old rector
Boldyryev was dismissed: Tchaadayev was turned into
an idle man. Granting that Ivan Kireyevsky could not
make boots, yet he could publish a magazine; he published two numbers, the magazine was forbidden; he
contributed an article to the *Dennitsa*, and the censor,
Glinka, was put in custody: Kireyevsky was turned into
a superfluous man. N. Polevoy cannot, of course, be
charged with idleness; he was a resourceful man, and
yet the wings of the *Telegraph* were clipped, and, I
confess in my weakness, when I read how Polevoy told
Panayev that he, as a married man, handicapped by a
family, was afraid of the police, I did not laugh, but
almost cried.'

'But Byelinsky could write and Granovsky could give
lectures; they did not sit idle.'

'If there were men of such energy that they could
write and give lectures in sight of the police-chaise and the
fortress, is it not clear that there were many others of less
strength, who were paralysed and suffered deeply from
it?'

'Why did they not take to making boots or splitting
logs—it would have been better than nothing?'

'Probably because they had money enough not to be
obliged to do such dull work; I have never heard of any-
one taking to cobbling for pleasure. Louis XVI. is the
only example of a king by trade and a carpenter by
inclination. However, you are not the first to observe
this lack of practical work in these superfluous men; to
correct it, our watchful Government sent them to hard
labour.'

'My antediluvian friend, I see that you still look down upon work.'

'As on a far from entertaining necessity.'

'Why should they not have taken their share of the general necessity?'

'No doubt they should, but in the first place they were born, not in North America, but in Russia, and unluckily were not brought up to it.'

'Why were they not brought up to it?'

'Because they were born, not in the tax-paying classes of Russia, but in the gentry; perhaps that really is reprehensible, but, being at that period in the inexperienced position of unborn infants, they cannot, owing to their tender years, be held responsible for their conduct. And having once made this mistake in the choice of their parents, they were bound to submit to the education of the day. And by the way, what right have you to demand of men that they should do one thing or another? This is some new compulsory organisation of labour; something in the style of socialism adapted to the methods of the Ministry of Crown Estates.'

'I don't compel any one to work; I simply state the fact that they were idle, worthless aristocrats, who led an easy and comfortable life, and I see no reason for sympathising with them.'

'Whether they deserve sympathy or not, let every one decide for himself. Every human suffering, especially if it is inevitable, awakens our sympathy. And there is no sort of suffering to which one could refuse it. The martyrs of the early centuries of Christendom believed in redemption. They believed in a future life. The Roman Muhanovs, Timashevs, and Luzhins compelled the Christians to bow down in the dust before the august image of the Caesar; the Christians would not make this trivial concession, they were thrown to the beasts in the arena. They were mad, the Romans were half-witted, there is no place here for sympathy or admiration. . . . But if so, farewell, not only to Thermopylae and Golgotha, but also to Sophocles and Shakespeare, and incidentally the whole long and endless epic poem which is continually ending in frenzied tragedies and continually going on again under the title of history.'

As is usual in argument, our Daniel did not give in. I began to be tired of it and, taking advantage of my palaeontological importance, said to him: 'Have it your own way, but you know it is a silly business pitching into people who are either dead or not far off dying, and to pitch into them in a society where almost all the living—military and civilian, landowners and priests—are worse than they are; I tell you what, if you are so particularly attracted by *censura morum*, are so fond of the harsh duty of a moralist, do pick out something original. If you like, I can pick you out types more pernicious than any superfluous persons, dead or living.'

'What types?'

'Well, the literary ruffian, for instance.'

'I don't understand.'

'In our pale literature, maltreated by the censorship, there have been numbers of queer fishes of all sorts, but until lately they were for the most part clean, honest men. If there were any of the mercenary, the disingenuous, the dealers in false coin and genuine police reports, they were either on the side of the Government, or they scuttled about underground and never crawled into conspicuous places, like the London black beetles, which confine themselves to the kitchen and do not appear in the drawing-room. And so we have preserved a naive faith in the poet and the writer. We are not used to the thought that it is possible to lie in the spirit and trade in talents, as prostitutes delude with the body and sell their beauty. We are not used to the money-grubbers who make profit out of their tears over the people's sufferings, or the traders who turn their sympathy for the proletariat into a well-paid article. And there is a great deal that is good in this confidence, which has not existed for years in Western Europe, and we ought all to try and maintain it. Believe me, that the man who denounces duplicity, crying shame and curses upon the disgrace and decay of to-day, and at the same time locks up in his cash-box money evidently stolen from his friends, is in the present ferment of ideas, with our looseness and impressionability, more pernicious and contaminating than all the idle and superfluous people, all the embittered and the lachrymose!'

I do not know whether my Daniel agreed.

PRINCESS EKATERINA ROMANOVNA DASHKOV

'I VERY much wish,' Miss Katharine Wilmot writes to her relations in Ireland, from the Princess Dashkov's country estate, 'that you could see the Princess herself. Everything about her—dress, language, everything—is original; whatever she does, she is absolutely unlike any one else. It is not only that I have never seen such a creature, I have never even heard of one. She teaches the masons how to build walls, helps make the paths, goes to feed the cows, composes music, writes articles for the Press, knows the Church ritual perfectly and corrects the priest if he makes a mistake in the prayers, understands the theatre perfectly and corrects her serf-actors when they go wrong in their parts; she is a doctor, a chemist, a sick-nurse, a blacksmith, a carpenter, a judge, a legislator; every day she does the most opposite things in the world, and carries on a correspondence with her brother, who holds one of the foremost posts in the Empire, with savants, with literary men, with Jews, with her son, and with all her relations. Her conversation, charming in its simplicity, sometimes borders upon child-like *naïveté*. Without stopping to think she speaks at once French, Italian, Russian, and English, mixing all the languages together.

'She was born to be a minister or a general, her place is at the head of a State.'

All that is true, but Miss Wilmot forgets that, in addition to all that, Princess Dashkov was born a woman, and remained a woman all her life. She was exceptionally developed on the side of the heart, of tenderness, of feeling, of devotion.

For us that is particularly important. In Princess Dashkov the Russian woman, awakened by the revolution made by Peter the Great, emerges from her seclusion, displays her capacity, demands her share in politics, in science, in the civilisation of Russia, and boldly takes her stand beside Catherine the Great.

In Princess Dashkov we are conscious of that force, still formless, which was struggling into life and freedom from under the mildew of Moscow stagnation, something powerful, many-sided, active, something of Peter the Great and of Lomonossov, but softened by aristocratic breeding and womanliness.

Catherine 11., in making her President of the Academy, recognised the political equality of the sexes, which is perfectly consistent in a country which accepted the civic equality of woman before the law, while in Western Europe they still remain bound to their husbands or in perpetual tutelage.

The memoirs of a woman who took a foremost part in the *coup d'état* of 1762, and who was a close witness of all the events from the death of Elizabeth to the Peace of Tilsit, are exceedingly important in Russian history, so poor in striking individualities; they are the more so as we know very little of our eighteenth century. We like to go much further back in history. We see the Varangians, the men of Novgorod, and the men of Kiev, and they block out our view of yesterday; the turreted walls of the Kremlin screen the flat lines of the Peter-Paul fortress from us. Going carefully through the royal records, we know little of what was being written in bad Russian in the Government offices of Petersburg, while sedition and tumult were roaring under the windows of the Winter Palace, menacing its inhabitants with Siberia and death, and the throne had not yet the strength and security which it gained not more than seventy-five years ago. To repeat the story of that period is very profitable, both for the Government, that it may not forget, and for us, that we may not despair.

I should like, however briefly, to explain what I mean.

All Europe and, what is far worse, all Russians accept the power of the Tsar in its present form as an eternal and immutable element of Russian life, which has the right to jeer at all rash assaults on it and boldly withstands every onslaught, resting firmly and securely on roots that spread far into the earth.

The power of the Tsar has, on the contrary, been firmly established only very recently. Even to this day it carries the traces of its revolutionary origin; in it, as in the strata of the earth, the granite of ancient times, the alluvial sands, the fragments casually brought down from above, or thrust up from below, in places tightly compressed together, but not chemically united, are mingled chaotically to this day.

The Byzantine necklet of Monomah, the throne of the Tsar Ivan the Terrible, the Uspensky Cathedral, lead us astray. Did not Napoleon array himself in the mantle of Charlemagne and put the iron crown on his head at Milan? That is all forgery in the style of Chatterton; the venerated emblems of what is old and past are borrowed to invest the new with respect, and to persuade us of its durability, of its eternity, so to speak.

The Russian Imperial autocracy developed from the power of the Tsar in response to the acute need for a different manner of life. It is a military and civil dictatorship with far more resemblance to the Caesarism of Rome than to a feudal monarchy. A dictatorship may be very strong and may absorb every power, but it cannot be permanent. It exists so long as the circumstances that have called it forth remain unaltered and so long as it is true to its destiny.

Of course, when, on landing from a steamer, one meets a freshly pipe-clayed, spick-and-span regiment of Guards, an unquestioning bureaucracy, galloping couriers, motionless sentinels, Cossacks with whips, policemen with fists, half the town in uniform, half the town stand-

ing at attention, and the whole town hurriedly taking off
its hat, and when one reflects that they are all deprived
of every kind of independence, and simply acting as the
fingers, teeth, and nails of one man who combines in his
own person every form of authority—that of landowner,
priest and executioner, mother and sergeant—one may
turn giddy, be terrified, perhaps feel moved to take off
one's hat oneself, and to bow down while one's head is
still on one's shoulders. And it may even more forcibly
make one wish to return to the steamer and sail away
elsewhere. All that is so, and all that (except the last
item) was felt by the worthy Westphalian baron,
Haxthausen.

The Tsardom acquired this grimly gloomy, oppressive
aspect of brute force especially in the thirty years of
the reign of Nicholas; terrorism was with him a principle.
But here we cannot avoid asking why Nicholas could
not, in the course of those thirty years, forget the
'bad quarters of an hour' he spent during the defence
of the Winter Palace on the 14th of December 1825.
Why was it that he remembered that day on his deathbed and sent his thanks to the Guards for it?

It was because from the very beginning of his reign
he grasped that his throne was only strong through *force*.
By force alone he maintained his position, but he felt
that there was no lasting security in bayonets and physical
oppression; and he was seeking other means of support.
The allies to which he turned his attention could be
relied upon; beside autocracy he set orthodoxy and
nationalism. But this was a reaction against the movement inaugurated by Peter the Great, the whole gist of
which lay in the secularisation of the Tsardom and the
diffusion of European culture. Nicholas stood in direct
contradiction to the living principle of the Tsardom as
it had been from the time of Peter the Great, and so there
is nothing surprising in the fact that the immediate result

of his reign was a dumb breach between him and Russia. If he had lived another ten years, his throne would have collapsed of itself; everything was ceasing to work, everything had grown slack and begun to wilt; the spirit had gone out of everything, the irregularities of the administration had reached monstrous proportions. He understood that, had he followed Alexander's lead, he would inevitably have had to replace the autocratic power by more humane forms of government, but this he would not do, and he imagined that he was so far independent of the principles of Peter the Great that he could be another Peter without them.

He would have succeeded perhaps if the revolution wrought by Peter had really been, as Moscow Old Believers hold, the consequence of personal will and the caprice of genius. But it was not at all a matter of chance, it came in response to the instinctive craving of Russia to develop its forces. How else can its success be explained?

The political development of Russia moved slowly and was very late in coming. Russia lived from hand to mouth and, harried by Tatars, with difficulty gathered herself together into the ikon-like Suzdal-Byzantine kingdom of Muscovy; its political forms were clumsy and coarse, everything moved awkwardly, apathetically. The power of the Tsar was insufficient even for the defence of the country, and in 1612 Russia was saved without the help of the Tsar. And meanwhile something, that speaks to this day in the heart of every one of us, whispered that there was an immense vigour and strength under the old-fashioned burdensome garments. That something is youth, self-confidence, consciousness of strength.

The abrupt break with the old order wounded—yet pleased; the people liked Peter the Great; they put him into their legends and their fairy tales. It was as though the Russians divined that at all costs our sloth must be broken up and our slackness be braced by a strong political order. The inhuman discipline of Peter the Great, and of such of his successors as Bühren, aroused, of course, horror and loathing, but all that was borne with for the sake of the wide horizons of the new life. It was just as the Terror was endured in France.

The period initiated by Peter the Great was from the first more national than the period of the Muscovite Tsars. It has entered deeply into our history, into our manners, into our flesh and blood; there is something in it youthful and extraordinarily akin to us; the revolting mixture of barrack-room insolence and Austrian red-tape is not its chief characteristic. With that period the precious memories of our mighty growth, our glory, and our misfortunes are bound up; it has kept its word and created a powerful State. The people love success and strength.

One side of its ideal was accomplished when, in Paris, Alexander dictated the laws for all Europe. What was the next step? To go back again to the period before 1700, and combine a military despotism with a Tsardom bereft of everything human. This was what was desired by Nicholas and a dozen crazy Slavophils—and nobody else.

If the people hate the alien German Government, which fully deserves it, it does not follow that it loved the Muscovite rule; it forgot it in one generation and knows absolutely nothing about it.

After Peter the Great what hindered the return to the period that was only just over? The whole Petersburg system was hanging on a thread. Drunken and dissolute women, dull-witted princes who could scarcely speak Russian, German women and children, ascended the throne, and descended from it; the palace became the nearest way to Siberia and prison; the Government was in the hands of a handful of intriguers and *condottieri*.

Yet through all this chaos we see no special desire to return to the earlier period. On the contrary, what remains constant through all these convulsive changes, what develops in spite of them and gives them a striking unity, is precisely the fidelity to the ideas of Peter the Great. One party overthrows another, taking advantage of the fact that the new *régime* is not yet in working order; but whoever gained the day, no one touched the principles of Peter the Great, but all accepted them—Menshikov and Bühren, Minih and even the Dolgorukys, who wanted to limit the Imperial power, though not by the old Boyar Duma.[1] Elizabeth and Catherine 11. flatter orthodoxy, and flatter nationalism in order to possess the throne, but, once securely seated on it, they keep to the same way, Catherine 11. more so than any one.

The only opposition to the new order of things after its cruel installation we see in the unorthodox *raskolniks* and the passive lack of sympathy of the peasants. The obstinate grumblings of a few old men meant nothing. The crushed submission of all the 'Old Believers' was the admission of their impotence. If there had been anything living in their outlook there would certainly have been attempts, unsuccessful, impossible, impracticable perhaps, but they would have been made. All the Anna Leopoldovnas, the Anna Ivanovnas, the Elizabeth Petrovnas and Catherine Alexyevnas, found bold and devoted men ready to face the block and prison for their sakes. The Cossacks, faced with ruin, and the serfs, crushed under the heel of the nobility, had their Pugatchov, and Pugatchov his two hundred thousand lighting men; the Kirghiz-Kaisaks moved into China; the Crimean Tatars joined the Turks; Little Russia murmured loudly; everything injured or crushed by the Autocracy made its

[1] Of which Koshihin so picturesquely writes that the Boyars sat silent with their eyes fixed on their beards to show their profundity.—(*Author's Note.*)

protest, but the Old Russian party in Russia never did. It had neither voice nor devoted followers, neither a Polubotok nor a Mazeppa![1]

And it was not until one hundred and fifty years after Peter the Great that it found a representative and a leader, and that representative and leader was Nicholas. It would have been a calamity if he had, with the support of Church intolerance and nationalistic sentiment, succeeded in transforming the Autocracy, and changing it from a dictatorship into a purely monarchical or imperial government; but that was impossible. As soon as Nicholas was dead, Russia broke again into the path traced out by Peter the Great—not in the conquering or martial direction he had given it, but towards the development of its material and moral powers.

Peter the Great was one of the first of the leading figures of the great eighteenth century, and he acted in its spirit, he was saturated through and through with it, like Frederick 11. of Prussia, like Joseph 11. of Austria. His revolutionary realism gets the upper hand of his royal dignity—he is a despot, but not a monarch.

We all know how Peter crushed the old order and how he built up the new. To the burdensome, immovable Byzantine decorum he opposed the manners of the pot-house, the tedious Granovitaya Palata was transformed under him into a palace of debauchery; instead of the legal succession to the throne he, on one occasion, endowed the Tsar with the right of appointing his successor; on

---

[1] Polubotok was a candidate for the office of Hetman after Mazeppa's treason. Peter the Great appointed the weak Skuropadsky, saying that Polubotok was 'much too clever' and might be another Mazeppa. He owned more than two thousand peasant homesteads, and was one of the richest men in Little Russia; he did his utmost to defend the interests of his country against the encroachments of the Tsar's officials, and for some time with success, but in 1723 he was imprisoned in the Peter-Paul fortress, where he died a year later.—(*Translator's Note.*)

another occasion, wrote to the Senators that they should themselves select the most suitable one in case he should perish in a Turkish prison, and thereupon took the crown from his own son to give it to the servant-girl who, after passing through many men's hands, had come into his. He left vacant the post of the most holy Patriarch, forbade the display of holy relics, and wiped dry all the sorrowing tears of the wonder-working ikons. In the land of un-alterable precedence, he placed above all the rest the plebeian Menshikov, he associated with foreigners, even with negroes, got drunk in the company of skippers and sailors, rioted in the streets—in fact, in every way out-raged the rigid propriety of the Old Russian life and the dignified formality of a Tsar.

He set the tone. His successors maintained it, exaggerating and distorting it; for half a century after him, there was one unbroken orgy of drink, blood, and debauchery—*l'ultimo atto*, as an Italian writer expresses it, *d'una tragedia representata nel un lupanar*.

Where was orthodoxy, where was the principle of monarchy and chivalry, in all this?

If in the second half of the reign of Catherine the tragic character pales, the *locale* remains the same; the history of Catherine 11. cannot be read aloud before ladies. Versailles, corrupted in the monarchical style, looked with as much astonishment at the debauchery of the Russian court as at the philosophical liberalism of Catherine 11., for the French court did not understand that the foundations of the Imperial power in Russia were utterly different from those on which the Royal power of France was founded.

When Alexander said at Tilsit to Napoleon that he did not agree with the significance which the latter ascribed to the hereditary character of the Tsardom, Napoleon thought that he was deceiving him. When he said to Madame de Staël that he was only a 'happy accident,' she took it for a phrase. But it was a profoundly true saying.

Moved to wrath by the cowardice of the German sovereigns, the Emperor Alexander said in his proclamation of 22nd February 1813 to their subjects: 'Terror restrains your Governments, do not let that hold you back; if your sovereigns, under the influence of cowardice and servility, do nothing, then the voice of their subjects must be heard and must compel the rulers who are leading their peoples into slavery and misery to lead them into freedom and honour.'

The fact is, that Alexander retained a full understanding of the tradition of Peter the Great; he was too close to the first period of Imperial rule to pose as the military pope of all the reactions. Indeed, it was with obvious doubt and uncertainty that he read the police reports of Sherwood and Mayboroda.

With no doubt and no reflection, Nicholas sat down in his place and made of his power a machine which was to turn Russia back in her tracks. But the Tsardom ceased to be strong as soon as it became conservative. Russia had given up everything human, she had given up peace and freedom, and had gone into the German bondage only to escape from the cramped and stifling condition which she had outgrown. To turn her back by the same means was impossible.

It is only by going forward towards real objects, it is only by more and more actively promoting the development of the national forces with humane education, that the Tsardom can maintain itself. The oil with which the engines on the new railways are greased will be better for anointing the Tsars at their coronation than the holy unguents of the Uspensky Cathedral.

Whether our interpretation of the Imperial rule is correct will be clearly and vividly shown by the excellent memoirs of Princess Dashkov.

Our object will be fully attained if our brief sketch of its contents drives readers to open the book itself.

In the year 1744, the Empress Elizabeth and the Grand Duke Peter stood godfather and godmother to Ekaterina, the baby daughter of Count Roman Vorontsov, brother of the great Chancellor. The Vorontsovs belonged to that small number of oligarchic families which, together with the paramours of the Empresses, ruled Russia at that time as they liked, while the country passed abruptly from one reign to another. They played the master in the Empire, just as nowadays in the houses of wealthy landowners house-serfs govern districts far and near.

The Empress Elizabeth was loved, not at all because she deserved it, but because her predecessor, Anna Ivanovna, had kept Bühren, a German, as steward, and we Russians cannot endure German stewards. She was nearer to the people than Anna Ivanovna and Anna Leopoldovna; in addition to the blood of Peter, she had all the defects of the Russian character—that is, she sometimes had regular drinking bouts, and every evening drank till she could not wait for her maids to undress her, but ripped her laces and her dresses off. She used to go on pilgrimages, fasted, was superstitious and passionately fond of fine clothes—she left fifteen thousand dresses; above all, she loved precious stones, as our wealthy merchants' wives do, and probably had just as much taste as they, of which we can judge by the fact that she had a whole room decorated with amber.

The gentry in those days lived on quite a different footing with their serfs from now; there was a certain intimacy and familiarity between them, and, in spite of outbursts of domineering, they felt the novelty of their power and the necessity of support.

All of a sudden, for instance, Elizabeth takes Shuvalov

and drives with him to Count Vorontsov's to drink tea, to try on his Hungarian jacket, to gossip with him a little, while if any one told lies too wildly she would clip or cut out his tongue according to the degree of his guilt; and all this in a motherly, homely way without fuss, while she refused from motives of humanity to sign a single death-warrant.

When the Empress's god-daughter had reached the age of fourteen she had measles: measles and smallpox were no joke in those days, and almost reached the proportions of a political crime; measles or smallpox might attack Paul, that future hope of all Russia! A special Imperial decree forbade families in which there was this terrible illness to have any contact with the court. Our sick countess was hurriedly packed up and sent off into the country some fifty miles away; it must be assumed that the air there was not bad for the measles. With the countess were sent an old German lady and the rigidly decorous widow of a Russian major: the clever, plucky, and lively girl, on recovering from measles, almost died of boredom with her two companions; luckily, she found in the country a fairly good library. At fourteen our young countess knew four languages besides Russian, which she did not know, but after her marriage learnt thoroughly to please her mother-in-law. She did not attack novels but Voltaire, Bayle, and so on. Reading became a passion with her, yet books did not dispel her depression; she pined, and went back to Petersburg languid and unwell. The Empress sent her own doctor to her—and that doctor was Boerhaave; he said there was nothing wrong, that she was physically well, but that her imagination was ailing—in fact, that she was fourteen.

After Boerhaave, relations from all parts pounced on the poor girl, and with inexhaustible cruelty undertook to entertain her, to distract her mind, to feed her up; they tormented her with questions and advice. While she only asked for one thing, to be left in peace; she was at the time reading Hélvetius' *De l'Entendement.*

The remedy soon arrived of itself.

One evening the young countess, who was fairly free to make her own arrangements, went to Madame Samarin's and stayed to supper, ordering the carriage to be sent to fetch her home. At eleven o'clock the carriage drove round and she came out; but the night was so fine and there was no one in the streets, so she went home on foot, accompanied by Madame Samarin's sister. At the corner they met a tall graceful, man, who was acquainted with her companion; he began talking to the latter, and addressed a few words to the young countess.

The countess arrived home and dreamed of the handsome officer. The officer arrived home in love with the handsome countess.

No need to lose precious time; the countess was no longer a child (it was 1759), and she was fifteen; the officer was young, handsome, brilliant, and very tall, he was in the Preobrazhensky regiment, and belonged to an old family. The relations blessed the match, the Empress sanctioned it, and they were married. And so our young countess became Princess Dashkov.

A year and a half after their wedding, being on the eve of her second confinement, she remained alone in Moscow, while her husband went to Petersburg. His furlough was over, and he was asking for an extension of leave. The Grand Duke was at that time in command of the Preobrazhensky regiment; he would have given Dashkov the extension of leave at once, but the position was serious, and he wanted to make friends with his officers. The Empress was almost breathing her last; the Shuvalovs, the Razumovskys, and the Panins were intriguing with and without the Grand Duchess in favour of Paul, even in favour of the luckless Ivan—and most of all in their own favour. The Grand Duke was not liked; he was not a bad man, but he had every quality that the Russian temperament detests in the German — *gaucherie*, a coarse heartiness, a vulgar tone, a pedantry and a haughty self-complacency bordering on contempt for everything Russian. Elizabeth, though herself perpetually tipsy, could not forgive him for being drunk every evening. Razumovsky hated him for wanting to make Gudovitch Hetman; Panin for his guard-room manners; the Horse Guards for preferring his Holstein soldiers to them; the ladies for his inviting actresses and German women of all sorts to sit down at his banquets beside them; while the clergy detested him for his undisguised contempt for the Orthodox Church. Seeing that Elizabeth's end was near, and afraid of being deserted by every one, the tactless Peter attempted to make up to his officers and win their favour, and set about it with excessive clumsiness. Among others he wanted to make sure of Dashkov, who was in command of a company; and therefore, without refusing him his leave, he invited him to Oranienbaum.

Dashkov, after his interview with Peter, set off for Moscow; on the way he was taken ill with a sore throat and feverishness. Anxious not to worry his wife, he bade them take him to his aunt, Madame Novosiltsov, for he fancied that the pain in his throat was somewhat easier, and that his voice was coming back a little; instead of that, the illness turned out to be quinsy, and he was soon in a high fever.

At that very time, Prince Dashkov's mother, with her sister, Princess Gagarin, was sitting in our young princess's bedroom, together with a midwife, expecting the birth of the child in a few hours. The young mother was still able to move about, and she went to fetch something in another room, where her maid had long been awaiting her. The girl told her in secret of her sick husband's return, saying that he was at his aunt's, and begging her mistress not to betray her, as all were strictly forbidden to tell her the news. The young princess uttered a shriek at these unexpected tidings; recovering herself, she went upstairs to the bedroom, as though nothing had happened, assured them that they were all mistaken, that her confinement was not coming so soon, and persuaded them to go and rest, promising by all that was holy to send for them if anything should happen.

No sooner had the old ladies retired than the young princess flew with all the impetuosity of her character to entreat the midwife to take her to her husband. The kind-hearted German thought she had gone out of her mind, and began trying in her Silesian accent to dissuade her, continually adding: 'No, no, I shall have to answer to God afterwards for the slaughter of the innocent.' The princess told the midwife resolutely that, if she would not accompany her, she should go alone, and no force on earth should stop her. The old woman was worked upon by terror, but when the young lady told her that they must go on foot that her mother-in-law might not hear the crunch of the sledge-runners, she again resisted and stood motionless, 'as though her legs had sent down roots into the floor.' At last this difficulty, too, was overcome; but on the stairs the young princess's pains returned, and so violently that the midwife tried to dissuade her, but, clutching on to the stair-rail, she was not to be turned from her resolution.

They walked out of the gate, and in spite of the pains reached the Novosiltsovs 'house. Of the interview with her husband she remembered only that she saw him pale, ill, lying unconscious, that she only had time to take one look at him, and fell in a swoon on the floor. In this condition the Novosiltsovs' servants carried her on a stretcher home, where, however, no one had suspected her absence. Fresh and more acute pains restored her to consciousness, she sent for her husband's mother

and aunt, and an hour later gave birth to her son
Mihail.

At six o'clock in the morning her husband was brought
into the house; his mother put him in another room, forbidding any intercourse between the two sick-rooms on
the pretext that the young mother might catch the quinsy,
though in reality from a petty jealousy. The young
couple at once began a sentimental correspondence, which
was, of course, attended with much more risk for the
young mother than quinsy, which is not in the least
infectious, could be; they were writing notes to each
other at all hours of the day and night, till the old lady
found them out, scolded the maids, and threatened to
take away pens, pencils, and paper.

A woman who was capable of such love and such
determination in getting her own way in spite of danger,
fear, and pain was bound to play a great part in the times
in which she lived and in the circle to which she belonged.

On the 28th of July 1761, the Dashkovs moved to
Petersburg. 'The day,' she said, 'which twelve months
later became so memorable and so glorious for my
country.'

In Petersburg she found awaiting her an invitation
from the Grand Duke to move to Oranienbaum. She
did not want to go, and her father had difficulty in persuading her to take his summer villa not far from Oranienbaum. The fact is that by then she could not endure
the Grand Duke, while she was sincerely devoted to his
wife. Before she had left her father's house she had
been presented to the Grand Duchess; Catherine had
been gracious to her, the clever and highly cultured girl
had taken her fancy. With the smile, the *abandon* with
which Catherine for thirty years fascinated all Russia,
and the diplomatists and learned men of all Europe, she
won the devotion of Princess Dashkov for ever. From
the first interview the young girl loved Catherine passion-

ately, 'adored her' as schoolgirls adore their elder companions; she was in love with her as boys are in love with women of thirty.

On the other hand, she felt as genuine an aversion for her godfather, Peter. And a pleasant person he was, there is no denying. We shall see it directly.

Her own sister, Elizaveta Romanovna, was openly Peter's mistress. He considered that Saltykov and Poniatowski, the fortunate predecessors of the Orlovs, Vassiltchikovs, Novosiltsovs, Potyomkins, Lanskys, Yermolevs, Korsakovs, Zoritches, Zavodovskys, Mamonovs, Zubovs, and a whole phalanx of stalwart *virorum obscurorum* gave him the right not to be over-niggardly in his affairs of the heart, and not to conceal his preferences.

His attitude to his wife was already such that, on Princess Dashkov's first being presented to him, he said to her: 'Allow me to hope that you will bestow upon us no less time than upon the Grand Duchess.'

For her part the impetuous young princess did not dream of concealing her preference for Catherine. The Grand Duke observed it, and a few days later led the young princess aside, and said to her, 'in the simplicity of his head and the kindness of his heart,' as she puts it: 'Remember that it is safer to have to do with simple, honest people like your sister and me than with great intellects who squeeze every drop out of you and then throw you out of window like the skin of an orange.'

Princess Dashkov evasively observed that the Empress had expressed her urgent desire that they should show respect equally to the Grand Duchess and to His Highness.

Nevertheless, she could not avoid sometimes attending the Grand Duke's drinking-parties. These festivities were of a German barrack-room character, coarse and drunken. Peter, surrounded by his Holstein generals (that is, in her words, by corporals and sergeants of the Prussian army, sons of German artisans whose parents

did not know what to do with them, and sent them for
soldiers on account of their dissolute habits), with the
pipe always between his lips, sometimes went on drinking
till his flunkeys carried him out.

At one such supper-party in the presence of the Grand
Duchess and numerous visitors, the conversation turned
on Tchelishtchev, a sergeant of the Guards, and his
supposed *liaison* with the Countess Hendrikov, a niece
of the Empress.

Peter, who was already very drunk, observed that
Tchelishtchev ought to have his head cut off as a warning
to other officers not to get up love affairs with the female
relations of the royal family. The Holstein sycophants
expressed their approval and sympathy by every possible
token, while the young princess could not refrain from
observing that it seemed to her very inhuman to inflict
the death penalty for so trivial a crime.

'You are still a child,' answered the Grand Duke,
'your words prove it; otherwise you would know that
to be sparing with the death penalty means to encourage
insurbodination.'

'Your Highness,' answered Princess Dashkov, 'you
are trying to frighten us; with the exception of the old
generals, all of us who have the honour to be sitting at
your table belong to a generation which has never seen
the death penalty in Russia.'

'That does not signify,' retorted the Grand Duke;
'fine sort of order there has been in everything in consequence. I tell you, you are a child and know nothing
about these things.'

All remained silent. 'I am ready,' the young princess
replied, 'to acknowledge that I am incapable of understanding you; but I cannot help rejoicing when I think
that your aunt is still on the throne and is still well and
strong.'

All eyes were turned upon the bold young woman.

The Grand Duke did not answer in words; he confined himself to putting out his tongue—a charming trick to which he often resorted instead of a verbal reply, especially when he was in church.

This conversation, which was the beginning of Princess Dashkov's political career, was the more remarkable for the fact that these Nero-like speeches were uttered by the mildest man in the world, who had never put any one to death. There were a large number of the officers of the Guards and of the cadets sitting at the table, and Princess Dashkov's words were carried with lightning swiftness all over the town. They gave her a great notoriety, which at first she was far from appreciating, and which made of her one of the centres, and almost the principal one, round which discontented officers rallied. At first the young princess was delighted that the Grand Duchess was exceedingly pleased by her answer. 'Time,' she mournfully adds, 'had not then taught me how dangerous it is to tell the truth to sovereigns; if they can sometimes forgive it, their courtiers never do.'

Her affection for Catherine increased. Elizabeth was then living at Peterhof, and there the Grand Duchess was permitted *once a week* to see her son. On her way back from the Palace she usually drove to the Dashkovs', took the princess with her, and kept her for a whole evening. When it was impossible to visit her, Catherine wrote a brief note to her; from this there sprang up the friendly, intimate correspondence between them which lasted even after the Dashkovs had left the summer villa. They write about literature, about their day-dreams, about Voltaire, and about Rousseau, in verse and in prose.

'Such verse and such prose!' writes Catherine, 'and at seventeen! I entreat you not to neglect such a talent. Perhaps I am not altogether an impartial critic; your flattering attachment to me is to blame for your having chosen me for the subject of your poem. Blame me for pride if you like, but still I will say that it is long since I have read such correct and such poetical work.'

Catherine, too, sends her essays and very emphatically insists that they are to be shown to no one. 'In the circumstances under which I am compelled to live, everything serves as a ground for unpleasant suppositions.' She is so anxious that she begs Princess Dashkov to have letters addressed to her maid, Katerina Ivanovna, and burns them when she has read them. What she calls 'trifling grounds' may be surmised from one letter in which she again speaks of her manuscript. The young princess had returned it to her with much praise, assuring her that she had never let it go out of her own hands. Not a word is said of the contents of the manuscript, but it is evident from the following words (letter 21): 'You relieve me of my duties in regard to my son; I see in that a fresh proof of the goodness of your heart. I was profoundly agitated by the tokens of devotion with which I was greeted by the people on that day. I have never been so happy.'

That letter was written soon after Elizabeth's death, but we have not yet reached that stage of our narrative.

Towards the end of December 1761, there was a rumour that Elizabeth was very ill.

Princess Dashkov was lying in bed with a very bad cold when the news reached her. The thought of Catherine's danger struck her; she could no more lie still in bed with it than with the thought of her husband's illness; and so, wrapped in a fur coat, on the frosty night of the 20th of December, she set off for the wooden palace on the Moika, where the royal family lived at that time. Not wishing to be seen, she left the carriage at a little distance from the Palace, and walked towards the little entrance at the side of the Grand Duchess's apartments, though she did not know the way to them. Fortunately she met Katerina Ivanovna, the Grand Duchess's maid;

the latter said that the Grand Duchess was in bed; but Princess Dashkov insisted on being announced, saying that she absolutely must see her at once. The maid, knowing her and her devotion to the Grand Duchess, obeyed. Catherine, who knew the Princess Dashkov was seriously ill, and so would not have come out at night in the frost without specially important reasons, ordered her to be shown up.

At first she showered reproaches on the princess for not taking care of herself, and, seeing that she was cold, said to her: 'Dear princess, first of all you must get warm; come, get into my bed'; and only after tucking her up, she asked her at last what was the matter.

'In the present position of affairs,' said Princess Dashkov, 'when the Empress has only a few days, perhaps a few hours, to live, you must, without loss of time, take measures against the danger with which you are threatened and steps to avert it. For God's sake, trust me; I will show you that I am worthy of your trust. If you have any definite plan, make use of me, dispose of me, I am at your service.'

Catherine burst into tears and, pressing her friend's hand to her heart, said: 'I assure you that I have no plan whatever; there is nothing I can do, and I imagine that all that is left me is to await the course of events with fortitude. I resign myself to the will of God, and rest all my hopes on Him alone.'

'In that case your friends must act for you. As for me, I fed I have strength and energy enough to carry them all with me; and believe me, there is no sacrifice which would hinder me.'

'For God's sake,' Catherine interrupted, 'do not expose yourself to danger in the hope of resisting evil which seems really inevitable. If you ruin yourself for my sake, you will only add an everlasting grief to my unhappy lot.'

'All that I can tell you is that I will not take a step which could possibly involve you, or put you in danger. Whatever happens, may it come upon me, and, if my blind devotion to you leads me to the scaffold, you shall never be its victim.'

Catherine would have protested, but Princess Dashkov[1] interrupting her, took her hand, pressed it to her lips, and, saying that she was afraid to continue the conversation, asked leave to withdraw. Deeply touched, they remained for some minutes in each other's arms, then the princess cautiously went out, leaving Catherine in great agitation.

We must add to this affecting scene that Catherine had all the same deceived the princess; she had not entrusted her fate to God alone, but also to Grigory Orlov, with whom she had thought out her plan, and Orlov was already secretly trying to enlist the co-operation of the officers.

At Christmas the Empress died. Petersburg received the news gloomily; and Princess Dashkov herself saw the Semyonovsky and Izmailovsky regiments march sullenly past her house with muffled murmurs.

Peter 111., proclaimed Emperor, paid no regard to decorum; the drinking bouts went on. A few days after Elizabeth's death he visited the father of Princess Dashkov, and through her sister announced his displeasure at not seeing her at court. There was no escaping it; she went. Peter 111., dropping his voice, began telling her that she would end by drawing upon herself his anger, and might very bitterly repent of it later on, 'because there may easily come a time when Romanovna' (that was what he called his mistress) 'will be in *that woman's* place.'

---

[1] Diderot, in his extremely interesting account of his acquaintance with Princess Dashkov, speaking of this interview, adds that Catherine said to her: 'You are either an angel or a demon.' 'Neither the one nor the other,' she answered; 'but the Empress is dying and you must be saved.' — (*Author's Note*.)

Princess Dashkov made a show of not understanding, and hurriedly took her place at Peter 111.'s favourite game. In this game (*campis*) each player has several counters; the player who keeps one till the last wins the game. Every one put down ten imperials, which, considering Princess Dashkov's income at that time, was not a trifling sum for her, particularly as, when Peter III. lost, he used to take a counter out of his pocket and lay it on the pool, so that he almost always won. As soon as the game was over, the Tsar proposed a second; she refused. He pestered her so much to play that, taking advantage of her 'position as spoilt child,' she told him that she was not rich enough to lose for certain, that if His Majesty played like other people she would, at any rate, have a chance of winning. Peter III. responded with his 'usual buffooneries,' and the princess made her bows and withdrew.

As she walked through the suite of rooms filled with courtiers and persons of various grades, she felt as though she were at a masquerade, there was no one she could recognise. She could not help laughing when she saw Prince Trubetskoy, who was seventy, for the first time in his life dressed up in a military uniform, standing at attention, in high boots with spurs, all ready, in fact, for the most desperate battle. 'The pitiful little old man,' she adds, 'pretending to be ill and suffering, as beggars do, lay in bed while Elizabeth was dying; he felt a little better when Peter III. was proclaimed, and, learning that everything had gone off well, he leapt up at once, armed himself from head to foot, and showed himself like a hero in the Izmailovsky regiment to which he was attached.'

Apropos of uniforms, the fatal passion for them was handed down from Peter III. to Paul, from Paul to all his children, to all the generals, staff and higher officers; Panin, who supervised the education of Paul, complained that Peter III. was never present at his examinations. The Holstein princes, his uncles, persuaded Peter to attend

one at least; he was very much pleased, and promoted
Panin to be a general in the infantry. To perceive the
full absurdity of this, one must picture the pale, sickly
figure of Panin, who liked to be correctly dressed and
scrupulously groomed, and was rather like a courtier of
the days of Louis xiv. Panin detested Peter iii.'s
barrack-room tone, he hated uniforms and all that nonsense. When Melgunov brought him the joyful tidings
that he was a general, Panin would have fled to Switzerland and lived there in preference to wearing the uniform.
News of this reached Peter iii.; he transferred him to
the corresponding civilian grade. He never got over
his surprise at Panin. 'Why,' he used to say, 'I always
thought Panin was a sensible man!'

While Peter iii. was dressing his courtiers up as heroes,
the usual funeral ceremonies were taking place. The
Empress did not leave her rooms, and only appeared at
the requiem service. Peter iii., too, only rarely showed
himself, and then always behaved improperly, whispering
with the ladies, laughing with his adjutants, mocking at
the clergy, scolding the officers, and even the common
soldiers, over buttons or some such trifle. 'The new
Emperor,' the English ambassador, Keith, said to Prince
Golitsyn, 'is beginning his reign imprudently; if he goes
on like this he will come to be despised by his people
and afterwards to be hated by them.'

Peter iii. did everything as though on purpose to arouse
this hatred. One evening, when Princess Dashkov was
present, the Tsar was holding forth, as his habit was, on
the subject of his respect for Frederick ii., and suddenly
turning to the Secretary of State, Volkov, who had been
Chief Secretary of the Privy Council under Elizabeth, he
asked him whether he remembered how they used to
laugh over the perpetual failure of the secret instructions
sent to the army in the field. Volkov, who together with
Peter, then Grand Duke, had communicated to the

Prussian King all the army orders, and so stultified them, was so taken aback by Peter 111.'s words that he almost fainted. But the Tsar went on, jocosely describing how in time of war they had betrayed to the enemy the country in which he was heir to the throne.

At the conclusion of the peace with the Prussian King, in which he shamefully yielded everything that had been won by Russian blood, there was no end to the delight and rejoicing. There was festivity after festivity. Among others Peter 111. gave a great dinner, to which all the ambassadors and members of the three first grades were invited. After dinner the Tsar proposed three toasts, which were drunk to the firing of cannon—to the health of the Imperial Family, to the health of the Prussian King, to the permanence of the peace that had been concluded.

When the Empress drank the toast to the Imperial Family, Peter 111. sent his adjutant, Gudovitch, who was standing by his chair, to ask her why she did not stand up. Catherine answered that since the Imperial Family consisted only of her husband, her son, and herself, she had not supposed that it would be His Majesty's pleasure that she should stand up. When Gudovitch repeated her answer, the Tsar bade him go back and tell the Empress that she was 'a fool,' and ought to know that his uncles, the Holstein princes, belonged to the Imperial Family too. This was not enough; afraid that Gudovitch would soften his rudeness, he repeated what he had said across the table, so that the greater number of the guests heard it. For the first minute the Empress could not refrain from shedding tears, but, anxious to end the scandal as quickly as possible, she turned to the *kammerherr*, Strogonov, who was standing behind her chair, and begged him to begin some conversation. Strogonov, who was himself deeply shocked, began babbling something with a show of liveliness. As he

went out of the palace, he received the command to
go to his country estate, and not to leave it without
permission.

This incident was exceedingly prejudicial to Peter III.
Every one pitied the unfortunate woman, who had been
grossly insulted by a drunken boor. Princess Dashkov
was naturally bound to take advantage of this state of
public feeling. She became a desperate conspirator,
persuading, sounding, enlisting sympathisers, and at the
same time she went to balls and danced to avoid arousing
suspicion. Prince Dashkov, insulted by Peter III., made
him some answer on parade. The princess, afraid of
the consequences, succeeded in procuring him a commission to Constantinople, and gave him the advice to
'make haste slowly' with it. Having sent him off, she
surrounded herself with officers who put the fullest
confidence in their eighteen-year-old leader.

There were other people about Peter III. who were
dissatisfied, but owing to their age and position took no
part in the conspiracy; they were glad to take advantage
of a change, but the risk of losing their heads on the
scaffold was too much for a Razumovsky or a Panin.
The real conspirators were Princess Dashkov with her
officers, and Orlov with his adherents.

Of Razumovsky Princess Dashkov says: 'He loves
his country as much as the apathetic man can love anything. Sunk in the bog of wealth, surrounded by marks
of respect, well received at the new court, and liked by
the officers, he has dropped into indifference and grown
sluggish.'

Panin was a statesman and looked further ahead than
the rest; his aim was to proclaim Paul Tsar and Catherine
Regent. So doing he hoped to curtail the power of the
Autocracy. Moreover, he thought to attain his object
by legal means through the Senate.

All this was far from being approved by Princess

Dashkov. Moreover, the dissatisfaction and murmuring among the soldiers were growing. The disgraceful peace, on the one hand, and the insane war with Denmark which with no serious object Peter III. wanted to wage over Holstein, exasperated men's minds. This war became an insane obsession with him; even Frederick II. tried by letter to persuade him to defer it.

It is said that the young conspiratress used peculiarly eloquent weapons to induce stubborn Panin to co-operate with her party. Panin was so attracted by her intelligence, her energy, and, above all, her beauty, that, old as he was, he fell passionately in love with her. Princess Dashkov rejected his love with mirth, but finding no other means of persuading him she made up her mind to bribe him with herself. After this Panin was in her hands. It is only just to say that in two passages of her memoirs she denies this rumour with indignation.[1]

Although the conspirators could reckon on Razumovsky and Panin, and, what was more, on the Archbishop of Novgorod, and although a number of officers adhered to the conspiracy, they had no definite plan of action. Though at one in a common object, they could not agree on the steps to be taken; Princess Dashkov, devoured by burning energy, was angry with their deliberateness, did not know what to do, and at last went off to her summer villa at Krasny Kabak. This summer villa was the first possession she had entirely of her own: she at once set to work rebuilding, digging ditches, laying out gardens. 'In spite,' she said, 'of the affection I had for that first bit of ground which was my own, I did not want to give it my name, as I wished to dedicate it to the name of the saint on whose day success crowns our great enterprise.' 'Make haste and give a name to my villa,'

---

[1] Diderot in the above-mentioned essay relates that Princess Dashkov told him of this rumour with the greatest resentment.— (*Author's Note.*)

she writes to the Empress, when laid up with a fever, which she had caught through riding up to her waist in a bog. Catherine could make nothing of it, and thought that her friend was delirious.

But it was Peter III. who was really delirious; while Princess Dashkov was planting acacias and clearing paths, he was moving rapidly on his downward path; one folly succeeded another, one unseemly vulgarity was followed by another twice as unseemly. Keith's prophecy was coming true: public feeling was passing from contempt into hatred.

The Austrian persecution of the Greek Church in Serbia had driven many Serbs to appeal to the Empress Elizabeth, begging her to assign them lands in the south of Russia. In addition to lands, Elizabeth ordered a considerable sum of money to be given them for the expenses of their moving and resettlement. One of their agents, Horvat, a wily, intriguing fellow, took possession of the lands and money and, instead of carrying out the conditions on which the land was given, began to dispose of the emigrants as though they were his serfs. The Serbs presented a complaint, Elizabeth ordered an enquiry, but before it was over she died. Horvat, hearing of her death, went to Petersburg and began by giving two thousand gold pieces to each of the three persons who were in closest relations with Peter III.— L. Naryshkin, who was something in the way of a court buffoon, General Melgunov, and the Prosecutor-General Glyebov. The two latter went to the Tsar and told him straight out of the bribe. Peter III. was much pleased at their openness, he praised them for it, and added that if they would give him half he would go himself to the Senate and command them to decide the case in favour of Horvat. They divided the spoils, the Tsar kept his word, and for two thousand gold pieces lost hundreds of thousands of new settlers; seeing that their comrades had been cheated by the Government, those who had not yet started did not venture to move.

When the case was over, Peter III. heard that Naryshkin had concealed his bribe, and, to punish him for this lack of friendly confidence, took the whole sum from him. And for a long time afterwards he used to tease Naryshkin by asking him what he was doing with Horvat's gold pieces.

Here is another charming anecdote of Peter III. One day the Tsar returned home with Razumovsky after parade, much pleased with the Izmailovsky regiment; suddenly he heard a noise a little way off; his favourite negro was fighting with the fencing-master. At first Peter III. was delighted with the spectacle, but all at once he pulled a solemn face and said: 'Narcisse exists no longer for us.' Razumovsky, who could make nothing of it, asked what had so suddenly distressed His Majesty. 'Why, don't you see,' he cried, 'that I cannot keep a man about me who has fought with a fencing-master? he is disgraced, disgraced for ever.' Razumovsky, pretending to enter into these deep considerations, observed that the negro's honour might be restored by passing him under the flag of the regiment. This idea delighted Peter III.; he at once called the negro, bade him pass under the flag, and, feeling this was not quite sufficient, ordered that he should be scratched with the lance of the flag that he might wash out his offence with his own blood. The poor negro almost died of fright, the generals and the officers could hardly restrain their indignation and laughter. Only Peter III. performed the whole ritual of the negro's purification with perfect solemnity throughout.

And this buffoon was Tsar! . . . But not for long!

On the evening of the 27th of June Grigory Orlov came to Princess Dashkov to tell her that Captain Passek, one of the most desperate conspirators, was arrested-Orlov found Panin with her; to lose time, to procrastinate, was now impossible. Only the lymphatic, slow, and cautious Panin counselled waiting till the morrow, and first finding out how and why Passek was arrested. This did not please Orlov or her. The former said that he would go to find out about Passek. Princess Dashkov asked Panin to leave her, pretending that she was excessively tired. As soon as Panin had driven off, she threw on a man's grey overcoat and set off on foot to see Roslavlev, one of the conspirators.

Not far from home she met a man on horseback galloping full speed. Although she had never seen Orlov's brothers, she guessed that it was one of them; when she reached him, she called his name. He pulled up the horse, and she made herself known to him. 'I was coming to you,' he said. 'Passek has been seized as a political criminal. There are four sentries at the doors and two at the window. My brother has gone to Panin, and I have been to Roslavlev.'

'Is Roslavlev much alarmed?'

'He is indeed.'

'Send word to our men, Roslavlev, Lasunsky, Tchertkov, and Bredihin to gather at once to the Izmailovsky regiment, and to make ready to receive the Empress. Then say that I advise your brother or you to ride as fast as you can to Peterhof for the Empress; tell her that I have a carriage ready, tell her that I beseech her not to delay, but to drive full speed to Petersburg.'

On the previous evening Princess Dashkov, who had heard from Passek of the great discontent of the soldiers, and was afraid that something might happen, had by way of precaution written to the wife of Catherine's *kammerdiener*, Shkurin, telling her to send a carriage with four post-horses to her husband at Peterhof, and to bid him await her in his yard. Panin laughed at this unnecessary fuss, supposing that the *coup d'état* was not so imminent; events proved how necessary Princess Dashkov's precautions were.

On parting from Orlov, she returned home. In the evening a tailor was to have brought her a man's dress, but did not bring it, and she was not free enough dressed as a woman. To avoid rousing suspicion, she dismissed her maid and went to bed; but half an hour had not passed before she heard a knock at the outer door. It was the youngest Orlov, who had been sent by his elder brothers to ask her whether it was not too soon to disturb the Empress; Princess Dashkov was beside herself, and showered reproaches upon him and all his brothers: 'As though it were a question,' she said, 'of disturbing the Empress; better bring her unconscious, fainting, to Petersburg than expose her to imprisonment or to sharing the scaffold with us. Tell your brothers that some one must go this very minute to Peterhof.'

The young man agreed with her.

Then followed agonising hours of solitude and suspense; she trembled for her Catherine, and pictured her pale, worn out, in prison, going to be beheaded, and all 'through our fault.' Exhausted and feverish, she waited for news from Peterhof. At four o'clock it came: the Empress had gone to Petersburg.

How Alexey Orlov went in the night to the pavilion to where Catherine was calmly asleep; how, though, like Princess Dashkov, she did not know the younger Orlov by sight, she instantly determined to set off in the carriage that was waiting for her at Shkurin's; how Orlov sat on the box-seat as coachman, and knocked the horses up by his driving, so that the Empress was obliged to walk with her maid; how they afterwards met an empty cart; how Orlov hired it, and brought Catherine to Petersburg in democratic style—all that is well known.

The soldiers of the Izmailovsky regiment received Catherine with enthusiasm; they were told that Peter III. had tried that night to kill her and her son. With shouts and uproar the soldiers escorted her from the barracks

to the Winter Palace, proclaiming her the reigning
Empress as they passed through the streets; they met
with no hindrance of any kind. The people flocked in
crowds to the Palace, the leading noblemen gathered
together in the Cathedral, and the Archbishop, surrounded
by clergy, awaited the new sovereign with holy water.

When, after terrific efforts, Princess Dashkov succeeded
in reaching Catherine, they rushed into each other's arms,
and could only say: 'Well, thank God, thank God!'
Then Catherine told her how they had driven from
Peterhof, then they fell to embracing each other again.
'I do not know,' writes Princess Dashkov, 'whether a
mortal has ever been happier than I was at that minute!'

'And,' she adds, 'when I think by what extraordinarily small means this revolution was effected, with no
thought-out plan, by men who were not agreed among
themselves, who had different aims in view, and were
not in the least alike either in breeding or character, it is
clear to me that the finger of Providence was in it.'

The revolution, of course, was essential, but if the
finger of Providence was so directly concerned in it, then
the divine hands were far from being clean on that day.

After they had kissed each other to their hearts' content,
Princess Dashkov noticed that the Empress was wearing
the Catherine and not the Andrew ribbon; she ran at
once to Panin, took off his ribbon, put it on the Empress,
and put the Catherine ribbon and star in her pocket.

The Empress expressed a desire to put herself at the
head of the troops and to march to Peterhof. At the
same time she ordered the princess to accompany her.
The Empress took a uniform from Captain Talyzin,
Princess Dashkov one from Sergeant Pushkin. Both
uniforms were of the old Preobrazhensky pattern. As
soon as the Empress had arrived in Petersburg, the soldiers
had, of their own initiative, cast off their new uniforms
and put on their old ones.

While Princess Dashkov was changing her dress, Catherine was presiding over an Extraordinary Council, consisting of the highest dignitaries and senators who happened to be on the spot. The sentinels stationed at the doors admitted to it a young officer with a bold carriage and reckless air. No one but the Empress recognised him as Princess Dashkov; she went up to Catherine and said that the guard was very inefficient, that they would perhaps admit Peter III. himself if he should suddenly appear (how little even she knew the buffoon!); the guard was immediately strengthened; meanwhile, the Empress, who was dictating a manifesto to Tyeplov, broke off to tell the members of the Council who this young officer was who had come up *sans façon*, and begun whispering to her. All the senators stood up to greet her. 'I blushed to my ears at this honour,' says the charming sergeant, 'and indeed I was rather embarrassed by it.

'Then, after taking the necessary measures to ensure the tranquillity of the capital, we mounted our horses, and on the road to Peterhof reviewed ten thousand men, who cheered the Empress with enthusiasm.'

At Krasny Kabak the insurrectionary army halted: the men, who had been on their legs for twelve hours, needed a rest. Catherine and Princess Dashkov, who had not slept at all the last few nights, were much exhausted. The princess took an overcoat from Colonel Kar, spread it over the solitary sofa in the little room they had taken at the inn, and stationed sentries; then she and Catherine stretched themselves on the sofa, not taking off their uniforms, but firmly resolved to get a little sleep; they could not sleep, however, but spent the whole time talking, making plans, and entirely forgetting the danger they were in.

There is no denying that there is something extraordinarily fascinating in this daring exploit of two women, who changed the destinies of an empire, in this revolution wrought by a handsome, clever woman, surrounded by young men in love with her, and with the leading figure among them a beauty of eighteen on horseback in the Preobrazhensky regiment, with a sabre in her hand.

The unlucky Peter was meanwhile driving from Oranienbaum to Peterhof, and from Peterhof to Oranienbaum, unable to think what to do or to decide upon anything. He looked for Catherine through all the rooms of the pavilion, behind doors and cupboards, as though she were playing 'hide-and-seek' with him, and, not without complacency, repeated to 'Romanovna': 'There, you see I was right; I was sure she wuld do something; I always said that woman was capable of anything.'

The old champion, Minih, still stood by him, all Russia and part of Petersburg was still not against him, but he had already lost his head entirely. Displaying incredible cowardice at Cronstadt, he bade the Imperial yacht sail not to the fleet, but back to Oranienbaum; the ladies were afraid of sickness and the sea, he was afraid of everything. It was a calm moonlight night; the pitiful Tsar hid in the cabin with his courtiers, while the two heroes, Minih and Gudovitch, sat in gloomy brooding on deck, with shame and anger and sorrow in their hearts; they saw that there is no saving people against their will. At four o'clock in the morning they reached Oranienbaum again, and crestfallen stealthily returned to the Palace. Peter sat down to write a letter to Catherine.

At the same time two fiery steeds were being saddled, one for Catherine, the other for Princess Dashkov, and again, full of gaiety and energy, they were at the head of their soldiers, who set off on the march at five o'clock, and halted to rest at the Troitsky Monastery. Then Peter's envoys began appearing one after another, bringing pro-

posals each more foolish than the last; he abdicated
from the throne, begged leave to go to Holstein, and
owned himself to blame and unfit to rule. Catherine
insisted on his unconditional surrender to avert greater
troubles, and promised in return to arrange his life as
comfortably as possible in whichever he preferred of
the palaces away from the town.

Catherine's troops calmly occupied Peterhof; Orlov,
who had ridden on to reconnoitre, had found no one
there. The Holsteiners, who were about Peter in
Oranienbaum and were devoted to him, were ready to
die for him, but he told them to make no defence; he
meant to flee, ordered a horse to be brought, but did not
mount it; instead, he got into a carriage with Romanovna
and Gudovitch, and mournfully went to surrender to his
guilty wife. He was led secretly into a remote room of
the Palace. Gudovitch, who even then behaved with
extraordinary dignity, was arrested, together with
Romanovna; Peter was given food and drink, and taken
to Ropsha in the escort of Alexey Orlov, Passek, Baryatinsky, and Baskakov. He selected Ropsha himself; it
had belonged to him when he was Grand Duke. Other
authorities state, however, that he did not go to Ropsha
at all, but was on the estate of Razumovsky.

Princess Dashkov saw his letters to Catherine. In
one he speaks of his abdication, in another of the persons
he would like to keep about him, and enumerates everything he needed for his daily life, making special mention
of a store of Burgundy and tobacco. He asked further,
it is said, for a violin, a Bible, and various novels, adding
that he meant to become a philosopher.

On the evening of the day when Peterhof was taken,
Princess Dashkov, coming back from the Princess of
Holstein's to the Empress's apartments, came upon Orlov,
who was lying at full length on a sofa in one of the
Empress's inner rooms. He apologised for doing so,

alleging that he had hurt his foot. He was opening a big envelope; Princess Dashkov had seen such envelopes in the hands of her uncle, the Vice-Chancellor; they were used for the most important affairs of state communicated from the Privy Council to the Tsar.

'What are you doing?' she asked, with amazement.

'The Empress told me to.'

'Impossible,' she answered. 'You have no official status for doing it.'

At that moment word was brought that the soldiers had broken into the cellars, and were drinking Hungarian wine in their helmets, taking it for mead. Orlov did not stir. Princess Dashkov at once went downstairs, assumed a threatening air, and with her thin girlish voice restored discipline. Pleased with her success, she distributed among them all the money she had on her; then, turning her purse inside out, told them that her means were less than her goodwill, but that on their return to Petersburg they should have leave to drink at the Government's expense; after this she went back.

Beside the sofa on which Orlov was lying she found a table laid for three. The Empress came in, took her seat, and invited the princess to sit down. All this so impressed the latter that she could not conceal her emotion. The Empress noticed it, and asked her what was the matter.

'Nothing,' she answered; 'most likely I am tired from sleepless nights and excitement.'

Catherine, wishing to draw the princess into being civil to Orlov, told her that in spite of her urgent wishes he was giving up military service, and begged the princess to help her to dissuade him. 'I shall be charged,' she said, 'with horrible ingratitude if he leaves the army.' But Princess Dashkov, mortified by her discovery, answered that Her Majesty had so many means of rewarding his services that she had no need to constrain him.

'It was only then,' she adds, 'that I was convinced there was *une liaison* between them.'

It has been thought that she was mortified at this through jealousy, and it is not a mistake. Only, she was not jealous on Orlov's account; she never liked and never respected either him or his brothers; she was jealous over the Empress; she liked neither the choice nor the tone; moreover, her dreams of exclusive confidence, of romantic friendship, of all-powerful influence, paled and vanished at her discovery. And as a fact, from that evening she had a rival and an enemy; she felt that the very day after the *coup d'état*.

Crazy Peter's saying about the orange skin began coming true with extraordinary rapidity. The very day after ascending the throne the Empress began appraising and rewarding Princess Dashkov's services, she began to be grateful—that is, ceased to be her friend.

After her triumphal entry into Petersburg, Princess Dashkov went away to see her father, her uncle, and, most of all, to have a look at her little one. It must not be forgotten that our Preobrazhensky sergeant had a little daughter Nastya, whom she passionately loved, and with whom she longed to play, after having played enough with the Tsar's crown. Her father's house was full of soldiers, stationed there partly for his protection, and partly because 'Romanovna' had been brought to his house. Vadkovsky sent to ask the officer on duty whether all the guard was needed; Princess Dashkov, speaking to him in French, told the officer that half of the soldiers were not needed, and that she was dismissing them.

When she went back to the Palace, Catherine received her with a look of displeasure; the officer of the guard was present and was talking to Orlov. The Empress reprimanded Princess Dashkov for acting on her own initiative, and even observed that she had spoken French before the soldiers. The princess, deeply wounded, listened to the reprimand, made no reply, and, to change the conversation, gave Catherine the ribbon and the order which she had put in her pocket the day before.

'Not so fast, not so fast,' said the Empress. 'I had to reprimand you for your impetuosity—you had no right to dismiss the soldiers on your own authority; but I must also reward you for your services.' With this she put around her neck the ribbon that had been restored.

Instead of kneeling down before the Empress, as is done on such occasions, Princess Dashkov said to her sorrowfully: 'Your Majesty, forgive me for what I want to say; the time is coming when truth must be banished from your presence; before it comes, I beg you to take back that order: as a decoration I cannot sufficiently value it; if it is a reward—however great it might be, it could not reward my services, they cannot be paid by anything, for they were not to be bought.'

'But,' said the Empress, embracing her, and leaving the ribbon, 'friendship has its claims; surely I am not deprived of them now?'

Princess Dashkov, pleased again, kissed her hand, and the spirits of a girl of eighteen got the upper hand; half a century later she does not forget to add with pleasure: 'Fancy me in a uniform, with a spur on one high boot, looking like a boy of fifteen, with the red Catherine ribbon across my shoulder.' The new cavalier galloped back again to Nastya, to show herself to the baby, to be present at her supper, and at last undressing flung herself into bed; but this time, too, sleep fled from her fretted nerves, or terrified her with dreams: the amazing scenes of the preceding days, which she had not merely lived through, but had partly brought about, passed incessantly before her imagination.

The Empress herself did not deny the important share Princess Dashkov had taken in the revolution of the 28th of June; on the contrary, when the wily old

Bestuzhev was presented to her, she said to him: 'Who could have imagined that the daughter of Roman Vorontsov would have helped me to ascend the throne!'

The news of the murder of Peter filled Princess Dashkov with horror and aversion; she was so distressed and revolted by this stain on the 'revolution which has not cost one drop of blood,' that she could not bring herself to go next day to the Palace. She omits in her memoirs all the details of the revolting proceeding, in which three officers, one of whom was of gigantic stature, were at work for half an hour stifling with a napkin the poisoned prisoner, as though they could not wait for a quarter of an hour. She assumed that Catherine did not know beforehand of Alexey Orlov's design;[1] it is more probable that she simply had no idea of the connivance of Catherine, who could carefully conceal her wishes. Not only Panin and the other conspirators knew nothing of her intrigue with Grigory Orlov, but, as we have just seen, Princess Dashkov had not suspected it.

Catherine perceived what was in the latter's heart, and when she saw her began to speak with horror of what had happened.

'Yes, your Majesty,' answered Princess Dashkov, 'this death has come too quickly and too soon for your fame and for mine.'

As she walked through the drawing-room, she said in a loud voice before every one that, of course, Alexey Orlov would spare her his acquaintance. For over twenty-five years they did not bow nor say a word to each other.

It is very possible that Catherine had not given instructions to murder Peter. Alexander went further: he

---

[1] There are no grounds for supposing that Catherine knew of any plan to murder Peter; there is strong evidence, indeed, that she did not know, and that in fact there was no such plan. It is obvious that Peter was killed in a drunken scrimmage. —(*Translator's Note.*)

positively insisted that they should not *kill* Paul, when
he sent a gang of the rebel nobles to him. We know
from Shakespeare how these orders are given by a glance,
a hint, a silence. Why did Catherine entrust the care
of the pusillanimous Peter to his worst enemies? Passek
and Baskakov had meant to kill him several days before
the 27th of June, and did not she know that? And why
were the murderers so shamelessly rewarded?

Princess Dashkov quotes in Catherine's defence a letter
from Orlov, written immediately after the murder, which
the Empress showed her. This letter, she says, bore
unmistakable traces of uneasiness, distress, consternation,
and tipsiness. It was preserved by the Empress in a
special case, together with other important documents. After her death Paul ordered Prince Bezborodka
to go through these papers in his presence; when they
got to this letter, Paul read it aloud to the Tsarina in the
presence of Madame Nelidov.[1] Then he ordered
Rastoptchin to read it aloud to the Grand Dukes.

I have heard what the letter contained from a trustworthy man who had read it himself; it was in this style:
'Little Mother, Empress, how am I to tell you what we
have done! such a misfortune has happened! We came
to see your husband, and were drinking with him; you
know what he is like when he is drunk; word followed
word. He so insulted us that we came to blows. All
of a minute he dropped dead. What is to be done?
Take our heads if you like, or, merciful Little Mother,
think that what is done cannot be undone, and overlook
our offence.'[2]

Princess Dashkov, carried away by her love for

---

[1] A mistress of Paul's, and a friend of his wife's.—(*Translator's
Note.*)

[2] This is the drift of the letter; I cannot answer for the exact
words. I repeat what I heard long ago from memory.—(*Author's
Note.*)

Catherine, believed, or professed to believe, that Miro-vitch,[1] too, acted without her knowledge; and the worst, most disgraceful and loathsome story of her whole reign, the abduction by Alexey Orlov and De Ribasse of Princess Tarakanov,[2] she does not mention at all.

It was, among other things, because she believed and wanted to believe in the ideal Catherine that she could not maintain herself in favour. And she would have been a splendid minister. Though indisputably gifted with political insight, she had besides her enthusiastic tempera-ment two great defects which hindered her from making a career: she could not be silent, her tongue was sharp and biting, and it spared no one except Catherine; more-over, she was too proud, and she could not, and would not, conceal her antipathies—in short, she could not 'abase her personality,' as the Moscow Old Believers express it.

As a matter of fact, a friendship between Catherine and Princess Dashkov was impossible. Catherine wanted not only to be sovereign by the Imperial power, but to rule over every one in the world by her genius and her beauty; she wanted to attract the attention of all to herself alone; she had an insatiable desire to please. She was still in the full flower of her beauty, but she was thirty. She could probably have borne to have about her a weak woman, lost in the radiance of her glory and adoring her, not very handsome and not very clever. But she could not endure at her side the vigorous Princess Dashkov, who

---

[1] Mirovitch plotted to rescue Ivan VI. from the Schlüsselburg and put him on the throne. Ivan's jailers had been instructed by the Empress Elizabeth to kill him if any attempt were made to effect his escape—and did so. For an impartial account of Catherine's reign see Sir Bernard Pares' *History of Russia*.

[2] Princess Tarakanov was an adventuress who claimed to be one of the natural children of the Empress Elizabeth (there were several). Alexey Orlov captured her, by pretending to make love to her. She was imprisoned in the Peter-Paul fortress, where she died of con-sumption. —(*Translator's Notes.*)

spoke of *her own fame*, with her wit, her fire, and her nineteen years.

She withdrew herself from her with the rapidity of truly royal ingratitude. In Moscow, after the Coronation, the old sinner Bestuzhev proposed writing an address to the Empress, and begging her, in the name of all her subjects, to take another husband. Grigory Orlov, who had already been created a prince of the Empire, dreamed of being Tsar. This roused the indignation of all decent people. Chancellor Vorontsov asked for an audience, and warned Catherine, on the supposition that she did not know what was being done. Catherine was surprised, and wanted to reprimand Bestuzhev.

Hitrov, one of the devoted conspirators of the 27th of June, loudly declared that he would sooner kill Orlov, or go to the scaffold, than acknowledge him Emperor. It need hardly be said that Princess Dashkov's voice, too, was heard in the general murmur of displeasure; her words were carried to Catherine. Suddenly one evening, Tyeplov, the secretary of the Empress, came to Prince Dashkov and demanded to see him. The Empress had written him the following note: 'I sincerely desire not to be compelled to consign to oblivion the services of the Princess Dashkov on account of her imprudent behaviour. Tell her to remember this next time she permits herself an indiscreet freedom of language amounting to threats.'

Princess Dashkov did not answer a word to this letter; she held herself aloof, and after the death of her husband in 1768 asked leave to visit foreign lands. 'I might very well go without question,' she said (probably never dreaming that in another eighty years a stupid law would almost completely deprive Russians of the right of crossing the frontier, and still less, that the Government would force every traveller to pay ransom),'but my position as a lady of the court lays upon me the obligation to ask the sanction of the Most High.'

Receiving no answer, she went to Petersburg, and at her first reception asked Catherine to allow her to go abroad for the sake of her children's health.

'I am very sorry,' answered Catherine, 'that such a distressing cause obliges you to go. But, of course, Princess, you are perfectly free to make what arrangements you like.'

Where was the time when they had lain in one bed, under one quilt, and had wept and embraced each other, or, lying on Colonel Kar's overcoat, had dreamed for a whole night of political reforms?

Abroad Princess Dashkov revived, and became again the same proud, indefatigable, indomitable, active woman, interested in every one and throwing herself into everything.

On the wall in the hotel at Dantzig there hung a big picture representing some battle between Prussians and Russians, in which, of course, the Russians were being beaten. In the foreground there was a group of our soldiers on their knees before the Prussians begging for mercy. Princess Dashkov could not stand this. She induced two Russians to creep by night into the room, with oil-paints and brushes, locked the door, and set to work with her companions to repaint the uniforms, so that by the morning the Prussians were on their knees begging the Russians to spare them. When she had finished the picture, she sent for post-horses, and before the hotel-keeper had grasped the situation, she was racing along the road to Berlin, laughing at the thought of his amazement.

In Hanover she went to the Opera alone with Mlle. Kamensky. They were so unlike the worthy German women that the Prince of Mecklenburg, who was the chief authority in the town, sent to find out who they were. His adjutant went unceremoniously into the box in which there were also two German ladies, and asked our Russians whether they were not foreigners. Princess Dashkov said 'Yes.'

'His Highness,' added the adjutant, 'wishes to know with whom I have the honour of speaking.'

'Our name,' answered Princess Dashkov, 'can be of no interest either to you or to the Duke; as women we have the right not to say who we are, and not to answer your question.'

The adjutant went away in confusion. The German ladies, who had from the first felt involuntary respect for our ladies, gazed at them with awe when they heard Princess Dashkov's valiant answer. Seeing that the Germans took them for very great ladies, Princess Dashkov, turning courteously to them, said that though she would not answer the Prince's impudent question, she had no reason to conceal from them her identity. 'I am an opera-singer, and my friend is a dancer; we are both out of a job, and on the look-out for a good engagement.' The German ladies opened their eyes wide, blushed to their ears, and not only abandoned their polite attentions, but tried so far as the size of the box permitted to sit with their backs turned on them.

In Paris Princess Dashkov was surrounded by all the celebrities and made friends with all of them except Rousseau; him she would not go to see on account of his hypocritical humility and affected originality. Diderot, on the other hand, became an intimate friend, spent whole evenings *tête-à-tête* with her, and discussed everything under the sun with her. Princess Dashkov proved to him that serfdom was not so bad as was supposed, trapped him into contradictory statements, and the susceptible Diderot was ready to agree with her instantly.

A servant came in and announced that Madame

Necker[1] and Madame Geoffrin[2] had arrived. 'Don't receive them!' cried Diderot, without asking Princess Dashkov's wishes; 'say that she is not at home.'

'There is not a better woman in the world than Madame Geoffrin, but she is the greatest gossip in Paris; I positively won't have her talking all sorts of nonsense about you before she has time to know you properly. I won't have blasphemy against my idol.' And Princess Dashkov sent word that she was unwell.

Rulhière,[3] who was writing about Russia and the year 1762, also urgently wished to see her. Diderot would not have him received either: he wanted to keep Princess Dashkov to himself.

In London Princess Dashkov made the acquaintance of Paoli, but she did not like his 'Italian grimaces,' which were unbecoming in a great man. In Geneva she visited Voltaire and marvelled at him, though she could not help laughing with some doctor over the way Voltaire lost his temper at losing a game of draughts, and at the killing faces he made. The doctor, observing that it was not only Voltaire who could make such faces, bade his dog lift up his head, and Princess Dashkov could not control her laughter at the extraordinary resemblance. From Geneva she went to Spa; there she made great friends with Mrs. Hamilton[4] and, when she parted from her, romantically swore to come again in five years to see her, if they did not meet before, and, what was even more romantic, actually came.

[1] Madame Necker, wife of the great minister of finance and mother of Mme. de Staël.

[2] Madame Geoffrin, a lady noted for her wit, whose salon was the favourite resort of the philosophers of the day.

[3] Rulhière, Claude de (1735-1791), a French historian and poet.

[4] Hamilton, Elizabeth (1758-1816), a Scotswoman, authoress of *Letters of a Hindoo Rajah, Letters on Education,* and also *On the Moral and Religious Principle,* and *The Cottagers of Glenburnie.*—(*Translator's Notes.*)

The feeling of the most ardent, most active affection was almost the strongest emotion in this proud and strong-willed woman. Deeply wounded by Catherine's treatment of her,[1] she looked prematurely old. Diderot says that she looked nearly forty, though she was at that time twenty-seven. Whether she loved any man after her husband's death, or was beloved by one, is not to be seen from her Memoirs; but it may be said for certain that no man played a significant part in her life. After Catherine she attached herself, with all the ardour of a hungry heart, to Mrs. Hamilton. And in her old age an infinitely tender motherly affection brought warmth into her life; I am speaking of Miss Wilmot, who edited her Memoirs.

From Spa she went back to Moscow to the house of her sister, Madame Polyansky; this sister, with her humble, prosaic name, was no other than the notorious 'Romanovna,' who, if she had not been Madame Polyansky, might easily have been Empress of all the Russias.

The clouds which had overcast Princess Dashkov's sky were beginning to clear away. The influence of the Orlovs had waned. The Empress, hearing of her arrival, sent her sixty thousand roubles to buy an estate.

But the princess was utterly unable to get on with the favourites, and there was no real intimacy between her and the court. Now she began to be deeply absorbed in the education of her son; an ardent admirer of England

---

[1] An impartial reader of the Memoirs of both ladies will probably be surprised at Catherine's forbearance with Princess Dashkov, whose tediously reiterated insistence on her own virtue and impeccability must have been a severe tax on the quick-witted Empress's patience and good nature. Only on one occasion she permitted herself the gentle retort: 'Dear princess, your reputation is better established than that of the whole calendar of saints,' the irony of which was probably not apparent to Princess Dashkov. — (*Translator's Note.*)

and English institutions, she made up her mind to go
with her son to Edinburgh. Moreover, she saw that she
was completely superfluous in the Winter Palace.

While she was preparing for this journey she betrothed her daughter to Shtcherbinin. On the way to
the estate of the young man's brother, to which she was
going with the whole party, a servant fell off the box, and
three sledges passed over him; he was badly hurt and
stunned; he had to be bled, but how? Princess
Dashkov had with her a case of surgical instruments
bought in London; she took out a lancet, but no one
would undertake to use it; the injured man lay unaided
until, overcoming an intense feeling of disgust, she opened
his vein, and after successfully performing the operation,
almost sank into a swoon herself.

In Edinburgh she was soon surrounded by the leading
celebrities, Robertson, Blair, Adam Smith, Fergusson.
She wrote long letters to Robertson, and explained to him
in detail her plan of education; she wanted her son, who
was at that time fourteen, to complete his studies in two
years and a half, and then, after making a tour of the
whole of Europe, to go into the Service.

Robertson presumed that he would need four years; the
mother thought that was too much. She wrote out in
detail what her son knew already, and what he must know.

'*Languages:*

Latin. — The initial difficulties are overcome.

English. — The prince has a very good understanding of prose, and to some extent of verse.

German. — He understands it perfectly.

French. — He knows like his mother tongue.

'*Literature:* He is familiar with the best classical
works. His taste is more formed than is
common at his age. He has an excessive tendency to be critical, which is perhaps his only
defect.

'*Mathematics:* A very important branch of study. He has been fairly successful in the solution of advanced problems, but I should like him to go further in algebra.

'*Civil and Military Architecture:* I want him to make a particular study of these subjects.

'*History and Political Institutions:* He has a knowledge of general history, and particularly of Germany, England, and France, but he ought to go through a course of history more in detail; he can study it at home with a tutor.

'Now this is what I want him to study: 1. Logic and the Philosophy of Reasoning. 2. Experimental Physics. 3. A little Chemistry. 4. Philosophy and Natural History. 5. Natural Law, International Law, public and private Law in its application to the legal systems of European nations. 6. Ethics. 7. Politics.'

This extensive programme she divides into five sessions, and then, as always, carries it out exactly. Her son passed his M.A. examination in 1779; it is commonly said that she exhausted him, and, certainly, he never did anything; moreover, he died very young, but whether his education is to blame for that it is hard to say.

After the examination Princess Dashkov went at once to Ireland, queened it in Dublin society, and composed church music, which was sung in the Chapel of Magdalen in the presence of a vast concourse of people, 'desirous,' as she expresses it, 'of hearing how the bears of the North compose.' Probably it was a successful experiment, for later on she was busy negotiating with David Garrick for the performance on the stage of her musical works. She was also writing long instructions to her son in the style of the counsels of Polonius concerning the conduct of his travels. . . .

From England she went to Holland; in Haarlem she

went to see a doctor of her acquaintance, and there met Prince Orlov, by now married and out of favour. The same day Orlov came to call on her, and just at dinner-time. His visit was to Princess Dashkov 'as unexpected as it was disagreeable.'

'I have come to you not as an enemy, but as a friend and ally,' said Orlov, sitting down in a low chair. Then followed a silence on both sides. He looked intently at young Dashkov, and observed: 'Your son is enrolled in the Cuirassiers, and I am in command of a regiment of the Horse Guards; if you like, I will ask the Empress to transfer him to my regiment; that will give him promotion.'

Princess Dashkov thanked him for his kind suggestion, but said that she could not take advantage of his offer, because she had already written on his behalf to Prince Potyomkin, and did not want without good reason to do anything in opposition to him.

'What could there be disagreeable to him in it?' asked Orlov, feeling the sting of this. 'However, as you please; you may rely on me; your son will make a great career; it would be hard to find a *handsomer* young man.'

The mother flushed crimson with anger, and the conversation dropped. But at the next meeting Orlov, addressing young Dashkov, said: 'What a pity that I shall not be in Petersburg when you arrive! I am certain that you will oust the present favourite as soon as you appear at court; I should be pleased to carry out my present duties—comforting the forsaken.'

Beside herself with indignation, Princess Dashkov sent her son out of the room, and told Orlov that she thought it extremely improper to speak to a boy of seventeen in that way, and that in so doing Orlov was compromising the Empress, whom she had brought her son up to respect; that, as for favourites, she begged him to remember that she had never known and never recognised one of them.

After that they parted. Orlov went to Switzerland, Princess Dashkov to Paris. Then we meet her inspecting the French fortresses with her son and Colonel Samoylov, by special permission of Maréchal de Biron.[1] From France she went to Italy, and there was completely absorbed in pictures and statues, cameos and antiques, bought a picture of Angelica Kauffmann's as a present for the Empress, went to see the Pope and Abbé Galiani,[2] and finally returned to Russia through Vienna.

In Vienna she had a heated argument with Kaunitz, with whom she was dining. He called Peter the Great the political creator of Russia; Princess Dashkov observed that this was a European misconception. Kaunitz was not ready to yield his point; she was even less so. She admitted that Peter had done a very great deal for Russia, but thought that the material was ready, and that, together with his masterly use of it, he had inhumanly oppressed and distorted it.

'If he had really been a great statesman, he would by his intercourse with other nations, and by trade, have gained without haste what he attained by violence and cruelty. The nobility and the serfs were both left worse off through his unbridled passion for innovations; from the latter he took the protective tribunal to which alone hey could appeal in case of oppression, from the former he took all their privileges. And to what end was it all? To clear the way for a military despotism, that is, for the very worst of all existing forms of government. From simple vanity he was in such a hurry to build Petersburg that he sent thousands of workmen to die in

[1] The duc de Biron, afterwards a general in the service of the government of the Revolution, was beheaded in 1793.

[2] An Italian writer on philosophy, history, and economics (1728-1789). — (*Translator's Notes.*)

the marshes. He not only forced the landowners to provide a certain number of peasants, but compelled them to build themselves houses according to his own plans, without asking whether they needed them. One of his principal buildings, the Admiralty and Docks, which cost immense sums, was constructed on the bank of a river which no human efforts could make navigable even for merchant vessels, much less for ships of the Navy.'

'However,' observed Kaunitz, 'no one can help being touched at the sight of a monarch learning shipbuilding with the axe in his hand.'

The ruthless lady would not let this pass. 'Your Excellency,' she answered, 'is doubtless joking. Who can know better than you how precious is a monarch's time, and whether he has the leisure to practise a handicraft? Peter I. was in a position to command the services not only of shipbuilders, but even of admirals. To my mind, when he was wasting time in Saardam working with the axe and learning the slang of the Dutch market, and sailors' words with which he distorted the Russian language, he was simply neglecting his duty.'

I foresee how the good Orthodox souls of our Moscow Slavophils will rejoice at reading these words; they certainly ought, on days for commemorating the dead, to keep the memory of our princess with pancakes and lenten oil.

Joseph II. was ill, and wanted Princess Dashkov to remain a few days longer, but she had received an invitation from Frederick II. for herself and her son to be present at his manœuvres. She had, however, an informal interview with Joseph II. in the study he devoted to natural history.

A week later Princess Dashkov was at the manœuvres at which Frederick II. drilled forty-two thousand men, and to which he had never before admitted women, but she was specially invited. The Prussian Princess herself drove to fetch her, brought her to the spot where the King was to meet her, and asked her to get out of the carriage, saying: 'Dear Princess, as I have not the slightest desire to see the old grumbler, I will drive on,' and Princess Dashkov was left to an innocent *tête-à-tête* with Frederick 11., who took her and her son with him to a military inspection of the provinces.

In July 1782 she returned to Petersburg. The Empress appointed her President of the Academy of Science. Princess Dashkov was apparently for the first time in her life disconcerted, and wanted to decline the honour. She wrote a sharp letter to the Empress, and at twelve o'clock at night drove with it to Potyomkin. Potyomkin had gone to bed; however, he received her. He read the letter, tore it up and threw it on the floor, but, seeing that she was angry, said to her: 'Here are pen and paper, by all means write it again; only, it is all nonsense; why do you refuse? The Empress has been full of the idea for the last two days. In that position you will be frequently seeing her, and the fact is, to tell the truth, she is dying of boredom, perpetually surrounded by fools.'

Potyomkin's eloquence overcame her opposition; she went to the Senate to take the oath for her new duties, and from that moment became a consummate president. She asked old Euler, the great mathematician, to introduce her at the assembled Academy; she wanted to appear under the aegis of learning before the academicians. She presented herself to them not in silence, as Russian presidents usually do, but with a speech, after which, seeing that the first place next the president was occupied by Stehlin,[1] she turned to Euler and said: 'Sit where you prefer; whatever place you occupy will be the first.'

[1] The former tutor of Peter 111. — (*Translator's Note.*)

Then with her habitual energy she set to work to eradicate abuses, that is, thefts; she increased the number of the pupils, improved the printing-press, and finally proposed to the Empress the founding of a Russian Academy. Catherine appointed her president of this new academy too. Again Princess Dashkov made a speech. 'You all know, gentlemen,' she said, among other things, 'the wealth and splendour of our language. The powerful eloquence of Cicero, the measured grandeur of Virgil, the fascinating charm of Demosthenes, and the light language of Ovid, translated into Russian, lose nothing of their beauties. . . . But we are without exact rules, the limits and meanings of words have not been defined, and many foreign phrases have crept into our language,' and therefore she proposed that the Russian Academy should work at a grammar and dictionary of the language. She herself prepared to share the labours of the academicians, and did, in fact, work at the dictionary. The Empress seemed to be pleased with her. Her energy at this period was amazing. She undertook the publication of special geographical maps of the different provinces, and edited the periodical, *Lovers of the Russian Language*, to which the Empress herself, Von Vizin, Derzhavin, and others contributed.

Her relations with the Empress were unmistakably improved. A correspondence sprang up between them again; the letters deal with a review they were publishing and various literary subjects. These letters, which are of little general interest, are a striking proof of the degree to which good manners, culture, and humanity have since sunk in the Winter Palace. Catherine gives no orders, does not command in her notes, does not confine herself to set forms, is not afraid of jesting; she has confidence in herself, and the Empress often gives way to the woman of intelligence. The Prussian Gatchina tone, translated into official red tape by Nicholas, has replaced with brutal illiteracy the gentleness of cultured language.

All would have been well if only Princess Dashkov could have kept on good terms with the favourites; she got on better with Potyomkin than with any of the rest, perhaps because Potyomkin was the cleverest of them; with Lanskoy, and afterwards with Manonov, she was at daggers drawn. Zubov gossiped spitefully against her, and did her a great deal of mischief.

In the summer of 1783 she was in Finland with the Empress, who had an interview there with the King of Sweden. Lanskoy kept pestering her to know why in the news published under the auspices of the Academy her name was the only one mentioned of the persons who were with the Empress. Princess Dashkov explained to him that it was not her doing at all, that the Court news was sent and printed without alteration. Lanskoy went on sulking and grumbling till she was sick of it.

'You ought to know,' she said to him, 'that, though it is always an honour and a happiness to me to dine with the Empress, I cannot really be so much overwhelmed by it as to publish it in the papers. I am too much accustomed to it; as a little child I used to dine on the Empress Elizabeth's knee, as a little girl I sat at her table; it is so natural that it could not be a matter for boasting to me.'

Lanskoy grew heated, but Princess Dashkov, seeing that the room was beginning to fill up, raised her voice, and said: 'Sir, people whose whole life has been devoted to the public welfare are not always particularly powerful or happy, but they always have the right to insist on being treated without insolence. They quietly go their own way and outlive those meteors of a day which burst and fall, leaving no trace.'

The doors were flung open and the Empress walked in. Her arrival put an end to the conversation. How could

Lanskoy fail to hate her? It was as well for her that he died soon after.

On her return from Finland Princess Dashkov received her friend, Mrs. Hamilton, to stay with her. She took her to her new estate; there she kept a village holiday, met with bread and salt the peasants newly settled there, introduced them to the Englishwoman, and informed them that henceforth the new village would be called Hamiltonovo. After this she travelled with her to other estates in the provinces of Kaluga, Smolensk, Kiev, and Tambov.

The following year Princess Dashkov received a cruel blow in her personal life. Her son was in Rumyantsev's army, and she was glad that he was not in Petersburg. Latterly even Potyomkin had designs upon him. He once sent Samoylov to fetch him late one evening, and Samoylov gave the mother a hint of their project. She refused to have anything to do with it, and said that if it happened she would take advantage of her son's influence to obtain leave of absence abroad for many years. For this reason she was relieved that her son was away in Kiev. But there love had another arrow in store for him, aimed not from above, but from below.

One day, as she came out of the Empress's bedroom, she met Rebinder, who warm-heartedly congratulated her on her son's marriage. She was thunderstruck. Rebinder was disconcerted; he had had no idea that young Dashkov's wedding was a secret. She was wounded in her motherly feelings and in her pride; on the one hand, the *mésalliance*, on the other, the lack of confidence. It was a heavy blow, it made her ill.

Two months later her son wrote her a letter, asking for her permission to marry; this was a fresh blow—falsity, cowardice, deceit. Moreover, he had so little understanding of his mother's character that together with his own letter he sent one from Field-Marshal Rumyantsev obviously written at his request. Rumyantsev tried to persuade Princess Dashkov to sanction her son's marriage, spoke of the prejudices of aristocratic birth and of the instability of fortune, and, in her words, 'reached such a pitch of futility as to give advice in a matter of such gravity between mother and son, though nothing in their relations gave him a right to meddle.'

Wounded on two sides at once, she wrote a sarcastic letter to Rumyantsev, in which she explained to him that, 'among the various foolish ideas with which her head was filled, there was happily no exaggerated respect for aristocratic birth; but that, if she had been endowed with such remarkable eloquence as the Count, she would have used it to show the superiority of good breeding over bad.'

To her son her letter was strikingly simple; here it is: 'When your father intended to marry a Countess Vorontsov, he drove post-haste to Moscow to ask his mother's sanction. You are married; I knew this before you wrote, and I know, too, that my mother-in-law had done no more to deserve to have a friend in her son than I have.'

The discussions that followed this and other family affairs must have cost her much mortification. Her daughter parted from her husband. Miss Wilmot has omitted several pages in the Memoirs, after which Princess Dashkov goes on like this: 'All was black in the future and the present. . . . I was so worn out by suffering that I was at times visited by the thought of suicide.'

And so the demon of family troubles crushed her, as it has crushed many strong characters. Family misfortunes wound so deeply, because they steal upon one in silence and to combat them is almost impossible. Victory in the struggle makes it worse. They are like those poisons whose presence is only recognised when their effect is shown in pain, that is, when the man is already saturated with them.

Meanwhile, the French Revolution had come. Catherine, who was growing old, worn out by a life of vice, threw herself into reaction. This was no longer the conspirator of the 27th of June, who said to Betsky: 'I reign by the will of God and the election of the people,' not the Petersburg correspondent of Voltaire and the translator of Beccaria and Filangier,[1] who proclaimed in her famous *Nakaz*[2] the evils of the censorship and the advantage of an assembly of deputies from the whole realm of Russia. In 1792 we find her an old woman afraid of thought, a worthy mother of Paul. . . . And like a pledge that a savage reaction would crush for long years every branch of free development in Russia, Nicholas was born before her death. Catherine's dying hand was still there to caress this awful monster who was destined to cry *Halt!* to the epoch of Peter's reforms, and to delay the progress of Russia for thirty years.

Princess Dashkov, an aristocrat and an admirer of English institutions, could not sympathise with the Revolution; but still less could she share the feverish terror of free speech and applaud the punishment of thought.

Catherine was alarmed by Radishtchyev's pamphlet;[3] she saw in it the 'signal of revolution.' Radishtchyev was seized and sent without trial to Siberia. Princess Dashkov's brother, Alexandr Vorontsov, who loved Radishtchyev, and had been a benefactor to him, retired from the Service and went to Moscow.

Her own turn came next. Knyazhnin's[4] widow asked her, for the benefit of her children, to publish under the

[1] An Italian writer of the school of the physiocrats.

[2] See Pares' *History of Russia*, p. 241.

[3] The pamphlet referred to is *A Journey from Petersburg to Moscow*, an impassioned protest against serfdom. (See vol. v. p. 313.)

[4] Knyazhnin translated tragedies from the French and wrote imitations of them. This last one was called *Vadim of Novgorod.* —(*Translator's Notes.*)

auspices of the Academy her husband's last tragedy. The subject was taken from the history of the subjugation of Novgorod. Princess Dashkov directed that it should be published. Field-Marshal Saltykov, 'who,' as she says, 'could not be charged with ever having read a book of any sort,' read this one and talked to Zubov of its pernicious tendency. Zubov spoke to the Empress about it.

Next day the Petersburg police-master arrived at the Academy bookshop to seize the copies of the Jacobin Knyazhnin's inflammatory tragedy; and in the evening the Prosecutor-General, Samoylov, came himself to tell Princess Dashkov of the Empress's displeasure at the publication of the dangerous play. Princess Dashkov answered coldly that probably no one had read the tragedy, and that it was certainly less pernicious than the French plays which were being performed at the Hermitage.

The ex-liberal Catherine met her with a frowning face. 'What have I done,' she asked her, 'that you publish such dangerous books against me and my authority?'

'And does your Majesty really think that?' the princess asked.

'That tragedy ought to have been burnt by the hand of the hangman.'

'Whether it is burnt by the hand of the hangman or not is no concern of mine. I shall not have to blush for it. But for God's sake, madam, before you decide on an action so opposed to your character, read the whole play.'

At that the conversation ended. Next day Princess Dashkov attended a great court reception, and made up her mind that if the Empress did not send for her to her dressing-room, as she always did, she would resign her post. Samoylov came out from the inner apartments.

With a patronising air he went up to Princess Dashkov and told her not to be uneasy, that the Empress was not angry with her.

She could not brook this, and answered, as her habit was, in a loud voice: 'I have no reason to be uneasy, my conscience is clear. It would greatly distress me if the Empress retained an unjust feeling towards me; but I should not be surprised even then: at my age injustice and misfortune have long ceased to surprise me.'

The Empress was reconciled with her, and tried once more to explain why she had acted as she did. Instead of answering her, Princess Dashkov replied: 'A grey cat has run between us, madam: let us not awaken her again.'

But Petersburg was becoming distasteful to her; she was sick of it. She felt 'utterly alone in these surroundings, which became every day more hateful to her.' This feeling of repulsion was so great that she made up her mind to leave the court, Petersburg, her public activity, her Academy of Science, and her Russian Academy, and finally her Empress, and to go and live on her estate in the country.

'With deep sorrow I thought of parting, perhaps for ever, from the Sovereign whom I loved passionately, and loved long before she was on her throne, when she had less means of bestowing benefits on me than I found occasions for serving her. I still loved her, although she did not always treat me as her own heart, her own brain, would have prompted her.'

That is all! Not one word of anger, of condemnation for complete lack of heart, for ingratitude; even here she gives us to understand that it was not Catherine's fault, but other people's.

The parting of these women was remarkable. The Empress said to her drily, and with an angry face: 'I wish you a good journey.' Princess Dashkov was amazed; she did not understand it, and went away after kissing her hand. Next morning Troshtchinsky, the Secretary of the Empress, arrived, and in her name handed the princess an unpaid bill, the unpaid bill of a tailor who had done work for Shtcherbinin. The Empress sent word that she was surprised that the princess should leave Petersburg without carrying out her promise to pay her daughter's debts. Zubov, who hated Princess Dashkov, and was a patron of the tailor's, had carried these paltry details to the Empress. To crown it all, it appeared that the bill had nothing to do with her daughter, but had been incurred by her husband, Shtcherbinin, who was living apart from her.

Princess Dashkov, utterly revolted at this humiliation, firmly resolved to leave Petersburg for ever.

But people of her temperament do not fold their hands at a little over fifty, in the full possession of their faculties. She became a capital manager of her estates; she built houses, drew maps, and laid out parks. There was not a tree nor a bush in her garden which she had not planted or to which she had not at least assigned its position. She built four houses, and says with pride that her peasants were among the most prosperous in the neighbourhood. While she was engaged in these rustic pursuits, Serpuhovsky, the Marshal of the Nobility, suddenly arrived, looking distressed.

'What is the matter with you?' she asked.

'Don't you know?' answered the Marshal; 'the Empress is dead.'

Princess Dashkov's daughter rushed to her, thinking that she would faint. 'No, no, don't worry about me,' said her mother; 'I am quite well, though it would be happiness to die at this moment. My fate is worse; I am destined to see all the reforms that had been begun destroyed, and my country ruined and unhappy.'

With these words she fell into convulsions, and gave way to prolonged grief.

It was not long before she felt the heavy, weighty, autocratic hand of Peter's crazy son.[1] First she received a decree discharging her from her post; she asked the Prosecutor-General, Samoylov, to testify to the Tsar her gratitude for relieving her from the burden which had become too great for her strength.

A little later she went to Moscow, but the Governor-General of Moscow called on her at once and informed her that she should go back to the country immediately, and there think of the year 1762. She answered, 'that she never forgot that year, but that in accordance with the Tsar's will she would think of that time, which had left her neither stings of conscience nor remorse.'

Her brother Alexandr, anxious to soothe her, told her that Paul was doing all this now for the rehabilitation of his father's memory, but that after his coronation things would go better. On reaching Troitskoye she wrote to him: 'Dear brother, you write that Paul will leave me in peace after the coronation. Believe me, you are much mistaken in his character. When the tyrant has once struck his victim, he will repeat his blows until he has crushed the victim utterly. The consciousness of innocence and the feeling of indignation serve to give me courage to endure discomfort so long as his growing spite does not assail all of you, my relations, also. Of one thing you may rest assured, that no circumstances will compel me to do anything or say anything to demean myself.

'Examining my past life,' she adds, 'I am not without inner consolation, aware in myself of sufficient strength of character, tested by many calamities, to feel certain that I shall find again strength to endure misfortune.'

She correctly gauged the character of the relentless, petty, frenzied tyrant. Only a few days after she had

[1] Catherine's own Memoirs make it clear that, though crazy, Paul was not the son of Peter III.—(*Translator's Note.*)

reached Troitskoye, a courier from the Governor-General arrived from Moscow. Paul commanded Princess Dashkov to go at once to her son's estate in a remote district of the Novgorod Province, and there to await his further commands.

She answered that she was ready to obey the Sovereign's will, and that it was a matter of complete indifference to her where she ended her days, but that she knew nothing of the estate nor of the roads thither, that she would have to write from Moscow either for her son's steward or for a peasant from that village to guide her by the cross-country roads.

When she was ready and had obtained a guide, she drove off into her exile in the winter frost, travelling slowly with her own horses, surrounded by the spies of Arharov, and accompanied by her kind-hearted kinsman, Laptyev, whom she tried in vain to dissuade from coming and exposing himself to the persecution of the frenzied autocrat.

But as the foremost symptom of madness is inconsistency, she was here mistaken: when it was reported to Paul that Laptyev had accompanied her, he said: 'He is not such a petticoat as our young men; he knows how to wear the breeches.'

As a rule far more value is attached to such momentary flashes of humane feeling in Paul and others than they deserve. What would Paul have done if all the young men had known 'how to wear the breeches' like Laptyev? he had plenty of Arharovs, Araktcheyevs, and Obolyaninovs to torture them, fetter them in chains, and send them into exile. (Pahlen and Bennigsen[1] did show him, however, that there was an even better way to 'wear the breeches'!)

This approbation of the victim is the final outrage on

[1] By their successful conspiracy to assassinate Paul. —(*Translator's Note.*)

him, the miscreant sets his conscience at rest with it. On one occasion, in the presence of Ségur, Potyomkin gave some colonel a blow, and, recollecting himself, said to the ambassador: 'How is one to treat them differently when they put up with everything?'

And what would Potyomkin's answer have been, if the colonel had given him a blow or a challenge?

Princess Dashkov settled in a peasant's hut. She took another for her daughter, and a third as a kitchen. To add to the discomforts of this life in the wilds in winter, exiles from Petersburg to Siberia were brought by her windows. The figure of one young officer haunted her long afterwards; he was some distant relative of hers. Learning that she was here, he wanted to see her. Risky as such an interview was, she received him. She was shocked to see the convulsive twitching of his face, and how ill he looked; this was the result of the tortures in which his limbs had been twisted and dislocated. What had this criminal done? He had said something about Paul in the barracks, and some one had informed against him. Yet perhaps he, too, knew how to 'wear the breeches,' till his arms were wrenched out of their sockets.

Before the spring flooding of the rivers, which would have cut off Princess Dashkov from all communication for a long period, she wrote a letter to the Empress Marya Feodorovna, and enclosed in it a request for permission to move to her Kaluga estate. Paul could not have liked the tone of her letter; she said in it that it was as little to her honour to write this letter as it was to her Majesty's to read it, but that religion and humanity compelled her to make a final effort to save all her people from this cruel exile.

Paul, as usual, flew into a fury, and gave orders that pen and paper should be taken from Princess Dashkov, that she should be forbidden all correspondence, be kept under stricter supervision, and I do not know what else.

'It is not so easy,' he said, 'to turn me off the throne.' With these orders a courier was despatched, but the Empress and Madame Nelidov induced the Grand Duke Michael Pavlovitch to beg his infuriated father for mercy, and the little boy, with the help of the wife and mistress, succeeded. Paul took up a pen and wrote: 'Princess Ekaterina Romanovna, since you desire to return to your Kaluga estate, I give you permission for the same. I remain well disposed to you.—PAUL.'

Arharov had to despatch another courier: fortunately the second overtook the first.

In 1798 Paul suddenly took a fancy to Prince Dashkov, showered undeserved favours of all sorts upon him, and made him the present of an estate. Dashkov asked Kurakin to submit to Paul that, instead of an estate, he would prefer permission for his mother to live where she chose. Paul gave the permission with the proviso that she should never remain in the same town where he was.

The mother was forgiven. Now came the son's turn. A certain Altesti was tried for misappropriation of public money, but really for being a friend of Zubov. Dashkov said to Lopuhin that Altesti was innocent. In the evening he received the following note: 'Since you meddle in affairs that have nothing to do with you, I have dismissed you from your duties.—PAUL.'

Dashkov, afraid of worse to follow, went off to his Tambov estate.

At last, on the 12th of March 1801, Paul's life 'came to an end,' as Princess Dashkov says. With deep emotion and intense joy she learned that this pernicious man had ceased to exist. 'How many times,' she goes on, 'have I thanked Heaven that Paul exiled me! by so doing he saved me from the humiliating obligation of appearing at the court of such a sovereign.'

She breathed freely again in the reign of Alexander . . . she could appear at his court without the loss of

her human dignity, but she did not feel at home in the
new surroundings. Many things had changed since
Catherine had sent her the tailor's bill. Princess
Dashkov, now an old woman, is angry with the younger
generation surrounding Alexander, and thinks that they
are all Jacobins or martinets.

One pure presence arrested her, and with respectful
love, with reverence, she looked upon her and attached
herself to her; sorrowful and unappreciated, this melancholy being moved thoughtfully through the halls of the
Winter Palace, and vanished like a shadow; she would
have been forgotten, if we did not sometimes come across
a well-known picture of the year 1815, in which the
Emperor Alexander and the Empress Elizabeth are
represented as the peacemakers of Europe.

Miss Wilmot has appended to Princess Dashkov's
Memoirs a well-drawn portrait of the Empress Elizabeth;
the unhappy woman is standing with her arms folded,
she looks out mournfully from the paper, a hidden grief
and a sort of perplexity can be seen in her eyes, the
whole figure expresses one thought: 'I am a stranger
here'; indeed, she is holding up her skirt and wraps as
though on the point of departure.

How strange was her destiny, and that of Anna Pav-
lovna, the wife of the Tsarevitch!

After the coronation Princess Dashkov saw that there
was really no place for her at the new court, and she
began making plans for repose at Troitskoye. In her
honoured seclusion she again became a power.

Friends and relations, celebrities whose fame was
waning, and rising stars visited her.

> 'Crossing your threshold
> I am back in Catherine's days.
> Taking no share in the world's hopes and fears,
> You at your window stand with mocking gaze
> To watch at times the flying wheel of change.

> E'en so, withdrawing from the busy whirl
> To court the Muses and their idle ease,
> In porphyry baths and marble palaces,
> Grandees in Rome endured their world's decay.
> And to them from afar the young men came, —
> Dictator, consul, tribune, warrior chief —
> To rest in peace, to heave luxurious sighs,
> Then off at once upon the road again.'

She often visited Moscow. There she was held in the highest respect; active and inexhaustible, she was seen at balls and dinners, and arrived there indeed earlier than any. Young ladies trembled at her criticisms and observations, men sought the honour of being presented to her.

At the other end of Moscow, not far from the Donsky Monastery, another living monument of the reign of Catherine was passing his last days in a palace surrounded by gardens. He led a gloomy life, retaining in spite of his age his athletic frame and savage energy of character. In 1796, with a scowling brow but unrepentant, he carried all over Petersburg the crown of the man whom he had murdered; hundreds of thousands of people pointed the finger at him; his companion, Prince Baryatinsky, turned pale and nearly fainted; old Orlov merely complained of his gout.

But his sombre life was not to pass uncheered. At his side a gentle, tender little girl, exceptionally graceful and talented, was growing up. The haughty old man began to live for her; he became her nurse, petted her, cared for her, waited on her, and loved her beyond all measure, as no one but her dead mother could have loved her.

Sitting on his sofa, he made his daughter dance gipsy and Russian dances, watched her movements with fond tenderness and unspoken pride, sometimes wiping a tear from eyes which had, dry and cold, looked on so many horrors.

At last the time came for the old man to bring his

treasure out into the world; but to whom was he to confide her, into what woman's care was he to entrust this cherished flower? There was, indeed, one woman whom he could have trusted, who with her marvellous tact might have directed her first steps; but they were not on good terms. She had not forgiven him for the stain he had brought on her revolution forty-two years before.

And now the haughty Alexey Orlov, the Orlov of Chesme,[1] whom even Paul could not crush, sought the favour of an interview with Princess Ekaterina Romanovna, and, receiving permission to present his daughter to her, joyfully hastened to take advantage of it and went with his Annushka to see her.

Princess Dashkov came in to greet him; bowing, the old man kissed her hand; both were agitated; at last Princess Dashkov said to him: 'So many years have passed since we have met, Count, and so many events have transformed the world in which we once lived that, indeed, I feel that we are meeting now as shades in the other world. The presence of this angel' (she added, feelingly pressing to her bosom the daughter of her former enemy) 'who has brought us together again makes that feeling even stronger.' In his delight Orlov kissed the hand of Miss Wilmot, who was afraid of him, in spite of the fact that she calls him 'a majestic old man,' and saw with surprise the portrait of Catherine on his breast, framed in nothing but diamonds, and the *heiduks* standing in the hall, and with them a dwarf dressed like a jester.

The Count invited Princess Dashkov, and gave one of those fabulous banquets of which we used to hear traditions in our childhood, feasts reminiscent of Versailles and the Golden Horde. The gardens were brilliantly lighted up, the house was thrown open,

[1] In 1770, Alexey Orlov, in command of the Russian fleet, defeated and burnt the Turkish fleet at Chesme Bay.—(*Translator's Note.*)

throngs of house-serfs in gorgeous masquerade costumes filled the rooms, an orchestra played, the tables groaned under the viands; in short, a royal banquet. He had some one now to whom to entrust his daughter!

At the height of the festivities, the father called her, the guests formed a circle, and she danced, danced with a shawl and danced with a tambourine in the Russian style. The old father beat time and watched Princess Dashkov's face; the old lady was pleased, the crowd was silent through respect for the father's rank and the daughter's extraordinary grace. 'She danced,' says Miss Wilmot, 'with such simplicity, such natural charm, such dignity and expression, that her movements seemed her language.'

After each dance, she ran to her father and kissed his hand. Princess Dashkov praised her; her father bade her kiss the princess's hand too. But he fancied that she was overheated, and with his own hands wrapped her in a shawl that she might not take cold. At supper, with a blare of trumpets and kettledrums, the Count, standing, drank the health of Princess Dashkov. Then followed her favourite Russian songs accompanied by a full orchestra. Then the strains of the polka were heard, and Orlov led Princess Dashkov into the drawing-room, where the music of the wind instruments astonished our Irish girl, who had never before heard serfdom put to the service of art. At last Princess Dashkov got up to take leave, and the Count, bowing and kissing her hand, thanked her for honouring his poor house.

This was how Orlov of Chesme celebrated his reconciliation with old Princess Dashkov, and this was how the grim, harsh man loved his daughter.

I, too, like Princess Ekaterina Romanovna, am almost reconciled to him. Savage were the days in which he lived, and savage were his actions; the Russia of Peter's creation was still in the melting-pot: let us not judge him more severely than Princess Dashkov did, and, if the prayers of parents can do much in the next world, let us forgive Orlov much in this for his love for his daughter.

Her fate, too, was a strange one.

As a boy I saw her once or twice, then I saw her again in 1841 at Novgorod; she was living near the Yurev Monastery. Her whole life was one prolonged, sorrowful penitence for a crime that she had not committed, one prayer for the remission of her father's sins, one act of atonement for them. She could not overcome the horror inspired in her by the murder of Peter III., and was crushed at the thought of her father's eternal punishment. All her mind, all her Orlov energy, she fixed on this one object, and little by little abandoned herself completely to gloomy mysticism and superstition. Called by birth, by wealth, and by talent to one of the foremost positions not only in Russia, but in Europe, she spent her days with tedious monks, with old bishops, with all sorts of paralytics, sanctimonious hypocrites, crazy saints. I am told that after 1815 German hereditary princes sought her hand; Alexander showed her marked attention; she withdrew from the court. Her palace grew emptier and emptier, and at last sank into complete silence; neither the clatter of old-fashioned goblets nor the choruses of singers were heard in it, and no one cared about the cherished racehorses. Only the black figures of bearded monks moved gloomily about the garden avenues and looked at the fountains, as though Count Alexey's funeral were not yet over—and, indeed, the prayer for the repose of his soul still went on.

In the drawing-room, where she had spun and twirled in the gipsy dance in her girlish purity, innocent of the significance of the ardent movements of the Asiatic dance, where smoothly, with downcast eyes, she had danced with modestly raised hand our languid feminine dances, and where her terrible father had gazed at her with tears in his eyes, the bigoted fanatic, Foty,[1] sat now uttering incoherent speeches, and bringing even greater horror into her crushed soul; the daughter of the haughty conqueror of Chesme meekly listened to his sinister words, carefully covering her feet with a shawl, perhaps the very one in which her father had wrapped her!

'Anna,' Foty would say, 'fetch me water,' and she ran for water. 'Now sit and listen,' and she sat and listened. Poor woman!

Her palace and gardens in Moscow she presented to the Tsar. What for? I do not know. The immense estates, the stud-farms, all went to adorn the Yurev Monastery; thither she transferred, too, her father's coffin; there in a special vault a lamp for ever burned, and a prayer was muttered over him, there her own sarcophagus, still empty when I saw it, was prepared. In the church twilight, the wealth of the Orlovs, transformed into rubies, pearls, and emeralds, glitters mournfully in the settings of ikons and the caps of archimandrites. With them the luckless daughter tried to bribe the Heavenly Judge.

Catherine had robbed the monasteries of their estates and distributed them among the Orlovs and her other lovers. What a nemesis!

Princess Dashkov's Memoirs fail us about this time. The very details of her interview with Orlov we have taken from the letters of the two Wilmot sisters.

Miss Mary Wilmot, grieving for the loss of her brother and dull at home, received an invitation from Princess Dashkov to spend a year or two with her. Miss Mary did not know the princess personally, but (she was Mrs. Hamilton's niece) she had from her childhood heard of this wonderful woman, had heard how at eighteen

---

[1] The archimandrite of the Yurev Monastery, famous for his fanaticism and ascetic exploits. Alexander I. once had an interview with him, but was repelled by his crassness.—(*Translator's Note.*)

she had been at the head of a conspiracy, how she had
dashed on horseback before revolting troops, how afterwards she had lived in England and stayed in Ireland, had
been President of the Academy, and had written passionate letters to Mrs. Hamilton. The young girl imagined
her something fantastic, 'a fairy and partly a witch, and
for that very reason decided, in 1803, to go to her.

When she reached Troitskoye, however, she felt so
scared and homesick that she would have been glad to
return if it had been possible.

A short old lady, in a long dark cloth dress with a
star on the left side, and something like a peaked hat, came
to meet her. Round her neck she had a shabby old kerchief—one damp evening, when out for a walk, twenty
years earlier, Mrs. Hamilton had given her that kerchief,
and from that time forward she had kept it as a holy relic.
But if her attire really was suggestive of a witch, the noble
features of her face and the expression of infinite tenderness in her eyes fascinated the Irish girl from the first
moment. 'There was so much truth, so much warmth,
dignity, and simplicity in her manner, that I loved her
before she said anything.'

Miss Mary was completely under her influence from
the first day, was surprised at it, and angry with herself,
but could not resist the attraction of the splendid old
lady. She liked everything in her, even her broken
English, which gave something childlike to her words.
'Tears and life,' she says, 'have given serenity and
softness to her features, and their expression of pride,
of which slight traces still remain, has been replaced by
indulgence.'

But how Princess Dashkov loved her! She loved her
passionately, as she had once loved Catherine. Such
freshness of feeling, such feminine tenderness, such
craving for love, such youthfulness of heart, are astound-
ing at sixty. The solicitude of a mother, the solicitude

of a sister, a lover, are what Miss Mary found at Troitskoye; for her entertainment Princess Dashkov went to Moscow, took her to balls, showed her monasteries, presented her to Empresses, adorned her room with flowers, spent evenings with her reading the letters of Catherine and other celebrities.

Miss Wilmot begged and besought her to write her Memoirs. 'And what I would never do for my relatives or my friends, I am doing for her.'

She wrote her Memoirs for her, and dedicated them to her.

In 1805 Princess Dashkov invited Miss Mary's sister, Miss Katharine, who was then in France and was obliged to leave that country, being persecuted as an Englishwoman. The sisters were not in the least alike. Mary was a soft, tender creature, delighted to have some one to protect her, and to nestle under some one's wing; she attached herself to Princess Dashkov, as the weak twig to a strong old tree; she calls her 'my Russian mother'; she came to her from a little town, and had seen nothing before except her 'Emerald Isle.' Her sister, who had lived in Paris, was lively and hot-tempered, independent in her opinions, clever and ironical, not particularly loving or tolerant, and rather free in her speech. Moreover, there was a great deal in Russia that she positively disliked—and so her letters have for us a special interest of their own.

'Russia,' she says, 'is like a girl of twelve—wild and awkward, who has been dressed up in a fashionable Parisian hat. We are living here in the fourteenth or fifteenth century.'[1]

She was far more shocked by serfdom than her kind-

---

[1] Miss Wilmot meant to say something biting, but paid us a compliment. It is only a pity that she does not see how old the girl is now! It is not something to be reckoned by years.—(*Author's Note.*)

hearted sister. In vain Princess Dashkov pointed out to her the prosperity of her peasants.

'They are well off,' writes Miss Katharine, 'while the princess lives, but what will happen to them afterwards?' Every landowner seems to her an iron link in the fetters of Russia.

In the pitiful cringing, the shameless servility of our society she very correctly sees the reflection of slavery. With amazement she sees again in assembly halls and drawing-rooms slaves devoid of all moral feeling and personal dignity. She is astonished at visitors who dare not sit down, and stand for hours at a time at the door, shifting from one foot to the other, till they are dismissed with a nod. 'The conceptions of good and evil are in Russia mixed up with the idea of being in favour or out of favour. A man's worth is easily ascertained from the address calendar, and it depends on the Tsar whether a man is unreservedly taken for a snake or an ass.'

The Moscow grandees did not overawe her with the galaxy of their stars, with their ponderous dignity and boring dinners.

'I feel,' she writes after the festivities of 1806, 'that I have been floating all this time among the shades and spirits of Catherine's palace. Moscow is the imperial political Elysium of Russia. All the personages of power and authority in the reigns of Catherine and Paul, who have long ago been succeeded by others, retire into the luxurious idleness of this lazy city, maintaining a supposed consequence which is allowed them out of courtesy. Influence and power have passed years ago to another generation; nevertheless, the *oberkammerherr* of the Empress Catherine, Prince Golitsyn, is still hung all over with orders and decorations under the burden of which his ninety years are weighed down to the ground; still, as in the palace of Catherine, a diamond key is tied to his skeleton, which is dressed in an embroidered kaftan, and he still majestically accepts tokens of respect from his companion shades who once shared power and honour with him.

'By his side is another gaudy *revenant*, Count Osterman, once the great Chancellor; he is hung with ribbons of every possible colour, red, blue, and striped; eighty-three years are piled upon his head, but still he drives his skeleton about with the bones rattling behind a team of six horses, dines with *heiduks* waiting at his table, and keeps up the solemn etiquette by which he was surrounded when he was in power.' Among the shades she saw, too, Count Alexey Orlov.

'The hand that murdered Peter III. is studded with diamonds, among his gifts from royalty the portrait of the Empress is particularly conspicuous; Catherine smiles from it in everlasting gratitude.'

Miss Wilmot mentions, too, Korsakov, 'who might have been taken for a glittering vision of diamonds,' Prince Baryatinsky and some other figures from this world of the past, 'from which they have retained the habit of court gossip about important nonentities, haughtiness, vanity, and the empty bustle in which they find their joy and their sorrow.'

And she concludes with indignation: 'And yet the open coffin stands at their tottering feet threatening to consign their paltry existences to speedy oblivion.'

'All these old grandees are surrounded by wives, daughters, and granddaughters, dressed up to the nines, and sitting in gilded apartments, in patriarchal fashion making their maids dance for their amusement, and incessantly regaling one on jam. There is something French in their appearance, and, being brought up by Frenchwomen, they speak that language well and dress in the latest Parisian mode. But there is very little real politeness in these ladies; their education is absolutely superficial, and there is not a trace here of the charming lightness of French society. When a Moscow lady has scanned you from head to foot and kissed you five or six times (though twice, one would think, would be more than enough), has assured you of her everlasting affection, told you to your face that you are sweet and charming, asked you the price of everything you have got on, and babbled about the coming ball at the Hall of the Nobility, she has nothing more to say.'

Both sisters were greatly shocked by the vulgar habit of wearing other people's diamonds at balls. Moreover, every one knew whose they were; thus a Princess Golitsyn used to lend her friends a girdle of diamonds and a head-dress of marvellous beauty that was known to the whole town. On one occasion she adorned the shoulders of a niece of Princess Dashkov's with her jewels; the young lady had completely forgotten that the princess was to be present; the stern and implacable old lady, it need hardly be said, detested these displays of other people's wealth. The young lady was so terrified at the sight of Princess Dashkov that she kept out of sight all the evening. But the fatal hour of supper arrived; Miss Mary, feeling cold, put on her shawl; this struck the young lady as a way of salvation, and she took hers to conceal the rivers of diamonds from Princess Dashkov. They sat down, the aunt opposite; the soup tureen screened the niece a little, but her headdress burnt her like fire. Princess Dashkov stared at it. Red patches came out on the poor girl's face and tears came into her eyes. The princess said not a word.

The sisters, who in many ways disagreed over people and incidents, are completely at one whenever Princess Dashkov is spoken of. Miss Katharine's sarcastic pen loses all its venom when writing of the princess. We have put her description of her at the beginning of this account. In it she has shown least appreciation of the tender, womanly side, for which love was a necessity.

This side of her nature was far better understood by Miss
Mary, and yet she abandoned her.

In 1807 Miss Katharine went away. Mary meant
to leave a little later. She was detained by a terrible
blow which fell upon Princess Dashkov. ✦

Though the latter loved her son devotedly, she had
never quite forgiven his marriage, and would never
receive his wife; she was in correspondence with her son,
however, but did not see him. In spite of all entreaties,
and in particular those of Miss Wilmot, whose influence
was so immense, the mother's wounded heart, which they
had not known how to soften immediately after the
marriage, could not do violence to itself and be fully
reconciled. In 1807, immediately after Princess Dashkov
had arrived in Moscow, her son was taken ill, and a few
days later he died.

This was a terrible blow for her, it shortened her life;
repentance too late laid all its irrevocable burden of regret
upon her. She sent for her daughter-in-law. And
these women, who had done each other so much harm,
who had never met and had openly and senselessly hated
each other, fell sobbing in each other's arms, and were
reconciled for ever beside the coffin of the man whom
they had so much loved.

Life was shattered for the princess. One consolation
was left her—that was her child, her friend, her 'Irish
daughter,' and *she* was preparing to leave her.

Why she went away I do not understand. It is hard
to restrain a feeling of vexation, seeing how unnecessarily
Miss Wilmot abandoned Princess Dashkov for the sake of
her Irish relatives, who played an extremelylimited part in
her life, and with whom she must have been very dreary.

Princess Dashkov, frightened of her isolation, wanted
to go with her to Ireland, there to end her existence,
'which has no heirs and must die out.' Miss Wilmot
persuaded her not to go and promised to come back to

her. The old woman felt it bitterly. Miss Mary, to spare her, set off secretly, but, detained in Petersburg by the departure of the ship and the incredibly stupid police measures taken against the English on account of the war which had then been declared, she made up her mind to go back for some months to Moscow; the figure of the old lady with tears in her eyes rent her heart; she wrote to her of her intention.

Princess Dashkov's joy and gratitude knew no bounds, and how did she celebrate the news? She sent to the prison for five men who were there for debt to be released, and charged them to celebrate a thanksgiving service for her.

But the bitterness of separation was only deferred; the obstinate Miss Mary would have her way, and went after all. Princess Dashkov, heartbroken at parting from her friend, had gone to bed. At night Miss Wilmot stole quietly once more into her room. The princess, who had been weeping the whole day, had fallen asleep: 'The expression of her face was serene as a child's. I softly kissed her and went away.' They never saw each other again.

The last days of our princess were passed in complete emptiness, through which those dreary 'shades' flitted from time to time, covered with stars and powder, and growing still more decrepit. Her thoughts were concentrated on the young girl with a sorrow and dreamy tenderness which makes the heart ache; one has a distinct feeling that this grief must go uncomforted.

'What am I to say to you, my beloved child, not to grieve you?' she writes on the 25th of October 1809. 'I am sad, very sad, tears are flowing from my eyes, and I cannot get used to our separation. I have built a few bridges. I have planted a few hundred trees, I am told successfully; all that distracts me for a minute, but my sadness comes back again.'

On the 29th of October she writes: 'And how changed everything is in Troitskoye since you left! The theatre is shut up, there has not been a single performance, the pianos are mute, and even the maids do not sing. But why am I telling you this? you are surrounded by your kinsfolk, you are happy, contented. . . .'

She writes her a few more lines on the 6th of November, and ends her letter with the English words: 'God bless you!' Did Mary know that that blessing came from a dying hand? Less than two months later, on the 9th of January 1810, Princess Ekaterina Romanovna was no more.

Five years before her death, on the 22nd of October 1806, she concluded her Memoirs with these words: 'With an honest heart and pure intentions I have had to endure many calamities; I should have been crushed under them if my conscience had not been clear . . . now I look forward without fear and uneasiness to my approaching dissolution.'

What a woman! What a rich and vigorous life!

BAZAROV

Letter 1

INSTEAD of a letter, dear friend, I am sending you a dissertation, and an unfinished one too. After our conversation I read over again Pisarev's article on Bazarov, which I had quite forgotten, and I am very glad I did—that is, not that I had forgotten it, but that I read it again. The article confirms my point of view. In its one-sidedness it is more true and more worth consideration than its opponents have supposed. Whether Pisarev has correctly grasped the character of Bazarov as Turgenev meant it, does not concern me. What does matter is that he has recognised himself and his comrades in Bazarov, and has added to the portrait what was lacking in the book. The less Pisarev has adhered to the narrow framework in which the exasperated 'Father' has tried to confine the obstinate 'Son,' the more freely has he been able to treat him as the expression of his ideal.

'But what interest can Mr. Pisarev's ideal have for us? Pisarev is a smart critic, he has written a great deal, he has written about everything, sometimes about subjects of which he had knowledge, but all that does not give his ideal any claim on the attention of the public.'

The point is that it is not his own individual ideal, but the ideal which both before and since the appearance of Turgenev's Bazarov has haunted the younger generation, has been embodied not only in various heroes in novels and stories, but in living persons who have tried to take Bazarovism as the basis of their words and actions. What Pisarev says I have seen and heard myself a dozen times; in the simplicity of his heart, he has let out the cherished thought of a whole circle and, focussing the scattered rays on one centre, has shed a light on the typical Bazarov.

To Turgenev, Bazarov is more than alien; to Pisarev, more than a comrade; to study the type, of course, one must take the view which sees in Bazarov the desideratum.

Pisarev's opponents were frightened by his lack of caution; while denouncing Turgenev's Bazarov as a caricature, they repudiated even more violently his transfigured double; they were displeased at Pisarev's having put his foot in it, but it does not follow from this that he was wrong in his interpretation·

Pisarev knows the heart of his Bazarov through and through; he makes a confession for his hero. 'Perhaps,' he says, 'at the bottom of his heart Bazarov does accept a great deal of what he denies in words, and, perhaps, it is just what is accepted and concealed that saves him from moral degradation and from moral insignificance.'

We regard this indiscreet utterance, which looks so deeply into another soul, as very important.

Further on, Pisarev describes his hero's character thus: 'Bazarov is extremely proud, but his pride is not noticeable' (clearly this is not Turgenev's Bazarov) 'just because it is so great. Nothing would satisfy Bazarov but an *eternity of ever-widening activity and ever-increasing enjoyment.'*[1]

Bazarov acts everywhere and in everything only as he wishes, or as he thinks advantageous and convenient; he is guided only by his personal desire or personal calculation· He acknowledges no Mentor above him, without himself nor within himself. Before him is no lofty aim, in his mind is no lofty thought, and with all that his powers are immense. If Bazarovism is a malady, it is a malady of our age, and will have to run its course in spite of any amputations or palliatives.

---

[1] Youth is fond of expressing itself in all sorts of incommensurables, and striking the imagination by images of infinite magnitude. The last sentence reminds me Vividly of Karl Moor, Ferdinand, and Don Carlos. — (*Author's Note.*)

Bazarov looks down on people, and rarely gives himself the trouble, indeed, to conceal his half-contemptuous and half-patronising attitude to those who hate and to those who obey him. He loves no one. He thinks it quite unnecessary to put any constraint on himself whatever. There are two sides to his cynicism, an internal and an external, the cynicism of thought and feeling and the cynicism of manner and expression. The essence of his inner cynicism lies in an ironical attitude to feeling of every sort, to dreaminess, to poetical enthusiasm. The harsh expression of this irony, the causeless and aimless roughness of manner, are part of his external cynicism. Bazarov is not merely an empiricist; he is also an unkempt Bursch. Among the admirers of Bazarov there will doubtless be some who will be delighted with his rude manners, the vestiges left by his rough student life, and will imitate those manners, which are in any case a defect and not a virtue.[1] Such people are most often evolved in the grey environment of hard work: stern work coarsens the hands, coarsens the manners, coarsens the feelings; the man is toughened, casts off youthful dreaminess, and gets rid of tearful sentimentality; there is no possibility of dreaming at work; the hard-working man looks upon idealism as a folly peculiar to the idleness and soft self-indulgence of the well-to-do, he reckons moral sufferings

[1] The prophecy has now been fulfilled. This mutual interaction of men on books, and books on men, is a curious thing. The book takes its whole shape from the society in which it is conceived; it generalises, it makes it more vivid and striking, and afterwards is outdone by reality. The originals caricature their vividly drawn portraits, and actual persons live in their literary shades. At the end of last century all young Germans were a little after the style of Werther, while all their young ladies resembled Charlotte; at the beginning of the present century the university Werthers had begun to change into 'Robbers,' not real ones, but Schilleresque robbers. The young Russians who have come on the scene since 1862 are almost all derived from *What Is to be Done?* with the addition of a few Bazarov features. — (*Author's Note.*)

as imaginary, moral impulses and heroic deeds as far-fetched and absurd. He feels a repulsion for high-flown talk.'

Then Pisarev draws the genealogical tree of Bazarov: the Onyegins and Petchorins begat the Rudins and the Beltovs,[1] the the Rudins and the Beltovs begat Bazarov. (Whether the Decembrists are omitted intentionally or unintentionally I do not know.) The bored and dis-illusioned are succeeded by men who strive to act, life rejects them both as worthless and incomplete. 'It is sometimes their lot to suffer, but they never succeed in getting anything done. Society is deaf and inexorable to them. They are incapable of adapting themselves to its conditions, not one of them ever rises so high as head clerk of a government office. Some are consoled by becoming professors and working for future generations. Their negative usefulness is incontestable. They increase the numbers of men incapable of practical activity, in consequence of which practical activity itself, or more precisely the forms in which it usually finds expression now, slowly but steadily sink lower in public esteem.'

'It seemed (after the Crimean War) that Rudinism was over, that the period of fruitless ideals and yearnings was succeeded by a period of seething and useful activity. But the illusion has faded. The Rudins have not become practical workers, and a new generation has come forward from behind them and taken up a reproachful and ironical attitude towards its predecessors. "What are you whining about, what are you seeking, what are you asking from life? You want happiness, I suppose? I daresay you do! Happiness has to be fought for. If you are strong, take it. If you are weak, hold your tongue; we feel sick enough without your whining!" A gloomy, concentrated energy is expressed in this un-

[1] The hero of Herzen's novel, *Who Is to Blame?*—(*Translator's Note.*)

friendly attitude of the younger generation to their Mentors. In their conceptions of good and evil the young generation and the best men of the preceding one are alike, the sympathies and antipathies of both are the same; they desire the same thing, but the men of the past generation were in an everlasting fuss and ferment. The men of to-day are not in a fuss, they are not trying to find anything, they will not give in to any compromise, and they hope for nothing. They are as helpless as the Rudins, but they recognise their helplessness. "I cannot act now," each of these new men thinks, "and I am not going to try. I despise everything that surrounds me, and I am not going to conceal my contempt. I shall enter on the battle with evil when I feel myself strong." Having no possibility of acting, men begin to reflect and investigate. Superstitions and authorities are torn to shreds, and the philosophy of life is completely cleared of all sorts of fantastic conceptions. It is nothing to them whether the public is following in their footsteps. They are full of themselves, of their own inner life. In short, the Petchorins had will without understanding, the Rudins understanding without will, the Bazarovs both understanding and will. Thought and action are blended in one firm whole.'

As you see, there is everything here (if there is no mistake), both character-drawing and classification. All is brief and clear, the sum is added up, the bill is presented, and perfectly correctly from the point of view from which the author has attacked the question.

But we do not accept this bill, and we protest from our premature coffins which have not yet arrived, though bespoken. We are not Charles v., and have no desire to be buried alive.

How strange has been the fate of *Fathers and Children*! That Turgenev created Bazarov with no idea of patting him on the head is clear; that he meant

to do something for the 'Fathers' is clear too. But
when he came to deal with such pitiful and worthless
'Fathers' as the Kirsanovs, Turgenev was carried away
by Bazarov in spite of his harshness, and instead of
thrashing the son he chastised the fathers.

And so it has come to pass that some of the younger
generation have recognised themselves in Bazarov. But
we entirely fail to recognise ourselves in the Kirsanovs,
just as we did not recognise ourselves in the Manilovs
nor the Sobakevitches, although Manilovs and Sobakevitches existed all over the place in the days of our
youth, and are existing now.

Whole herds of moral freaks live at the same date in
different layers of society and in its different currents;
undoubtedly they represent more or less general types,
but they do not represent the most striking and characteristic side of their generation, the side which most fully
expresses its force. Pisarev's Bazarov is, in a one-sided
sense, to a certain extent the extreme type of what
Turgenev called the 'Sons'; while the Kirsanovs are
the most commonplace and ordinary representatives of
the 'Fathers.'

Turgenev was more of an artist in his novel than is
thought, and that is why he turned out of his course, and
to my thinking he did well in so doing—he meant to go
one way, and he went another and a better one.

He might just as well have sent his Bazarov to London.
That insignificant creature, Pisemsky, did not shrink from
travelling expenses for his sorely tried freaks. We could
perhaps have shown Bazarov on the banks of the Thames
that, without rising to the post of head clerk of an office,
one might do quite as much good as any head of a department; that society is not always deaf and inexorable when
the protest finds a response; that action does sometimes
succeed; that the Rudins and the Beltovs sometimes have
will and perseverance; and that, seeing the impossibility

of carrying on the work to which they are urged by their inner impulse, they have forsaken many things, gone abroad, and without 'fuss and ferment' have established a Russian printing-press, and are carrying on a Russian propaganda. The influence of the London press from 1856 to the end of 1863 is not merely a practical fact, but an historical fact. It cannot be effaced, it has to be accepted. In London Bazarov would have seen that it was only from a distance that we seemed to be waving our arms in despair, and that in reality we were keeping our hands hard at work. Perhaps his wrath would have been changed to lovingkindness, and he would have given up treating us with 'reproach and irony.'

I frankly confess this throwing of stones at one's predecessors is very distasteful to me, I repeat what I have said already: 'I should like to save the younger generation from historical ingratitude, and even from historical error. It is high time that the fathers gave up devouring their children like Saturn, but it is time the children ceased to follow the example of those savages who slaughter their old people. Surely it is not right that only in natural science the phases and degrees of development, the variations and the deviations, even the *avortements*, should be studied, accepted, considered *sine ira et studio*, while as soon as one approaches history the physiological method is abandoned, and the methods of the Criminal Court and the House of Correction are adopted.'

The Onyegins and Petchorins have passed away.

The Rudins and the Beltovs are passing.

The Bazarovs will pass . . . and very quickly, as a matter of fact. It is a too artificial, bookish, over-strained type to persist for long.

A type has already tried to thrust himself forward to replace him, one rotten in the spring of his days, the type of the orthodox student, the conservative patriot trained at Government expense, in whom everything loathsome in Imperial Russia was incarnate, though even he felt embarrassed after serenading the Iversky Madonna, and singing a thanksgiving service to Katkov.

All the types that arise pass, and all, in virtue of the law of the conservation of energy which we have learnt to recognise in the physical world, persist and will spring up in different forms in the future progress of Russia and in her future organisation.

And so would it not be more interesting, instead of pitting Bazarov against Rudin, to analyse what are the salient points connecting them, and what are the reasons of their appearing and their transformation? Why have precisely these forms of development been called forth by our life, and why have they passed one into the other in this way? Their dissimilarity is obvious, but in some respects they are alike. Typical characters readily pounce on distinctions, exaggerate the angles and prominent features for the sake of emphasising them, paint the barriers in vivid colours, and tear apart the bonds. The shades are lost and unity is left far away, hidden in mist, like the plain that joins the foot of the mountains, whose tops, far apart from each other, are brightly lighted up. Moreover, we load on the shoulders of these types more than they can carry, and ascribe to them in life a significance they have not had, or have only in a limited sense. To take Onyegin as the finest type of the intellectual life of the period between 1820 and 1830, as the integral of all the tendencies and activities of the class then awakening, would be quite a mistake, although he does represent one of the aspects of the life of that time.

The type of that period, one of the most splendid types of modern history, was the Decembrist and not Onyegin. He could not be touched by Russian literature for all these forty years, but he is not the less for that.

How is it the younger generation have not the clearness of vision, the imagination, or the heart to grasp the grandeur and the virtue of those brilliant young men who emerged from the ranks of the Guards, those spoilt darlings of wealth and high rank who left their drawing-rooms and their piles of gold to demand the rights of man, to protest, to make a statement for which—and they knew it—the hangman's rope and penal servitude awaited them? It is a melancholy and puzzling question.

To resent the fact that these men appeared in the one class in which there was some degree of culture, of leisure, and of security, is senseless. If these 'princes, boyars, voyevods,' these secretaries of state and colonels, had not been awakened by moral hunger, but had waited to be aroused by bodily hunger, there would have been no whining and restless Rudins, nor Bazarovs, priding them-selves on their combination of will and knowledge: in their place there would have been a regimental doctor who would have done the soldiers to death, robbing them of their rations and medicines, and have sold the death certificate to a Kirsanov's bailiff when he had flogged a peasant to death, or there would have been a court clerk taking bribes, for ever drunk, fleecing the peasants of their quarter-roubles, and handing overcoat and goloshes to his Excellency, a Kirsanov and Governor of the province; and what is more, serfdom would not have received its death-blow, nor would there have been any of that under-ground activity under the heavy heel of authority, gnawing away the imperial ermine and the quilted dressing-gown of the landowners. It was fortunate that, side by side with men who found their gentlemanly pastimes in the kennels and the serfs' quarters, in outraging and flogging at home and in cringing servility in Petersburg, there were some whose 'pastime' it was to tear the rod out of their hands and fight for freedom, not for licence but freedom for mind, for human life. Whether this pastime of theirs was their serious work, their passion, they showed on the gallows and in prison . . . they showed it, too, when they came back after thirty years spent in Siberia.

If the type of the Decembrist has been reflected at all in literature, it is—faintly but with kindred features—in Tchatsky.[1]

His exasperated, bitter feeling, his youthful indignation, betray a healthy impulse to action; he feels what it is he is displeased with, he beats his head against the stone wall of social conventions and tries whether the prison bars are strong. Tchatsky was on the straight road for penal servitude, and if he survived the 14th of December he certainly did not turn into a passively suffering or proudly contemptuous person. He would have been more likely to rush into some indignant extreme, like Tchaadayev, to become a Catholic, a Slav-hater or a Slavophil, but he would not in any case have abandoned his propaganda, which he did not abandon either in the drawing-room of Famussov or in his entrance-hall, and he would not have comforted himself with the thought that 'his hour had not yet come.' He had that restless energy which cannot endure to be out of harmony with what surrounds it, and must either crush it or be crushed. This is the ferment which makes stagnation in history impossible and clears away the scum on its flowing but dilatory wave.

If Tchatsky had survived the generation that followed the 14th of Decemberin fear and trembling, and grown up crushed by terror, humiliated and suppressed, he would have stretched across it a warm hand of greeting to us. With us Tchatsky would have come back to his natural surroundings. These *rimes croisées* across the generations are not uncommon even in zoology. And it is my profound conviction that we should meet Bazarov's children with sympathy and they us 'without bitterness and sarcasm.' Tchatsky could not have lived with his hands

---

[1] The hero of *Woe from Wit.*—(*Translator's Note.*)

folded, neither in capricious peevishness nor in haughty self-admiration; he was not old enough to find pleasure in grumbling sulkiness, nor young enough to enjoy the conceit and self-sufficiency of adolescence. The whole character of the man lies in this restless ferment, this leaven of energy. But it is just that aspect that displeases Bazarov, it is that that incenses his proud stoicism. 'Keep quiet in your corner if you have not the strength to do anything; it is sickening enough as it is without your whining,' he says; 'if you are beaten, well, stay beaten. . . . You have enough to eat; as for your weeping, that 's just an idle diversion'. . . and so on.

Pisarev was bound to speak in that way for Bazarov; the part he played required it.

It is hard not to play a part so long as it is liked. Take off Bazarov's uniform, make him forget the jargon he uses, let him be free to utter one word simply, without posing (he so hates affectation!), let him for one miriute forget his bristling duty, his artificially frigid language, his role of castigator, and within an hour we should understand each other in all the rest.

In their conceptions of good and evil the new generation are like the old. Their sympathies and antipathies, says Pisarev, are the same; what they desire is the same thing . . . at the bottom of their hearts the younger generation accept much that they reject in words. It would be quite easy then to come to terms. But until he is stripped of his ceremonial trappings Bazarov consistently demands from men who are crushed under every burden on earth, outraged, tortured, deprived both of sleep and of all possibility of action when awake, that they should not speak of their misery; there is a smack of Araktcheyev about it.

What reason is there to deprive Lermontov, for instance, of his bitter lamentation, his upbraidings of his own generation which sent a shock of horror through so many? Would the prison-house of Nicholas be really any better if the gaolers had been as irritably nervous and carping as Bazarov and had suppressed those voices.

'But what are they for? What is the use of them?'

'Why does a stone make a sound when it is hit with a hammer?'

'It cannot help it.'

And why do these gentlemen suppose that men can suffer for whole generations without speech, complaint, indignation, cursing, protest? If complaint is not of use for others, it is for those who complain; the expression of sorrow eases the pain. '*Ihm*,' says Goethe, '*gab ein Gott zu sagen, was er leidet.*'

'But what has it to do with us?'

Nothing to do with you, perhaps, but something to do with others, maybe; moreover, you must not lose sight of the fact that every generation lives for itself also. From the point of view of history it leads on to something else, but in relation to itself it is the goal, and it cannot, it ought not to endure without a murmur the afflictions that befall it, especially when it has not even the consolation which Israel had in the expectation of the Messiah, and has no idea that from the seed of the Onyegins and the Rudins will be born a Bazarov. In reality, what drives our young people to fury is that in our generation *our* craving for activity, *our* protest against the existing order of things was *differently* expressed from theirs, and that the motive of both was not always and completely dependent on cold and hunger.

Is not this passion for uniformity another example of the same irritable spirit which has made of formality and routine the one thing of consequence and reduced military evolutions to the goose-step? That side of the Russian character is responsible for the development of Araktcheyevism, civil and military. Every personal, individual manifestation or deviation was regarded as disobedience, and excited persecution and incessant bullying. Bazarov leaves no one in peace; he provokes every one with his scorn. Every word of his is a reproof from a superior to a subordinate. There is no future before that. 'If,' says Pisarev,' Bazarovism is the malady of our age, it will have to run its course.' By all means. This malady is only in place before the end of the university course; like teething, it is quite unseemly in the full-grown.

The worst service Turgenev did Bazarov was putting him to death by typhus because he did not know how to get rid of him. That is an *ultima ratio* which no one can withstand; had Bazarov been saved from typhus, he would certainly have grown out of Bazarovism, at any rate in science, which he loved and prized, and which does not change its methods, whether frog or man, embryology or history, is its subject.

'Bazarov rejected every sort of convention, and was nevertheless an extremely uncultured man. He had heard something about poetry, something about art, and, without troubling himself to think, abruptly passed sentence on the subject of which he knew nothing. This conceit is characteristic of us Russians in general; it has its good points, such as intellectual daring, but at times it leads us into crude errors.'

Science would have saved Bazarov; he would have ceased to look down on people with deep and unconcealed contempt. Science even more than the Gospel teaches us humility. She cannot look down on anything, she does not know what superiority means, she despises nothing, is never false for the sake of a pose, and conceals nothing to produce an effect. She stops short at the facts to investigate, sometimes to heal, never to punish, still less with hostility and irony.

Science—I anyway am not compelled to keep some

words hidden in the silence of the spirit—science is love, as Spinoza said of thought and vision.

Letter 2

What has been leaves an imprint by means of which science sooner or later restores the past in its fundamental features. All that is lost is the particular atmosphere in which it has occurred. Apotheoses and calumnies, partialities and envies, all fade and are blown away. The faint track on the sand vanishes; the imprint which has force and persistence stamps itself on the rock and will be brought to light by the honest investigator.

Connections, degrees of kinship, testators and heirs, and their mutual rights, will all be revealed by the heraldry of science.

Only goddesses are born without predecessors, like Venus from the foam of the sea, Minerva, more intelligent, sprang from the ready head of Jupiter.

The Decembrists are our noble fathers, the Bazarovs our prodigal sons.

The heritage we received from the Decembrists was the awakened feeling of human dignity, the striving for independence, the hatred for slavery, the respect for Western Europe and for the Revolution, the faith in the possibility of an upheaval in Russia, the passionate desire to take part in it, the youth and freshness of our energies.

All that has been recast and moulded into new forms, but the foundations are untouched.

What has our generation bequeathed to the coming one? Nihilism.

Let us recall the position of affairs a little.

Somewhere about 1840 our life began to force its way out more vigorously, like steam from under a closed lid.

A scarcely perceptible change passed all over Russia, the change by which the doctor discerns before he can fully account for it that there is a turn for the better, that the patient's strength, though very weak, is reviving—there is a different *tone*. Somewhere inwardly in the moral invisible world there is the breath of a different air, more stimulating and healthier. Externally everything was deathlike under the ice of Nicholas's government, but something was stirring in the mind and the conscience— a feeling of uneasiness, of dissatisfaction. The terror had grown weaker, men were sick of the twilight of the kingdom of darkness.

I saw that change with my own eyes, when I came back from exile, first in Moscow, afterwards in Petersburg. But I saw it in the literary and scientific circles.

Another man, whose Baltic antipathy for the Russian movement places him beyond the suspicion of partiality, described not so long ago how, returning at that period to the Petersburg aristocracy of the barracks after an absence of some years, he was puzzled at the decline of discipline. Aides-de-camp and colonels of the Guards were mur- muring, were criticising the measures taken by the Government, and were displeased with Nicholas him- self. He was so overwhelmed, distressed, and alarmed for the future of the Autocracy that in the tribulation of his spirit he felt when dining with the aide-de-camp B., almost in the presence of Dubbelt himself, that Nihilism had been born between the cheese and the dessert. He did not recognise the new-born spirit, but the new-born spirit was there. The machine wound up by Nicholas had begun to give way; he turned the screw the other way and every one felt it; some spoke, others kept silent and forbade speech, but all knew that things were really going wrong, that every one was oppressed, and that this oppression would bring no good to any one.

Laughter played its part too; laughter, never a good

companion for any religion, and Autocracy is a religion. The vileness and degradation of the lower ranks of the officials had reached such a pitch that the Government abandoned them to the satirist. Nicholas, roaring with laughter in his box at the Mayor and his Derzhimorda,[1] helped the propaganda, never guessing that after the approval of the Most High the mockery would soon be promoted to the higher ranks.

It is difficult to apply Pisarev's rubrics to this period without modification. Everything in life consists of *nuances*, hesitations, cross-currents, ebbing and flowing, and not of disconnected fragments. At what point did the men of will without knowledge cease to be and the men of knowledge without will begin?

Nature resolutely eludes classification, even classification by age. Lermontov was in years a contemporary of Byelinsky; he was at the university when we were, but he died in the hopeless pessimism of the Petchorin movement, against which the Slavophils and ourselves alike rose in opposition.

And by the way, I have mentioned the Slavophils. Where are Homyakov and his brethren to be put? What had they—will without knowledge, or knowledge without will? Yet the position they filled was no trifling one in the modern development of Russia, they left a deep imprint on the life of that time. Or in what levy of recruits shall we put Gogol, and by what standard? He had not knowledge, whether he had will I don't know, I doubt it; but he had genius, and his influence was colossal.

And so, leaving aside the *lapides crescunt, planta crescunt et vivunt* . . . of Pisarev, let us pass on.

There were no secret societies, but the secret agreement of those who understood was immense. Circles consist-

---

[1] The reference is to the performance of Gogol's *The Government Inspector.*—(*Translator's Note.*)

ing of men who had felt the bear's claw of the Government on their own persons, more or less, kept a vigilant watch on their membership. Every action was impossible, even a word must be masked, but great was the power of speech, not only of the printed but even more of the spoken word, less easily detected by the police.

Two batteries were quickly moved forward. Journalism became propaganda. At the head of it, in the full flush of his youthful strength, stood Byelinsky. University lecture-rooms were transformed into pulpits, lectures into the preaching of humane culture; the personality of Granovsky, surrounded by young professors, became more and more prominent.

Then all at once another outburst of laughter. Strange laughter, terrible laughter, the laughter of hysteria, in which were mingled shame and pangs of conscience, and perhaps not the tears that follow laughter, but the laughter that follows tears. The absurd, monstrous, narrow world of *Dead Souls* could not endure it; it sank and began to disappear. And the propaganda went on gathering strength . . . always unchanged; tears and laughter and books and speech and Hegel[1] and history—all roused men to the consciousness of their position, to a feeling of horror for serfdom and for their own lack of rights, everything pointed them on to science and culture, to the purging of thought from all the litter of tradition, to the freeing of conscience and reason. That period saw the first dawn of Nihilism—that complete freedom from all established conceptions, from all the inherited obstructions and barriers which hinder the Western European

---

[1] Hegel's dialectic is a terrible battering-ram, in spite of its double-facedness and its Prussian Protestant cockade; it dissolved everything existing and dissipated everything that was a check on reason. Moreover, that was the period of Feuerbach, *der kritischen Kritik.*—(*Author's Note.*)

mind from advancing in its historical fetters, from taking a step forward.

The silent work of the 'forties was cut short all at once. A time even blacker and more oppressive than the beginning of Nicholas's reign followed upon the revolution of February. Byelinsky died before the beginning of the persecution. Granovsky envied him and wanted to leave Russia.

A dark night that lasted seven years fell upon Russia, and in it that intellectual outlook, that way of thinking that is called Nihilism, took shape, developed, and gained a firm hold on the Russian mind.

Nihilism (I repeat what I said lately in *The Bell*) is logic without structure, it is science without dogmas, it is the unconditional submission to experience and the resigned acceptance of all consequences, whatever they may be, if they follow from observation, or are required by reason. Nihilism does not transform something into nothing, but shows that nothing which has been taken for something is an optical illusion, and that every truth, however it contradicts our fantastic ideas, is more wholesome than they are, and is in any case what we are in duty bound to accept. Whether the name is appropriate or not does not matter. We are accustomed to it; it is accepted by friend and foe, it has become a police label, it has become a denunciation, an insult with some, a word of praise with others. Of course, if by Nihilism we are to understand destructive creativeness, that is, the turning of facts and thoughts into nothing, into barren scepticism, into haughty passivity, into the despair which leads to inaction, then true Nihilists are the last people to be included in the definition, and one of the greatest Nihilists will be Turgenev, who flung the first stone at them, and another will be perhaps his favourite philosopher, Schopenhauer. When Byelinsky, after listening to one of his friends, who explained at length that the *spirit* attains self-consciousness in man, answered indignantly: 'So, I am not conscious for my own sake, but for the spirit's? . . . Why should I be taken advantage of? I had better not think at all; what do I care for its consciousness? . . .' he was a Nihilist.

When Bakunin convicted the Berlin professors of being afraid of negation, and the Parisian revolutionaries of 1848 of conservatism, he was a Nihilist in the fullest sense.

All these discriminations and jealous reservations lead as a rule to nothing but artificial antagonism.

When the Petrashevsky group were sent to penal servitude for 'trying to uproot all laws, human and divine, and to destroy the foundations of society,' in the words of their sentence, the terms of which were stolen from the inquisitorial notes of Liprandi, they were Nihilists. Since then Nihilism has broadened out, has to some extent become doctrinaire, has absorbed a great deal from science, and has produced leaders of immense force and immense talent. All that is beyond dispute. But it has brought forth no new principles. Or if it has, where are they? I await an answer to this question from you, or perhaps from some one else, and then I will continue.

THE RUSSIAN PEOPLE AND SOCIALISM

A Letter to J. Michelet

This letter was first published at Nice in 1851, but only circulated in Piedmont and Switzerland, as the French police seized almost the whole edition in Marseilles.

DEAR SIR,—You hold so high a position in the esteem of all thinking men, and every word which comes from your noble pen is received by the European democracy with such complete and deserved confidence, that I cannot keep silent in a matter that touches upon my deepest convictions. I cannot leave unanswered the description of the Russian people which you have included in your legend of Kosciuszko.[1]

This answer is necessary for another reason also. The time has come to show Europe that when they speak about Russia they are not speaking of something absent, defenceless, deaf and dumb.

We who have left Russia, only that free Russian speech may be heard at last in Europe, we are on the spot and deem it our duty to raise our voice when a man wielding an immense and deserved authority asserts that 'Russia does not exist, Russians are not men, they are devoid of moral significance.'

If by this you mean official Russia, the parade-Tsardom, the Byzantine-German Government, then you are right. We agree beforehand with everything that you tell us; it is not for us to play the part of champion there. The Russian Government has so many agents in the press that there will never be a lack of eloquent apologies for its doings.

---

[1] It appeared in a feuilleton of the journal *l'Événement*, 1851, and was later on included in a volume entitled *Democratic Legends.*— (*Note to Russian Edition.*)

But not official society alone is dealt with in your work; you touch on a deeper question; you speak of the people itself.

Poor Russian people! There is no one to raise a voice in its defence! Judge whether I can in duty be silent.

The Russian people, my dear sir, is alive, strong, and not old; on the contrary, indeed, very young. Men do die even in youth, it does happen, but it is not the normal thing.

The past of the Russian people is obscure, its present is terrible, but it has claims on the future. It does not *believe* in its present position; it has the temerity to expect the more from time, since it has received so little hitherto.

The most difficult period for the Russian people is drawing to its close. A terrible conflict awaits it; its enemies are making ready.

The great question, 'to be or not to be,' will soon be decided for Russia, but it is a sin to despair of success before the fight has begun.

The Russian question is assuming immense and fearful proportions; it is the object of interest and anxiety to all parties; but I think that too much attention is paid to Imperial Russia, to official Russia, and too little to the Russia of the people, to voiceless Russia.

Even looking at Russia solely from the point of view of its Government, do you not think it would be as well to become more closely acquainted with this incon- venient neighbour who makes himself felt throughout the whole of Europe, in one place with bayonets, in another with spies? The Russian Government extends its influence to the Mediterranean by its protection of the Ottoman Porte, to the Rhine by its protection of its German uncles and connections, to the Atlantic by its protection of *order* in France.

It would not be amiss, I maintain, to appraise at its true value this universal protector, to inquire whethe this strange realm is destined to play no other part than the repulsive one assumed by the Petersburg Government, the part of a barrier continually thrown up on the path of human progress.

Europe is approaching a terrible cataclysm. The mediaeval world is falling into ruins. The feudal world is drawing to a close. Political and religious revolutions are flagging under the burden of their impotence; they have accomplished great things, but have not carried out their tasks. They have destroyed faith in the Throne and the Altar, but have not established freedom; they have kindled in men's hearts desires which they are incapable of satisfying. Parliamentarianism, Protestantism, are only stop-gaps, temporary havens, weak bulwarks against death and resurrection. Their day is over. Since 1849 it has been grasped that petrified Roman law, subtle casuistry, thin philosophic deism, and barren religious rationalism are all equally powerless to hold back the workings of destiny.

The storm is approaching, it is impossible to avert it. Revolutionaries and reactionaries are at one about that. All men's minds are perturbed; the oppressive, vital question lies heavy on the hearts of all. With growing uneasiness all men ask themselves whether there is still strength for recovery in old Europe, that decrepit Proteus, that decaying organism. The answer to that question is awaited with horror, and the suspense is terrible.

Indeed, it is a fearful question! Will old Europe have the power to infuse new blood into its veins and fling itself into the boundless future to which it is drawn by an invincible force, to which it is being borne headlong, the path to which is perhaps over the ruins of its ancestral home, over the fragments of past civilisations, over the trampled riches of modern culture?

On both sides the full gravity of the moment has been

understood; Europe is plunged in dim, stifling gloom, on the eve of the momentous conflict. It is not life, but an oppressive, agitating suspense. There is no regard for law, no justice, no personal freedom even; everywhere the sway of the secular inquisition is supreme; instead of order upheld by law, there is a state of siege, all are governed by a single feeling—fear, and there is plenty of it. Every question is thrown into the background before the all-devouring interests of the reaction. Governments, apparently most hostile, are united into a single world-wide police. The Russian Emperor, without concealing his hatred for the French, rewards the Prefect of the Parisian police; the King of Naples bestows a decoration on the President of the Republic. The Prussian King, donning the Russian uniform, hastens to Warsaw to embrace his foe, the Emperor of Austria, in the gracious presence of Nicholas; while the latter, the schismatic of the one Church of salvation, proffers his aid to the Pope of Rome. In the midst of these Saturnalia, in the midst of this Sabbath of the reaction, nothing is left to safeguard freedom from the caprices of tyranny. Even the guarantees which exist in undeveloped societies, in China, in Persia, are no longer respected in the capitals of the so-called civilised world.

One can hardly believe one's eyes. Can this be the Europe which once we knew and loved?

Indeed, if it were not for free and haughty England, 'that jewel set in a silver sea,' as Shakespeare calls it, if Switzerland were, like Peter, in fear of Caesar, to renounce its principles, if Piedmont, that branch still left of Italy, that last refuge of freedom, which has been hunted beyond the Alps, and cannot cross the Apennines, were led astray by the example of her neighbours, if those three countries were infected by the spirit of death that breathes from Paris and Vienna, it might be thought that the Conservatives had succeeded already in bringing the old world to its final dissolution, that the days of barbarism had already returned in France and Germany.

In the midst of this chaos, in the midst of these pangs of death and agonies of birth, in the midst of a world falling into dust about the cradle of the future, men's eyes involuntarily turn to the East.

There a hostile, menacing empire is seen standing out behind the mists, like a dark mountain; at times it seems as though it is falling upon Europe like an avalanche, that like an impatient heir it is ready to hasten her tardy death.

This empire, absolutely unknown two hundred years ago, has suddenly made its appearance, and with no right to do so, with no invitation, has loudly and bluntly raised its voice in the council of European Powers, demanding a share in the booty, won without its assistance.

No one has dared to oppose its pretensions to interfere in the affairs of Europe. Charles XII tried to do so, but his sword, till then invincible, was broken; Frederick II. attempted to resist the claims of the Petersburg Court; Königsberg and Berlin became the prey of the foe from the North. Napoleon, with half a million men, penetrated to the very heart of the giant, and stole away alone in the first peasant sledge he came upon. Europe gazed with astonishment at Napoleon's flight, at the crowds of Cossacks racing in pursuit of him, at the Russian troops marching to Paris, and giving the Germans their national independence by way of alms on the road. Since then Russia has lain like a vampire over the fate of Europe, watching the mistakes of rulers and peoples. Yesterday she almost crushed Austria, assisting her against Hungary; to-morrow she will proclaim Brandenburg a Russian province to appease the Prussian King.

Is it credible that on the very eve of conflict nothing is known of this combatant? Yet he stands already menacing, fully armed, prepared to cross the frontier at the first summons of reaction. And meanwhile men scarcely know his weapons, or the colour of his flag, and are satisfied with his official speeches and the vague, incongruous tales that are told of him.

Some tell us only of the unlimited power of the Tsar, of the capricious tyranny of his Government, of the slavish spirit of his subjects; others assert, on the contrary, that the Imperialism of Petersburg has nothing in common with the people, that this people, crushed under the two-fold despotism of the Government and the landowners, bears the yoke, but is not resigned to it, that it is not crushed, but only unfortunate, and at the same time declare that it is this very people which gives unity and power to the colossal Tsardom that crushes it. Some add that the Russian people is a *contemptible rabble of drunkards and knaves*; others maintain that Russia is inhabited by a competent and richly. gifted race. It seems to me that there is something tragic in the senile heedlessness with which the old world mixes up the different accounts it hears of its antagonist. In this confusion of contradictory opinions there is apparent so much senseless repetition, such distressing superficiality, such petrified prejudice, that we are involuntarily moved to a comparison with the days of the fall of Rome.

Then, too, on the eve of catastrophe, on the eve of the victory of the barbarians, men loudly proclaimed the eternity of Rome, the impotent madness of the Nazarenes, and the insignificance of the movement that was arising in the barbarian world.

You have performed a great service: you first in France have spoken of the Russian people, you have, unawares, touched on the very heart, the very source of life. The truth would have been revealed to your eyes at once, if you had not, in a moment of anger, pulled back your outstretched hand, if you had not turned away from the source because its waters were not clear.

I read your bitter words with deep distress, with

melancholy, with anguish in my heart. I confess I looked in vain in them for the historian, the philosopher, and, above all, the tender-hearted man whom we all know and love. I hasten to explain, I fully understood the cause of your indignation; sympathy for unhappy Poland prompted your words. We, too, deeply cherish this feeling for our Polish brothers, and in us the feeling is not merely one of pity, but of shame, and pangs of conscience. Love for Poland! We all love her, but is it necessary to combine with that feeling hatred for another people as unhappy, a people forced to aid with its fettered hands the misdeeds of its savage Government? Let us be magnanimous, let us not forget that before our eyes the nation decked with all the trophies of recent revolution has consented to the establishment of *order* in Rome like that in Warsaw. And to-day . . . look yourself what is going on about you . . . yet we do not say that the French *have ceased to be men*.

It is time to forget this unhappy conflict between brothers. Among us there is no conqueror. Poland and Russia are crushed by a common foe. Even the victims and the martyrs turn their backs upon the past, which is equally sorrowful for them and for us. I, like you, appeal to your friend the great poet, Mickiewicz.

Do not say of the Polish bard's opinions that they are 'due to mercifulness, a sacred delusion.' No; they are the fruits of long and conscientious thought and a profound understanding of the destinies of the Slav world. The forgiveness of enemies is a glorious achievement, but there is an achievement still more glorious, more humane; that is, the understanding of enemies, for understanding is at once forgiveness, justification, reconciliation.

The Slav world is striving towards unity; that tendency became apparent immediately after the Napoleonic period. The idea of a Slavonic federation had already taken shape

in the revolutionary plans of Pestel and Muravyov.
Many Poles had a hand in the Russian conspiracy of
December 1825.

When the Revolution of 1830 broke out in Warsaw,
the Russian people displayed not the slightest animosity
against the disobedient subjects of their Tsar. The
young were in complete sympathy with the Poles. I
remember with what impatience we awaited tidings from
Warsaw; we cried like children at the news of the
memorial services held in the capital of Poland for our
Petersburg martyrs. Sympathy for the Poles exposed
us to the risk of cruel punishments, we were forced to
conceal it in our hearts and to be silent.

It may well be that during the war of 1830 a feeling of
exclusive nationalism and quite intelligible hostility
prevailed in Poland. But since those days the influence
of Mickiewicz, the historical and philological works of
many Slav scholars, a closer knowledge of other European
nations, purchased at the bitter price of exile, has given
a very different turn to Polish thought. The Poles have
come to feel that the battle is not between the Russian
people and themselves; they have learned that for the
future the only way they can fight is *for their and our
freedom*, the words inscribed on their revolutionary
banner.

Konarski, who was tortured and shot by Nicholas at
Vilna, called upon Russians and Poles without distinction
of race to rise in revolt. Russia showed her gratitude by
one of those almost unknown tragedies with which every
heroic action ends amongst us under the military heel of
our German rulers.

Korovazev, an army officer, resolved to save Konarski.
The day when he would be on duty was approaching,
everything was in readiness for the escape, when
the treachery of one of the Polish martyr's comrades
brought his plans to ruin. The young man was arrested

and sent to Siberia, and nothing has been heard of him since.

I spent five years in exile in the remote provinces of the Empire. There I met many Polish exiles. Almost in every district town there is either a whole group, or at least one of the luckless champions of independence. I would gladly appeal to their evidence; certainly they cannot complain of lack of sympathy on the part of the people around them. Of course, I am not speaking here of the police or members of the higher military hierarchy. They are nowhere conspicuous for their love of freedom, and least of all in Russia. I might appeal to the Polish students exiled every year to Russian universities to remove them from the influences of their native land; let them describe how they were received by their Russian comrades. They used to part from us with tears in their eyes.

You remember that when in 1847 the Polish emigrants in Paris celebrated the anniversary of their revolution, a Russian mounted their platform to beg for their friendship, and forgiveness for the past. That was our unhappy friend Bakunin. . . . But not to quote my fellow-countrymen, I will pick out one of those who are reckoned our enemies, a man whom you have yourself mentioned in your legend of Kosciuszko. For evidence on this subject I will refer you to one of the veterans of the Polish democracy, Bernacki, one of the ministers of revolutionary Poland. I boldly appeal to him, though long years of grief might well have embittered him against everything Russian. I am convinced that he will confirm all that I have said.

The solidarity binding Russia and Poland to each other and to the whole Slav world cannot be denied; it is obvious. What is more, there is no future for the Slav world apart from Russia; without Russia it will not develop, it will fell to pieces and be swallowed up by the German element; it will become Austrian and lose its independence. But in our opinion that is not its fate, not the end for which it is destined.

Following the gradual development of your idea, I must confess that I cannot agree with your view of Europe as a single individual in which every nationality plays the part of an essential organ.

It seems to me that all the German-Latin nationalities are necessary in the European world, because they exist in it, in consequence of some necessity. Aristotle long ago drew a distinction between pre-existent necessity and the necessity involved in the sequence of events. Nature is subject to the necessity of the accomplished fact, but her hesitation between various possibilities is very marked. On the same principle the Slav world can claim its right to unity, especially as it is made up of one race.

Centralisation is alien to the Slav spirit—federation is far more natural to it. Only when grouped in a league of free and independent peoples will the Slav world at last enter upon its genuine historical existence. Its past can only be regarded as a period of growth, of preparation, of purification. The political forms in which the Slavs have lived in the past have not been in harmony with their national tendency, a tendency vague and instinctive if you like, but by that very fact betraying an extraordinary vitality and promising much in the future. The Slavs have until now displayed in every phase of their history a strange unconcern—indeed, a marvellous receptivity. Thus Russia passed from paganism to Christianity without a shock, without a revolt, simply in obedience to the Grand Duke Vladimir, and in imitation of Kiev. Without regret they flung their old idols into the Volhov and accepted the new god as a new idol.

Eight hundred years later, part of Russia in precisely the same way accepted a civilisation imported from abroad.

The Slav world is like a woman who has never loved,

and for that very reason apparently takes no interest in what is going on about her. She is a stranger to all, unwanted everywhere, but there is no answering for the future; she is still young, and already a strange yearning has taken possession of her heart and sets it beating faster.

As for the richness of the national spirit, we need only point to the Poles, the one Slavonic people which has been at once free and powerful.

The Slav world is not in reality made up of nationalities so different in kind. Under the outer crust of chivalrous Liberal and Catholic Poland, and of imperial enslaved Byzantine Russia, under the democratic rule of the Serb Voyevod, under the bureaucratic yoke with which Austria oppresses Illyria, Dalmatia, and the Banat, under the patriarchal authority of the Osmanlis and under the blessing of the Archbishop of Montenegro, live nations physiologically and ethnographically identical.

The greater number of these Slav peoples have never been enslaved by conquest. The dependence in which they are so often found has for the most part consisted only in the recognition of a foreign potentate and the payment of tribute. Such, for instance, was the character of the Mongol power in Russia. Thus the Slavs have through long centuries preserved their nationality, their character, their language.

Have we not therefore the right to look upon Russia as the centre of the crystallisation, the centre towards which the Slav world in its striving toward unity is gravitating, especially as Russia is so far the only nation of the great race organised into a powerful and independent state?

The answer to this question would be perfectly clear if the Petersburg Government had the faintest inkling of its national destiny, if that dull-witted, deadly despotism could make terms with any humane idea. But in the present position of affairs, what honest man will bring himself to suggest to the Western Slavs their union with an empire which is perpetually in a state of siege, an empire in which the sceptre has been turned into a bludgeon that beats men to death?

The Imperial Pan-Slavism, eulogised from time to time by men who have been suborned, or who have lost their bearings, has, of course, nothing in common with a union resting on the foundations of freedom.

At this point we are inevitably brought by logic to a question of primary importance. Assuming that the Slav world can hope in the future for a fuller development, are we not forced to enquire which of the elements that have found expression in its undeveloped state gives it grounds for such a hope? If the Slavs believe that their time has come, this element must be in harmony with the revolutionary idea in Europe.

You indicated that element, you touched upon it, but it escaped you, because a generous sentiment of sympathy for Poland drew your attention away from it.

You say that 'the fundamental basis of the life of the Russian people is *communism*,' you maintain that 'their strength lies in their agrarian law, in the perpetual re-division of the land.'

What a terrible *Mene Tekel* has dropped from your lips! . . . Communism—the fundamental basis! Strength resting on re-division of the land! And you were not alarmed at your own words?

Ought we not here to pause, to take thought, to look more deeply into the question, and not to leave it before making certain whether it is a dream or truth?

Is there in the nineteenth century an interest of any gravity which does not involve the question of communism, the question of the re-division of the land?

Carried away by your indignation you go on: ' They (the Russians) are without any true sign of humanity, of moral sensibility, of the sense of good and evil. Truth and justice have for them no meaning; if you speak of these things—they are mute, they smile and know not what the words signify. 'Who may those Russians be to whom you have spoken? What conceptions of *truth and justice* appeared beyond their comprehension? This is not a superfluous question. In our profoundly revolutionary epoch the words 'truth and justice' have lost all absolute meaning identical for all men.

The *truth and justice* of old Europe are falsehood and injustice to the Europe which is being born. Nations are products of Nature, history is the progressive continuation of animal development. If we apply our moral standards to Nature, we shall not get very far. She cares nought for our blame or our praise. Our verdicts and the Montyon prizes[1] for virtue do not exist for her. The ethical categories created by our individual caprice are not applicable to her. It seems to me that a nation cannot be called either bad or good. The life of a people is always true to its character and cannot be false. Nature produces only what is practicable under given conditions: all that exists is drawn onwards by her generative ferment, her insatiable thirst for creation, that thirst common to all things living.

There are peoples living a prehistoric life, others living a life outside history; but once they move into the broad stream of history, one and indivisible, they belong to *humanity*, and, on the other hand, all the past of humanity belongs to them. In history—that is, in the life of the active and progressive part of humanity—the aristocracy of facial angle, of complexion, and other distinctions is gradually effaced. That which has not become human cannot come into history: so no nation which has become part of history can be reckoned a herd of beasts, just as

---

[1] A philanthropist, Baron de Montyon (1733-1820) endowed prizes for virtue and literary distinction to be distributed by the Institut in Paris. — (*Translator's Note.*)

there is no nation which deserves to be called an assembly of the elect.

There is no man bold enough, or ungrateful enough, to deny the importance of France in the destinies of the European world; but you must allow me the frank confession that I cannot share your view that the sympathetic interest of France is the *sine qua non* of historical progress in the future.

Nature never stakes all her fortune on one card. Rome, the Eternal City, which had no less right to the hegemony of the world, tottered, fell into ruins, vanished, and pitiless humanity strode forward over its grave.

On the other hand, unless one looks on Nature as madness incarnate, it would be hard to see nothing but an outcast race, nothing but a vast deception, nothing but a casual rabble, human only through their vices, in a people that has grown and multiplied during ten centuries, that has obstinately preserved its nationality, that has formed itself into an immense empire, and has intervened in history far more perhaps than it should have done.

And such a view is the more difficult to accept since this people, even judging from the words of its enemies, is far from being in a stagnant condition. It is not a race that has attained social forms approximately corresponding to its desires and has sunk into slumber in them, like the Chinese; still less, a people that has outlived its prime and is withering in senile impotence, like the people of India. On the contrary, Russia is a quite new State—an unfinished building in which everything smells of fresh plaster, in which everything is at work and being worked out, in which nothing has yet attained its object, in which everything is changing, often for the worse, but anyway changing. In brief, this is the people whose fundamental principle, to quote your opinion, is communism, and whose strength lies in the re-division of land. . . .

With what crime, after all, do you reproach the

Russian people? What is the essential point of your accusation?

'The Russian,' you say, 'is a liar and a thief; he is perpetually stealing, he is perpetually lying, and quite innocently—it is in his nature.'

I will not stop to call attention to the sweeping character of your verdict, but will ask you a simple question: who is it that the Russian deceives, from whom does he steal? Who—if not the landowner, the Government official, the steward, the police officer, in fact the sworn foes of the peasant, whom he looks upon as heathens, as traitors, as half Germans? Deprived of every possible means of defence, the peasant resorts to cunning in dealing with his torturers, he deceives them, and he is perfectly right in doing so.

Cunning, my dear sir, is, in the words of the great thinker,[1] the irony of brute force.

Through his aversion for private property in land, so correctly noted by you, through his heedless and indolent temperament, the Russian peasant has gradually and imperceptibly been caught in the snares of the German bureaucracy and of the landowners' power. He has submitted to this humiliating disaster with the resignation of a martyr, but he has not believed in the rights of the landowner, nor the justice of the law-courts, nor the legality of the acts of the authorities. For nearly two hundred years the peasant's existence has been a dumb, passive opposition to the existing order of things. He submits to coercion, he endures, but he takes no part in anything that goes on outside the village commune.

The name of the Tsar still stirs a superstitious sentiment in the people; it is not to the Tsar Nicholas that the peasant does homage, but to the abstract idea, the myth; in the popular imagination the Tsar stands for a menacing avenger, an incarnation of Justice, an earthly providence.

[1] Hegel.

Besides the Tsar, only the clergy could possibly have an influence on orthodox Russia. They alone represent old Russia in governing spheres; the clergy do not shave their beards, and by that fact have remained on the side of the people. The peasantry listen with confidence to the monks. But the monks and the higher clergy, occupied exclusively with life beyond the grave, care little for the people. The village priests have lost all influence through their greed, their drunkenness, and their intimate relations with the police. In their case, too, the peasants respect the idea but not the person.

As for the dissenters, they hate both person and idea, both priest and Tsar.

Apart from the Tsar and the clergy every element of government and society is utterly alien, essentially antagonistic to the people. The peasant finds himself in the literal sense of the word an outlaw. The law-court is no protector for him, and his share in the existing order of things is entirely confined to the twofold tribute that lies heavy upon him and is paid in his toil and his blood. Rejected by all, he instinctively understands that the whole system is ordered not for his benefit, but to his detriment, and that the aim of the Government and the landowners is to wring out of him as much labour, as much money, as many recruits as possible. As he understands this and is gifted with a supple and resourceful intelligence, he deceives them on all sides and in everything. It could not be otherwise; if he spoke the truth he would by so doing be acknowledging their authority over him; if he did not rob them (observe that to conceal part of the produce of his own labour is considered theft in a peasant) he would thereby be recognising the lawfulness of their demands, the rights of the landowners and the justice of the law-courts.

To understand the Russian peasant's position fully, you should see him in the law-courts; you must see his hopeless face, his frightened watchful eyes, to understand that he is a prisoner of war before the court-martial, a traveller facing a gang of brigands. From the first glance it is clear that the victim has not the slightest trust in the hostile, pitiless, insatiable robbers who are questioning him, tormenting him and fleecing him. He knows that if he has money he will be acquitted; if not, he will be found guilty.

The Russian people speak their own old language, the judges and the attorneys write in a new bureaucratic language, hideous and barely intelligible; they fill whole folios with ungrammatical jargon, and gabble off this mummery to the peasant. He may understand it if he can and find his way out of the muddle if he knows how. The peasant knows what this performance means, and maintains a cautious demeanour. He does not say one word too much, he conceals his uneasiness and stands silent, pretending to be a fool.

The peasant who has been acquitted by the court trudges home, no more elated than if he had been condemned. In either case the decision seems to him the result of capricious tyranny or chance.

In the same way, when he is summoned as a witness he stubbornly professes to know nothing, even in face of incontestable fact. Being found guilty by a law-court does not disgrace a man in the eyes of the Russian peasant. Exiles and convicts go by the name of *unfortunates* with him.

The life of the Russian peasantry has hitherto been confined to the commune. It is only in relation to the commune and its members that the peasant recognises that he has rights and duties. Outside the commune everything seems to him based upon violence. What is fatal is his submitting to that violence, and not his refusing in his own way to recognise it and his trying to protect himself by guile. Lying before a judge set over him by unlawful authority is far more straightforward than a hypocritical show of respect for a jury tampered with by a corrupt prefect. The peasant respects only those institutions which reflect his innate conception of law and right.

There is a fact which no one who has been in close contact with the Russian peasantry can doubt. The peasants rarely cheat each other. An almost boundless good faith prevails among them; they know nothing of contracts and written agreements.

The problems connected with the measurement of their fields are often inevitably complicated, owing to the perpetual re-division of land, in accordance with the number of taxpayers in the family; yet the difficulties are got over without complaint or resort to the law-courts. The landowners and the Government eagerly seek an opportunity of interference, but that opportunity is not given them. Petty disputes are submitted to the judgment of the elders or of the commune, and the decision is unconditionally accepted by all. It is just the same thing in the *artels*. The *artels* are often made up of several hundred workmen, who form a union for a definite period —for instance, for a year. At the expiration of the year the workmen divide their wages by common agreement, in accordance with the work done by each. The police never have the satisfaction of meddling in their accounts. Almost always the *artel* makes itself responsible for every one of its members.

The bonds between the peasants of the commune are even closer when they are not orthodox but dissenters. From time to time the Government organises a savage raid on some dissenting village. Peasants are clapped into prison and sent into exile, and it is all done with no sort of plan, no consistency, without rhyme or reason, solely to satisfy the clamour of the clergy and give the police something to do. The character of the Russian

peasants, the solidarity existing among them, is displayed
again during these hunts after heretics. At such times
it is worth seeing how they succeed in deceiving the
police, in saving their comrades and concealing their
holy books and vessels, how they endure the most awful
tortures without uttering a word. I challenge any one to
bring forward a single case in which a dissenting commune
has been betrayed by a peasant, even by an orthodox one.

The peculiarity of the Russian character makes police
enquiries excessively difficult. One can but heartily
rejoice at the fact. The Russian peasant has no morality
except what naturally, instinctively flows from his communism; this morality is deeply rooted in the people;
the little they know of the Gospel supports it; the flagrant
injustice of the landowner binds the peasant still more
closely to his principles and to the communal system.[1]

The commune has saved the Russian people from

1 A peasant commune belonging to Prince Kozlovsky bought
their freedom. The land was divided amongst the peasants in proportion to the sum contributed by each to the purchase-money.
This arrangement was apparently most natural and just. The
peasants, however, thought it so inconvenient and inconsistent with
their habits that they decided to regard the purchase-money as a debt
incurred by the commune and to divide the lands according to their
accepted custom. This fact is vouched for by Baron von Haxthausen.
The author himself visited the village in question.

In a book recently published in Paris and dedicated to the
Emperor Nicholas, the writer says that this system of the
division of land seems to him unfavourable to the development of
agriculture (as though the object of it were the success of agriculture!); he adds, however: 'It is difficult to escape these disadvantages, because this system of land division is bound up with
the organisation of our communes, which it would be *dangerous to
touch*; it is established on the fundamental idea of the unity of the
commune, and the right of every member of it to a share in the
communal property in proportion to his strength, and so it supports
the communal spirit, that trusty prop of the social order. At the
same time it is the best defence against the increase of the proletariat
and the diffusion of communistic ideas.' (We may well believe that
for a people in actual fact possessing their property in common,

Mongol barbarism and Imperial civilisation, from the
Europeanised landlords and from the German bureaucracy. The communal system, though it has suffered
violent shocks, has stood firm against the interference of
the authorities; it has successfully survived *up to the
development of socialism in Europe*. This circumstance
is of infinite consequence for Russia.

The Russian Autocracy is entering upon a new phase.
Having grown out of an anti-national revolution,[1] it has
accomplished its destined task. It has created an
immense empire, a formidable army, a centralised government. Without real roots, without tradition, it was
doomed to ineffectiveness; it is true that it undertook a
new task—to bring Western civilisation into Russia; and
it was to some extent successful in doing that while it
still played the part of an enlightened government.

That part it has now abandoned.

The Government, which severed itself from the people
in the name of civilisation, has lost no time in cutting
itself off from culture in the name of autocracy.

communistic ideas present no danger.) 'The good sense with
which the peasants avoid the inconveniences of their system where
such are inevitable is extremely remarkable; so is the ease with
which they agree over the compensation for inequalities arising from
differences of soil, or the confidence with which every one accepts
the decisions of the elders of the commune. It might be expected
that the continual re-divisions would give rise to continual disputes,
and yet the intervention of the higher authorities is only necessary
in the very rarest cases. This fact, *very strange in itself*, can only
be explained through the system, with all its disadvantages, having
so grown into the morals and conceptions of the peasants that its
drawbacks are accepted without a murmur.'

'The idea of the commune is,' says the same author, 'as natural
to the Russian peasant, and as fully embodied in all the aspects of his
life, as the corporate municipal spirit that has taken shape in the
bourgeoisie of Western Europe is distasteful to his character.'—
(*Author's Note.*)

1 I.e., from the revolutionary changes made by Peter the Great.—
(*Translator's Note.*)

It renounced civilisation as soon as the tri-coloured phantom of liberalism began to be visible through its tendencies; it tried to turn to nationalism, to the people. That was impossible—the people and the Government had nothing in common; the former had grown away from the latter, while the Government discerned deep in the masses a new phantom, the still more terrible phantom of the Red Cock.[1] Of course, liberalism was less dangerous than the new Pugatchovism, but the terror and dislike of new ideas had grown so strong that the Government was no longer capable of making its peace with civilisation.

Since then the sole aim of Tsarism has been Tsarism. It rules in order to rule, its immense powers are employed for their mutual destruction, for the preservation of an artificial peace. But autocracy for the sake of autocracy in the end becomes impossible; it is too absurd, too barren.

It has felt this and has begun to look for work to do in Europe. The activity of Russian diplomacy is inexhaustible; notes, threats, promises, councils are scattered on all sides, its spies and agents scurry to and fro in all directions.

The Russian Emperor regards himself as the natural protector of the German Princes; he meddles in all the petty intrigues of the petty German courts; he settles all their disputes, scolding one, rewarding another with the hand of a Grand Duchess. But this is not a sufficient outlet for his energy. He undertakes the duty of chief gendarme of the universe; he is the mainstay of every reaction, every persecution. He plays the part of the representative of the monarchical principle in Europe, assumes the airs and graces of the aristocracy, as though he were a Bourbon, or a Plantagenet, as though his courtiers were Gloucesters or Montmorencys.

[1] To 'let fly the Red Cock' is the popular Russian phrase for arson.—(*Translator's Note.*)

Unhappily there is nothing in common between feudal monarchism with its definite basis, its past, and its social and religious ideas, and the Napoleonic despotism of the Petersburg Tsar with no moral principle behind it, nothing but a deplorable historic necessity, a transitory usefulness.

And the Winter Palace, like a mountain top toward the end of autumn, is more and more thickly covered with snow and ice. The vital sap artificially raised to these governmental heights is gradually being frozen; nothing is left but mere material power, and the hardness of the rock which still resists the onslaught of the waves of revolution.

Nicholas, surrounded by his generals, his ministers, and his bureaucrats, tries to forget his isolation, but grows hour by hour gloomier, more morose, more uneasy. He sees that he is not loved; he discerns the deadly silence that reigns about him through the distant murmur of the far-away tempest, which seems to be coming nearer. The Tsar seeks to forget, he proclaims aloud that his aim is the aggrandisement of the Imperial power.

That avowal is nothing new; for the last twenty years he has unwearyingly, unrestingly laboured for that sole object; for the sake of it he has spared neither the tears nor the blood of his subjects.

He has succeeded in everything: he has crushed Polish nationalism; in Russia he has suppressed liberalism.

What more does he want, indeed? Why is he so gloomy?

The Emperor feels that Poland is not yet dead. In place of the liberalism which he has persecuted with a savagery quite superfluous, for that exotic flower cannot take root in Russian soil, another movement menacing as a storm-cloud is arising.

The peasantry is beginning to murmur under the yoke of the landowners; local insurrections are continually breaking out; you yourself quote a terrible instance of this.

The party of progress demands the emancipation of the peasants; it is ready to sacrifice its own privileges. The Tsar hesitates and holds it back; he desires emancipation and puts hindrances in its way. He sees that freeing the peasants involves freeing the land; that this in its turn is the beginning of a social revolution, the proclamation of rural communism. To escape the question of emancipation is impossible, to defer its solution to the next reign is, of course, easier, but it is a cowardly resource, and only amounts to the respite of a few hours wasted at a wretched posting-station in waiting for horses. . . .

From all this you see how fortunate it is for Russia that the village commune has not perished, that personal ownership has not split up the property of the commune; how fortunate it is for the Russian people that it has remained outside all political movements, outside European civilisation, which would undoubtedly have undermined the commune, and which has to-day reached in socialism the negation of itself.

Europe, as I have said in another place, has not solved the problem of the rival claims of the individual and the State, but has set herself the task of solving it. Russia has not found the solution either. It is in this problem that our equality begins.

At the first step towards the social revolution Europe is confronted with the people which presents it with a system, half-savage and unorganised, but still a system, that of perpetual re-division of land among its cultivators. And observe that this great example is given us not by educated Russia, but by the people itself, by its actual life. We Russians who have passed through European civilisation are no more than a means, a leaven, mediators between the Russian people and revolutionary Europe.

The man of the future in Russia is the peasant, just as in France it is the workman.

But, if this is so, have not the Russian peasantry some claim on your indulgence, sir?

Poor peasant! Every possible injustice is hurled at him: the Emperor oppresses him with levies of recruits, the landowner steals his labour, the official takes his last rouble. The peasant endures in silence but does not despair, he still has the commune. If a member is torn from it, the commune draws its ranks closer. One would have thought the peasant's fate deserved compassion, yet it touches no one. Instead of defending, men upbraid him.

You do not leave him even the last refuge, in which he still feels himself a man, in which he loves and is not afraid; you say: 'His commune is not a commune, his family is not a family, his wife is not a wife; before she is his, she is the property of the landowner; his children are not his children—who knows who is their father?'

So you expose this luckless people not to scientific analysis but to the contempt of other nations, who receive your legends with confidence.

I regard it as a duty to say a few words on this subject.

Family life among all the Slavs is very highly developed; it may be the one conservative element of their character, the point at which their destructive criticism stops.

The peasants are very reluctant to split up the family; not uncommonly three or four generations go on living under one roof around the grandfather, who enjoys a patriarchal authority. The woman, commonly oppressed, as is always the case in the agricultural class, is treated with respect and consideration when she is the widow of the eldest son.

Not uncommonly the whole family is ruled by a grey-haired grandmother. . . . Can it be said that the family does not exist in Russia?

Let us pass to the landowner's relation to the family of his serf. For the sake of clearness, we will distinguish the rule from its abuses, what is lawful from what is criminal.

Jus primae noctis has never existed in Russia.

The landowner cannot legally demand a breach of conjugal fidelity. If the law were carried out in Russia, the violation of a serf-woman would be punished exactly as though she were free, namely by penal servitude or exile to Siberia, with deprivation of all civil rights. Such is the law, let us turn to the facts.

I do not pretend to deny that with the power given by the Government to the landowners, it is very easy for them to violate the wives and daughters of their serfs. By privation and punishment the landowner can always bring his serfs to a pass in which some will offer him their wives and daughters, just like that worthy French nobleman who, in the eighteenth century, asked as a special favour that his daughter should be installed in the Parc-aux-Cerfs.

It is no matter for wonder that honourable fathers and husbands find no redress against the landowners, thanks to the excellent judicial system of Russia. For the most part, they find themselves in the position of Monsieur Tiercelin, whose daughter of eleven was stolen by Berruyer, at the instigation of Louis xv. All these filthy abuses are possible; one has but to think of the coarse and depraved manners of a section of the Russian nobility to be certain of it. But as far as the peasants are concerned they are far indeed from enduring their masters' viciousness with indifference.

Allow me to bring forward a proof of it.

Half of the landowners murdered by their serfs (the statistics give their number as sixty to seventy a year) perish in consequence of their misdeeds in this line. Legal proceedings on such grounds are rare; the peasant knows that the judges show little respect for his complaints; but he has an axe; he is a master of the use of it, and knows that he is.

I will say no more about the peasants, but beg you to listen to a few more words about educated Russia.

Your view of the intellectual movement in Russia is no more indulgent than your opinion of the popular character; with one stroke of the pen you strike off all the work hitherto done by our fettered hands!

One of Shakespeare's characters, not knowing how to show his contempt for a despised opponent, says to him: 'I even doubt of your existence!' You have gone further, for it is not a matter of doubt to you that Russian literature does not exist. I quote from your own words:

'We are not going to attach importance to the attempts of those few clever people who have thought fit to exercise themselves in the Russian language and cheat Europe with a pale phantom of Russian literature. If it were not for my deep respect for Mickiewicz and his saintly aberrations, I should really censure him for the indulgence, one might even say charity, with which he speaks of this trifling.'[1]

I search in vain, sir, for the grounds for the contempt with which you greet the first frail cry of a people that has awakened in its prison-house, the groan suppressed by its gaoler.

Why are you unwilling to listen to the shuddering notes of our mournful poetry, to our chants through which a sob can be heard? What has concealed from your eyes our hysterical laughter, the perpetual irony behind which the deeply tortured heart seeks refuge, in which our fatal helplessness is confessed? Oh, how I long to make you a worthy translation of some poems of

[1] The last sentence is omitted in the version of the 'Légende 'in Michelet's Collected Works. — (*Translator's Note.*)

Pushkin and Lermontov, some songs of Koltsov! Then you would hold out to us a friendly hand at once, you would be the first to beg us to forget what you have said!

Next to the communism of the peasants, nothing is so deeply characteristic of Russia, nothing is such an earnest of her great future, as her literary movement.

Between the peasantry and literature there looms the monster of official Russia. 'Russia. the deception, Russia the pestilence,' as you call her. This Russia extends from the Emperor, passing from gendarme to gendarme, from official to official, down to the lowest policeman in the remotest corner of the Empire. Every step of the ladder, as in Dante, gains a new power for evil, a new degree of corruption and cruelty. This living pyramid of crimes, abuses, and bribery, built up of policemen, scoundrels, heartless German officials everlastingly greedy, ignorant judges everlastingly drunk, aristocrats everlastingly base: all this is held together by a community of interest in plunder and gain, and supported on six hundred thousand animated machines with bayonets. The peasant is never defiled by contact with this governing world of aggression; he endures its existence—only in that is he to blame.

The body hostile to official Russia consists of a handful of men who are ready to face anything, who protest against it, fight with it, denounce and undermine it. These isolated champions are from time to time thrown into dungeons, tortured, sent to Siberia, but their place does not long remain empty, fresh champions come forward; it is our tradition, our inalienable task. The terrible consequences of speech in Russia inevitably give it a peculiar force. A free utterance is listened to with love and reverence, because among us it is only uttered by those who have something to say. One does not so easily put one's thoughts into print when at the end of every page one has a vision of a gendarme, a troika, and, on the far horizon, Tobolsk or Irkutsk.

In my last pamphlet[1] I have said enough about Russian literature. Here I will confine myself to a few general observations.

Melancholy, scepticism, irony, those are the three chief strings of the Russian lyre.

When Pushkin begins one of his finest poems with these terrible words:

> 'All say—there is no justice upon earth. . . .
> But there is no justice—up above us either!
> To me that is as clear as A B C,'

does it not grip your heart, do you not through the show of composure divine the broken life of a man grown used to suffering? Lermontov, in his profound repulsion for the society surrounding him, turns in 1830 to his contemporaries with his terrible

> 'With mournful heart I watch our generation,
> Tragic or trivial must its future be.'

I only know one contemporary poet who touches the gloomy strings of man's soul with the same He, too, was a poet born in slavery and dying before the rebirth of his Fatherland; that is the singer of death, Leopardi, to whom the world seems a vast league of criminals ruthlessly persecuting a handful of righteous madmen.

Russia has only one painter who has won general recognition, Bryullov. What is the subject of his finest work which won him fame in Italy?

Glance at this strange painting.[2] On an immense canvas groups of terrified figures are crowded in confusion, seeking in vain for safety. They are perishing

---

[1] *Du Developpement des Idees révolutionnaires en Russia.*

[2] The picture is called 'The Last Day of Pompeii.'—(*Translator's Notes.*)

from an earthquake, a volcanic eruption in the midst of a perfect tempest of cataclysms. They are overwhelmed by savage, senseless, ruthless force, to which any resistance is impossible. Such are the conceptions inspired by the Petersburg atmosphere. The Russian novel is occupied exclusively in the sphere of pathological anatomy. In it there is a perpetual reference to the evil consuming us, perpetual, pitiless, peculiar to us. Here you do not hear voices from heaven, promising Faust forgiveness for sinful Gretchen—here the only voices raised are those of doubt and damnation. Yet if there is salvation for Russia, she will be saved only by this profound recognition of our position, by the truthfulness with which she lays bare before all her plight. He who boldly recognises his failings feels that there is in him something that has been kept safe in the midst of downfalls and backslidings; he knows that he can expiate his past, and not only lift up his head, but turn from 'Sardanapalus the profligate to Sardanapalus the hero.'

The Russian peasantry do not read. You know that Voltaire and Dante, too, were not read by villagers, but by the nobility and a section of the middle class. In Russia the educated section of the middle class forms part of the nobility, which consists of all that has ceased to be the peasantry. There is even a proletariat of the nobility which merges into the peasantry, and a proletariat of the peasantry which rises up into the nobility. This fluctuation, this continual renewal, gives the Russian nobility a character which you do not find in the privileged classes of the backward countries of Europe. In brief, the whole history of Russia, from the time of Peter the Great, is only the history of the nobility and of the influence of enlightenment upon it. I will add that the Russian nobility equals in numbers the electorate of France established by the laws of the 31st of May.

In the course of the eighteenth century, the new

Russian literature fashioned that rich, sonorous language which we possess now: a supple and powerful language capable of expressing both the most abstract ideas of German metaphysics and the light sparkling play of French wit. This literature, called into being by the genius of Peter the Great, bore, it is true, the impress of the Government—but in those days the banner of the Government was progress, almost revolution.

Till 1789 the Imperial throne complacently draped itself in the majestic vestments of enlightenment and philosophy. Catherine 11. deserved to be deceived with cardboard villages and palaces of painted boards. . . . No one could dazzle spectators by a gorgeous stage effect as she could. In the Hermitage there was continual talk about Voltaire, Montesquieu, Beccaria. You, sir, know the reverse of the medal.

Yet in the midst of the triumphal chorus of the courtiers' songs of praise, a strange unexpected note was already sounding. That was the sceptical, fiercely satirical strain, before which all the other artificial chants were soon to be reduced to silence.

The true character of Russian thought, poetical and speculative, develops in its full force on the accession of Nicholas to the throne. Its distinguishing feature is a tragic emancipation of conscience, a pitiless negation, a bitter irony, an agonising self-analysis. Sometimes this all breaks into insane laughter, but there is no gaiety in that laughter.

Cast into oppressive surroundings, and armed with a clear eye and incorruptible logic, the Russian quickly frees himself from the faith and morals of his fathers. The thinking Russian is the most independent man in the world. What is there to curb him? Respect for the past? . . . But what serves as a starting-point of the modern history of Russia, if not the denial of nationalism and tradition?

Or can it be the tradition of the Petersburg period? That tradition lays no obligation on us; on the contrary, that 'fifth act of the bloody drama staged in a brothel'1 sets us completely free from every obligation.

On the other hand, the past of the Western European peoples serves us as a lesson and nothing more; we do not regard ourselves as the executors of their historic testaments.

We share your doubts, but your faith does not cheer us. We share your hatred, but we do not understand your devotion to what your forefathers have bequeathed you; we are too downtrodden, too unhappy, to be satisfied with half-freedom. You are restrained by scruples, you are held back by second thoughts. We have neither second thoughts nor scruples; all we lack is strength. This is where we get the irony, the anguish which gnaws us, which brings us to frenzy, which drives us on till we reach Siberia, torture, exile, premature death. We sacrifice ourselves with no hope, from spite, from boredom. . . . There is, indeed, something irrational in our lives, but there is nothing vulgar, nothing stagnant, nothing bourgeois.

Do not accuse us of immorality because we do not respect what you respect. Can you reproach a foundling for not respecting his parents? We are independent because we are starting life from the beginning. We have no law but our nature, our national character; it is our being, our flesh and blood, but by no means a binding authority. We are independent because we possess nothing. We have hardly anything to love. All our memories are filled with bitterness and resentment. Education, learning, were given us with the whip.

What have we to do with your sacred duties, we

1 Quoted from the excellent expression of one of the contributors of *Il Progresso* in an article on Russia, August 1, 1851.—(*Author's Note*.)

younger brothers robbed of our heritage? And can we be honestly contented with your threadbare morality, unchristian and inhuman, existing only in rhetorical exercises and speeches for the prosecution? What respect can be inspired in us by your Roman-barbaric system of law, that hollow clumsy edifice, without light or air, repaired in the Middle Ages, whitewashed by the newly enfranchised petty bourgeois? I admit that the daily brigandage in the Russian law-courts is even worse, but it does not follow from that that you have justice in your laws or your courts.

The distinction between your laws and our Imperial decrees is confined to the formula with which they begin. Our Imperial decrees begin with a crushing truth: 'The Tsar has been pleased to command'; your laws begin with a revolting falsehood, the ironical abuse of the name of the French people, and the words Liberty, Equality, and Fraternity. The code of Nicholas is drawn up for the benefit of the Autocracy to the detriment of its subjects. The Napoleonic code has absolutely the same character. We are held in too many chains already to fasten fresh ones about us of our own free will. In this respect we stand precisely on a level with our peasants. We submit to brute force. We are slaves because we have no possibility of being free; but we accept nothing from our foes.

Russia will never be Protestant, Russia will never be *juste-milieu*.

Russia will never make a revolution with the object of getting rid of the Tsar Nicholas, and replacing him by other Tsars—parliamentary representatives, judges, and police officials. We perhaps ask for too much and shall get nothing. That may be so, but yet we do not despair; before the year 1848 Russia could not, and should not, have entered on a career of revolution, she had to learn her lesson—now she has learnt it. The Tsar himself observes it, and is ferociously brutal in his opposition to universities, to ideas, to knowledge; he is trying to cut Russia off from Europe, to destroy culture. He is doing his job.

Will he succeed in it? As I have said before, we must not have blind faith in the future; every seed has its claim to development, but not every one develops. The future of Russia does not depend on her alone, it is bound up with the future of Europe. Who can foretell the fate of the Slav world, if reaction and absolutism finally vanquish the revolution in Europe?

Perhaps it will perish.

But in that case Europe too will perish. . . .

And progress will pass to America.

After writing the above I received the last two instalments of your legend. My first impulse on reading them was to throw what I had written in the fire. Your warm and generous heart has not waited for some one else to raise a voice on behalf of the despised Russian people. Your heart was too tender for you to play the part you had undertaken of the *relentless* judge, the avenger of the outraged Polish people. You have been drawn into inconsistency, but it is the inconsistency of a noble mind.

I thought, however, on reading over my letter that you might find in it some new views on Russia and the Slav world, and I made up my mind to send it you. I confidently hope that you will forgive the passages in which I have been carried away by my Scythian impetuosity. It is not for nothing that the blood of the barbarians flows in my veins. I so longed to change your opinion of the Russian people, it was such a grief, such a pain to me to see that you were hostile to us that I could not conceal my bitterness, my emotion, that I let my pen run away with me. But now I see that you do not despair of us, that under the coarse smock of the Russian peasant you discern the man. I see this, and in my turn confess that I fully understand the impression the very name of Russia must produce on every free man. We often ourselves curse our unhappy Fatherland. You know it, you say yourself that everything you have written of the moral worthlessness of Russia is feeble compared with what Russians say themselves.

But the time for funeral orations on Russia is past for us too, and with you we say 'in that thought lies hid the spark of life.' You have divined that spark by the power of your love; but we see it, we feel it. That spark will not be quenched by streams of blood, by the ices of Siberia, nor the suffocating heat of mines and prisons. May it spread under its layer of ashes! The cold, deadly breath which blows from Europe cannot put it out.

For us the hour of action has not come; France may still be justly proud of her foremost position. That painful privilege is hers until 1852. Europe will doubtless before us reach the goal of the grave or of the new life. The day of action is perhaps still far away for us; the day of recognising the idea, the day of utterance, has already come. We have lived long enough in sleep and silence; the time has come to tell what we have dreamed, what conclusions we have reached.

And indeed whose fault is it that we have had to wait until 1847 for a German (Haxthausen) to *discover*, as you express it, the Russia of the peasantry, as unknown before his time as America before Columbus?

Of course, it is we who are to blame for it, we poor dumb creatures with our cowardice, our halting words, our terrified imagination. Even abroad we are afraid to confess the hatred with which we look upon our fetters. Convicts from our birth up, doomed to the hour of death to drag the chains riveted to our legs, we are offended when we are spoken of as though we were voluntary slaves, as though we were frozen negroes, and yet we do not openly protest.

Ought we to submit meekly to these denunciations, or to resolve to check them, lifting up our voice for Russian freedom of speech? Better for us to perish suspected of human dignity than to live with the shameful brand of slavery on our brow, than to hear ourselves charged with voluntary servility.

Unhappily, free speech in Russia arouses terror and amazement. I have tried to lift only a corner of the heavy curtain that hides us from Europe, I have indicated only the theoretical tendencies, the remote hopes, the organic elements of our future development; and yet my book of which you speak in such flattering phrases has made an unpleasant impression in Russia. Friendly voices which I respect condemn it. In it they see a denunciation of Russia, denunciation! . . . For what? for our sufferings, our hardships, our desire to force our way out of this hateful position. . . . Poor precious friends, forgive me this crime, I am falling into it again.

Heavy and dreadful is the yoke of years of slavery with no struggle, no hope at hand! In the end it crushes even the noblest, the strongest heart. Where is the hero who is not overcome at last by weariness, who does not prefer peace in old age to the everlasting fret of fruitless effort?

No, I will not be silent! My words shall avenge those unhappy lives crushed by the Russian autocracy which brings men to moral annihilation, to spiritual death.

We are bound in duty to speak, else no one will know how much that is fine and lofty is locked for ever in those martyrs' breasts and perishes with them in the snows of Siberia, where their criminal name is not even traced upon their tombstone, but is only cherished in the hearts of friends who dare not utter it aloud.

Scarcely have we opened our mouth, scarcely have we murmured two or three words of our desires and hopes, when they try to silence us, try to stifle free speech in its cradle! It is impossible. A time comes when thought reaches maturity and can no longer be kept in fetters by the censorship, nor by prudence. Then propaganda becomes a passion; can one be content with a whisper when the sleep is so deep that it can scarcely be awakened by an alarm-bell? From the mutiny of the Stryeltsy to the conspiracy of the Fourteenth of December there has been no political movement of consequence in Russia. The cause is easy to understand: there were no clearly defined cravings for independence in the people. In many things they were at one with the Government, in many things the Government was in advance of the people. Only the peasants, who had no share in the Imperial benefits and were more oppressed than ever, tried to revolt. Russia from the Urals to Penza and Kazan was, for three months, in the power of Pugatchov. The Imperial army was defeated, put to flight by the Cossacks, and General Bibikov, sent from Petersburg to take the command of the army, wrote, if I am not mistaken, from Nizhni: 'Things are in a very bad way; what is most to be feared is not the armed hordes of the rebels, but the spirit of the peasantry, which is dangerous, very dangerous.' After incredible efforts the insurrection was at last crushed. The people relapsed into numbness, silence, and submission. . . . .

Meanwhile the nobility had developed, education had begun to fructify their minds, and like a living proof of that political maturity, of that moral development which is inevitably expressed in action, those divine figures appeared, those heroes as you justly call them, who 'alone in the very jaws of the dragon dared the bold stroke of the Fourteenth of December.'

Their defeat and the terror of the present reign have

crushed every idea of success, every premature attempt. Other questions have arisen; no one has cared to risk his life again in the hope of a Constitution; it has been too clear that any stroke won in Petersburg would be defeated by the treachery of the Tsar; the fate of the Polish Constitution has been before our eyes.

For ten years no intellectual activity could betray itself by one word, and the oppressive misery has reached the point when men 'would give their life for the happiness of being free for one moment' and uttering aloud some part of their thoughts.

Some, with that frivolous recklessness which is only met with in us and in the Poles, have renounced their possessions and gone abroad to seek distraction; others, unable to endure the oppressive atmosphere of Petersburg, have buried themselves in the country. The young men gave themselves up, some to Pan-Slavism, some to German philosophy, some to history or political economy; in short, not one of those Russians whose natural vocation was intellectual activity could or would submit to the stagnation.

The case of Petrashevsky and his friends, condemned to penal servitude for life, and exiled in 1849, because they formed some political societies not two steps from the Winter Palace, proves by the insane recklessness of the attempt, and the obvious impossibility of its success, that the time for rational reflection had passed, that feeling was beyond restraint, that certain ruin had come to seem easier to endure than dumb agonising submission to the Petersburg discipline.

A fable very widely known in Russia tells how a Tsar, suspecting his wife of infidelity, shut her and her son in a barrel, then had the barrel sealed up and thrown into the sea.

For many years the barrel floated on the sea.

Meanwhile, the Tsarevitch grew not by days but by hours, and his feet and his head began to press against the ends of the barrel. Every day he became more and more cramped. At last he said to his mother: 'Queen-mother, let me stretch in freedom.'

'My darling Tsarevitch,' answered the mother, 'you must not stretch, the barrel will burst and you will drown in the salt water.'

The Tsarevitch thought in silence for a while, then he said: 'I will stretch, mother; better stretch for once in freedom and die.'

That fable, sir, contains our whole history.

Woe to Russia if bold men, risking everything to stretch in freedom for once, are no more to be found in her. But there is no fear of that. . . .

These words involuntarily bring to my mind Bakunin. Bakunin has given Europe the sample of a free Russian.

I was deeply touched by your fine reference to him. Unhappily, those words will not reach him.

An international crime has been committed; Saxony has handed over the victim to Austria, Austria to Nicholas. He is in the Schlüsselburg, that fortress of evil memory where once Ivan, the grandson of the Tsar Alexis, was kept caged like a wild beast, till he was killed by Catherine the Second,[1] who, still stained by her husband's blood, first ordered the captive's murder, then punished the luckless officer who carried out her command.

In that damp dungeon in the icy waters of Lake Ladoga there is no place for dreams or hopes! May he sleep the last sleep in peace, the martyr betrayed by two Governments, whose hands are stained with his blood. . . . Glory to his name! And revenge! But where is the

[1] This is not a correct version either of the murder of Peter III. or of Ivan VI. Catherine was certainly not directly responsible for either of those crimes. — (*Translator's Note.*)

avenger? . . . And we too, like him, shall perish with our work half done; but then lift up your stern and majestic voice, and tell our children once more that there is a duty before them. . . .

I will close with the memory of Bakunin and warmly press your hand for him and for myself.

NICE, *September* 22,1851.